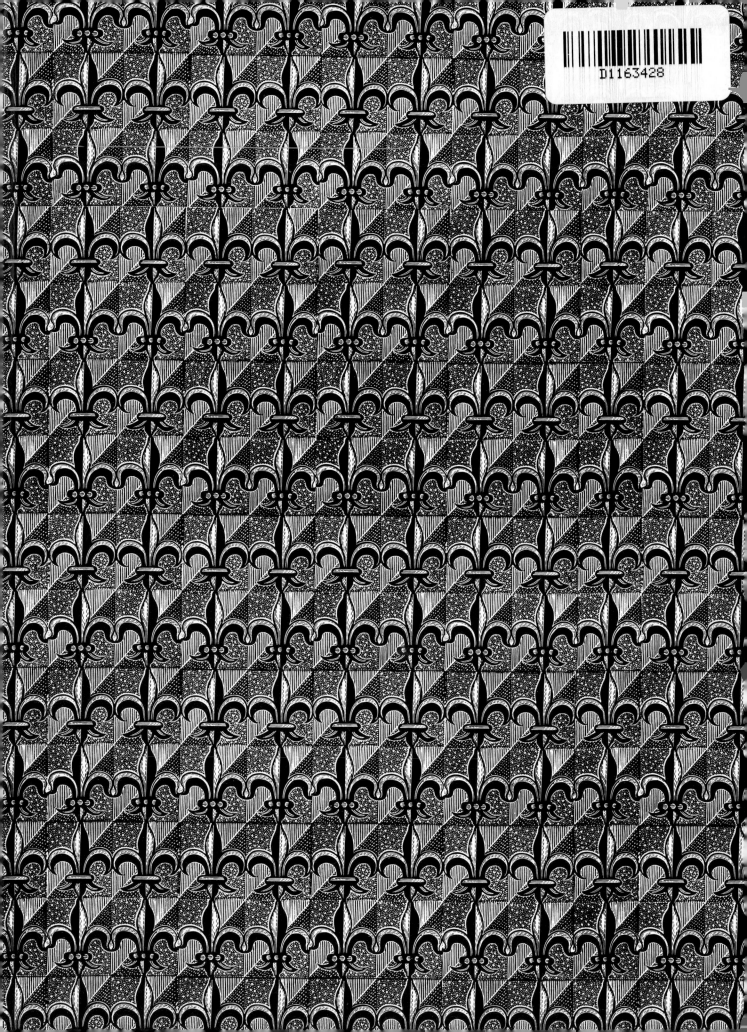

Ronald Searle

Ronald Searle

A biography

Russell Davies

Sinclair-Stevenson
LONDON

First published in Great Britain in 1990 by
Sinclair-Stevenson Limited
7–8 Kendrick Mews
London SW7 3HG

Copyright © 1990 by Russell Davies
Illustrations copyright © 1990 by Ronald Searle

A CIP catalogue record for this book
is available from the British Library

ISBN: 1 85619 004 8

Editor: Mark Bryant
Designer: Craig Dodd

Typeset by Butler & Tanner Limited
Printed and bound in Great Britain
by Butler & Tanner Limited, Frome and London

Half-title: Untitled, *Souls in Torment,*
London, 1953
*Clearly a satirist's pen, caught in a
moment of private grief for the world
depicted. 'Let there be gall enough in
thy ink, though thou write with a
goose-pen, no matter'* (Twelfth
Night).

Frontispiece: Ronald Searle in his
studio, 4 rue Antoine-Dubois,
Paris, 20 January 1973
For full caption see p. 163.

Contents

Acknowledgements

The author would like to thank Ronald Searle for supplying the bulk of the graphic work and photographs, and the following for individual items:

Olive Fenn: pp. 18, 19 (top), 30 (left); Gershon Ellenbogen: p. 35; George Sprod: p. 63; Kaye Webb: pp. 79, 87 (both); Paul Hogarth: p. 83; Kate Searle: p. 95, 'Crucifixion' (plate); Wendy Toye: pp. 100 (photograph), 112; Craig Dodd: p. 159; Godfrey Smith: p. 98; The National Gallery of Scotland: p. 23; Nottingham Castle Museum: p. 96 (top); Royal College of Art: p. 110; *Cambridge Daily News* (now *Cambridge Evening News*): pp. 32 (top), 40, 44, 75; *Granta*: p. 37; *Daily Express*: p. 46 (lower); *Tribune*: pp. 82, 84; *Punch*: pp. 91, 100, 104, 107, 108, 109, 126, covers (plates); *Le Canard enchaîné*: p. 121; *Life*: pp. 112, 133 (right), 135; *New Yorker*: p. 186, covers (plates); *Graphis*: cover (plate); Imperial War Museum: Changi Christmas card (plate); *New York Times*: poster (plate); American Express: illustration (plate).

The author and publishers have attempted to trace all copyright holders. Advice of omissions would be appreciated; these will be corrected in future editions.

Preface

No right-thinking individual strictly approves of biographies written within the lifetime of their subjects, but I was unable to resist the opportunity to write this one. In the course of the Introduction, I have suggested one or two reasons why a biography of Ronald Searle might be useful to have at this time, in spite of its inevitable incompleteness. The project was suggested by my editor, Mark Bryant, who had long been keen to explore the subject of Searle. By coincidence, Ronald Searle had been kind enough to help us get in touch with the widow of an earlier subject, the cartoonist Vicky, and when Mark approached Searle about a biography it emerged that he had read the Vicky book with enjoyment. And I was pleasantly surprised when he subsequently agreed to let his story be told in an illustrated volume, on the strict understanding that it be done from an independent point of view and not, as he put it, in the manner of 'an "authorised biography" (yuk)'. No more welcome proviso could have been uttered.

My independent point of view will give the impression, particularly towards the end of the book, that Searle has a strong sense of boundaries and guards his own fiercely, which is true. So I must make it absolutely clear at this point that he has tolerated and even encouraged my invasions into his life with the utmost kindness. At the start of my research, he provided a huge timetable of events, without which I simply could not have organized the material within his seventieth-birthday year, according to the publishers' wish. Documents have been unearthed, attributions supplied and explanations essayed not just with that appearance of enthusiasm of which we all are intermittently capable, but with a constant consideration and devotion to detail. Interviewing the Searles in 1977, Martin Amis wrote of being 'greeted as if my presence were a key part of some rare and complicated treat they had long promised themselves'. I had the same feeling, on a brief but vital visit to their home in southern France. So my first thanks go to Ronald and Monica Searle for all their help. Ronald Searle also kindly agreed to read the manuscript at the proof stage and correct errors of fact. No doubt he has allowed many impressionistic elisions of my own to remain. Biographers do like to convince themselves that one event led causally to another, because things look neater that way.

My strategy has been to consult the work first and the people later. The subject's sister, Mrs Olive Fenn, gave me many useful pointers in the beginning and was kind enough to lend early drawings, photographs and letters. Kaye Webb, Ronald Searle's first wife, similarly made available important materials, and answered my questions with admirable frankness. I am sorry that my visits must inevitably have stirred up some unwelcome feelings – an apology which applies equally, indeed, to Ronald Searle himself. His children, Katie and John, had every reason to avoid me, but did not; I am grateful to them for talking to me. Katie Searle also provided some rare items for reproduction from among the collection that is in her care.

I have been helped by many friends of Searle's, either by correspondence or in person. Valuable light was shed on the pre-war period by Miss Gee Horsley, his last surviving art teacher; Mrs Vera Piqué, one of his first colleagues at work; his *Granta* colleagues Gershon Ellenbogen and Professor Eric Hobsbawm; and his fellow art student, Philip Evett. Cécilé [Johnston] McLachlan, the first St Trinian's girl, supplied a touching memoir of the Kirkcudbright period, and letters relating to subsequent times. Survivors of the fall of Singapore have shown an eagerness to help which indicates their long-held respect for Searle. Bernard Campion, Philip Meninsky, John Wiggins, Klaas Kooy, Sir Alexander Fitzwilliam Barrington, Don Hosegood, Ronnie Horner and (from Australia) George Sprod all cheerfully revisited their pasts. The writings of Russell Braddon still provide the most dramatic first-hand evocation of life under the Japanese. For a dispassionate historical account, putting that experience in a fuller military context, I have consulted Kate Caffrey's *Out in the Midday Sun* (Deutsch, 1974); and am grateful to John Stewart for permission to quote briefly from his *To the River Kwai* (Bloomsbury, 1988). Alan Sunnucks kindly volunteered a description of his part in the Kyohara story, and provided a photograph of him. Jenny Wood of the Imperial War Museum patiently supervised my inspection of the Searle files there, and of the originals of *The Exile*. It was a pleasure, as usual, to deal with the staffs of the BBC Sound Archives and the BBC Written Archives Centre, Caversham.

Interviews kindly granted by David Arkell and Paul Hogarth illuminated the Forties, and after. Hogarth's *The Artist As Reporter* is a valuable history of its graphic genre. Arkell's fluent essay on Searle's life, published in *PN Review* No. 50 (1986) was my biographical starting-point. It is a pity that Arkell's unsurpassed collection of postcards 'enhanced' by Searle could not be represented in this volume. Wendy Toye gave me many enjoyable insights into her collaborations with Searle, and also access to her scrapbooks, from which a couple of fine photographs were detached. Three former secretaries of Searle, Mrs Louise Henderson, Mrs Janet Chivers and Mrs Kate Stout, have helped me form a picture of his working methods. William Hewison, an old friend from *Punch*, gave me all manner of useful information about greater days in the *Punch* office. I am especially grateful to him for bringing along a bottle of 'Stephens' Liquid Stains: Ebony', left behind by Searle in 1961. Amanda-Jane Doran and Miranda Taylor of the *Punch* library, last guardians of its tradition, found a Searle file which proved extremely useful.

To meet Searle's Parisian friends was a delight. Doreen and Lars Bo, Marcelle-Marie Methlin, Carmen Cassé of the Galerie Cassé, Mary Blume of the *International Herald-Tribune*, Deryk Mendel, and 'Tim' (Louis Mitelberg) of *L'Express* all gave generously of their time and hospitality. Jean-Pierre Desclozeaux, who looks after Searle's professional interests in Paris, proved himself not just a protector of humour but a generator of it. I much enjoyed my hours in his company. That Mme Charles David (Deanna Durbin) was prepared to suspend her rule of privacy and send me a charming account of her long friendship with the Searles must count as a great tribute to them. It is also pleasant to have the opportunity to thank my agent, Pat Kavanagh, not just for her usual professional care, but also for her memories of visits to the Searle abode in Paris, in company with Sid Perelman and others – and also for introducing me, once upon a time, to Sid himself.

In New York, John Locke was a most generous host. A day spent working through his records of Searle's American output proved invaluable. He introduced me to 'the incomparable Frank Zachary', as Searle has called him; and I also had most pleasurable meetings with Lola and Jimmy Owens, Steve Heller of the *New York Times*, and Barbara

Nicholls of the Nicholls Gallery, to whom I am also grateful for the loan of correspondence and a file of Searle's *New Yorker* covers. Lee Lorenz, current Art Editor of the *New Yorker*, helped me understand the selection processes the magazine operates, including the 'instinctive' evaluation practised by the latest Editor.

For various information received and accesses provided, I should like to thank my old friends Philip Speight and Alex Marengo of the BBC; Ivor Wood; Nick and Sue Webb; David H. Rawlings; Ian Hunt; B. and Theo Larsson; Gerald Scarfe; Michael Heath; Susan Jeffreys; Derek Gibbons of the Haunted Bookshop, Cambridge; Mel Calman of the Cartoon Gallery, London; Liz Ottaway of the Centre for the Study of Cartoons and Caricature at the University of Kent; and Mark Jones of the Department of Coins and Medals, British Museum.

To the many friends of Ronald and Monica Searle whose names do not appear in these pages, or occur in some apparently trivial context, I should say that the omission does not, of course, in the slightest way reflect upon the esteem in which the Searles hold them. They are not absent because I have been led to believe they belong to some secondary category of importance. It is simply a question of my having found it impossible, in the time and relatively short textual space available, to inflict myself on everybody. Most particularly does this apply to Searle's friends and colleagues in Germany, whose support for his work over the last thirty years has deserved a better tribute from me. It should be noted, in any case, that the place to keep up with the latest in exhibited Searles is the Neue Galerie Wien, Rotenturmstrasse 27, Vienna, his European gallery, where the proprietors are Hans and Elizabeth Schaumberger.

I can claim to have done all my own typing. This will not impress Mark Bryant, who has had to correct and edit it. My thanks, as ever, for his patience and regular supply of information on developments in the graphics world. Thanks also to Craig Dodd and Michael Brown for all their work on the design. James Woodall of Sinclair-Stevenson must be congratulated as well as thanked for the way he has seen the book through to publication amid all the novelties and uncertainties of a new imprint, including an office that has been virtually constructed around him. My wife, Judy Davies, was the first to read the manuscript and skim off one layer of ghastlinesses, but I thank her chiefly for putting up with the author.

Notes are arranged by page number. To any professional photographer whose copyright has been accidentally infringed by the use of unmarked prints, I apologize in advance. Responsibility for all inadequacies and inaccuracies of the text is my own, as are the opinions expressed by it, except where otherwise attributed.

Cambridge, 1990   R.D.

Right: At home, Haute-Provence, 1990

Ronald Searle at seventy, with a glass of champagne, his 'engine oil', and a pineapple included for composition rather than consumption.
(Photograph by Zbigniew Fitz.)

Introduction

Ronald Searle has often been called the foremost graphic artist of the modern age. His friend David Arkell has settled for the formulation 'arguably the finest graphic draughtsman of this century'. I don't particularly want to get into those arguments, or the game of definitions they entail. Searle is a superb comic draughtsman of international reputation. I do not personally know of any contemporary who approaches him in versatility, fecundity or the instant identifiability of his line. To have a 'unique' style should be no great claim in the graphics world; every artist ought to have such, and some (like, say, Ed Koren of the *New Yorker*, whose work Searle admires) have uniqueness in a hectic superabundance. But Searle has it not just in the overall 'feel' of his depictions, but built into his every pen-stroke, in the 'stammering' or 'hesitating' line for which there seems to be no more grandiose, Italianate term. One of the tasks of this book is to show, by means of a chronological continuum of graphic work – the choice modified and augmented by Searle himself – how the authority of his style has continued to develop, while retaining, if you look closely at the lines, a quality of nervousness, ricketiness, doubt. The beautiful flow of an outline may be built up by dozens of little halting jabs, which are sensed by the eye if not the whole brain. This effect has rendered the mature Searle virtually incapable of producing the instantly disposable laugh-and-pass-on cartoon. His merest gag is graphically ponderable (see the one discussed in the last pages of the text).

That Searle's work is funny I have tried as far as possible to take for granted. Nobody likes to be told all the time that he or she ought to be laughing. Essays making out an intellectual case for Searle's funniness, with reference to the social predicament of the satirist and the history of graphic fabulation, have been produced in the past. A book containing one such treatise has been lent to me; it has been edited, annotated and mutilated with impressive ferocity by a pencil-wielding Searle, and I am not surprised. I would rather use the space to examine why Searle is 'serious'. English critics for many years have accused him of perpetrating whimsy. They never say what they mean by this, and I suspect that 'whimsy' is a British code-word for any form of humour which does not happen to have tickled the reviewer that morning. If on the other hand we are keeping to a dictionary definition, like 'delicate, or affectedly delicate, fantasy' (Chambers), then my feeling is that Searle should plead loudly guilty. '*Affectedly* delicate fantasy' happens to suit some Searle creations particularly well, in the sense that he joins in happily with the affectations of his characters. His work is full of creatures – lobsters, snails, librarians, dictators – who put on preposterous airs, believing they are making an elegant or imposing impression, but only drawing attention to the terrible inadequacy of their natural equipment. (One thinks of the grand tableau 'Swine Lake', with its ballet-dancing pigs.) The beauty with which Searle invests such delusory scenes strikes me as too cruelly ironic to be merely whimsical; and of course, there is always a comment on human attitudes lurking within the animal prototype. If Searle's 'Cats' were just about cats, he would not have drawn them.

Searle's influence has been so widespread that an extra year's work would have been required to go chasing it. One of the world's most enjoyable theses (enjoyable to research, at any rate) awaits to be written around this topic. Special consideration will need to be given to artists – such as Arnold Roth – who started their careers as unmistakable Searle-followers; to young cartoonists who have passed through a period of seemingly helpless, slavish Searlism (Bill Hewison, in his time as Art Editor of *Punch*, had to beg one or two of them to desist); and the whole tradition of American political cartooning – now so much stronger than our own – whose leading exponents, such as Pat Oliphant and Jeff MacNelly, have given credit to Searle for reinvigorating the American scene with his magazine illustrations of thirty years ago. In a lovely example of unconscious irony, it was once reported in *Newsweek* that: 'To Oliphant's extreme annoyance, a growing number of cartoonists – he calls them "those bastards" – have begun to ape his neo-British, Ronald Searle style, right down to its distinctive signature.' Still, that's how evolution proceeds – apes of apes.

The most important developments in Searle's graphic career have occurred in work he has produced spontaneously, as expressions of what he personally wished to say. I have also mentioned some important instances of commissioned illustration work, including some advertisements; but there is a great deal more. The amount of advertising work will surprise many. 'It is a real horror story', Searle comments, and for admirers who prefer to imagine him as unentangled with commercial interests, I dare say it will all come as a shock. But Searle entered the profession at a time when every graphic humorist of any note, from Anton to David Langdon to Ernest Shepard, had some foothold in the advertising business. Searle has simply kept at it more tenaciously than most.

Some British readers of a patriotic cast of mind may feel that Searle is a bit hard on his homeland, if only because he denies it a proper look at his work. He has turned down many commissions on British topics, on the grounds that he is no longer familiar with our social scenery; and he has refused offers of retrospective exhibitions in this country – possibly in the belief (which he has seriously voiced to me) that he has fallen into the 'whatever happened to?' category as far as the British public is concerned. Just in case this impression of his is not so completely erroneous as I believe it to be, another useful function this book may fulfil, I hope, is to reintroduce Searle to British readers on new and expanded terms. If it does no more than discourage journalists from prefacing every mention of Searle with 'inventor of those incorrigible St Trinian's girls', or some equivalent phrase, I shall be satisfied.

While we are about it, I should take the opportunity to correct one misconstruction that has arisen over the last decade or so of journalistic interviews with Searle, and been passed on from profile to profile via the cuttings libraries. It concerns the belief that he systematically destroys his originals after publication. For clarity's sake I will quote his own explanation of how this myth arose:

> I may have said at some point that I retain the right to destroy any drawing that I either dislike, consider a 'miss', or would never wish to have circulated. True, I have destroyed some hundreds in my time. But only what I consider rubbish. A lot of people have told me that I shouldn't do this, but let posterity decide what is good and what is bad. But I prefer to exercise my own judgment before posterity can get

its dirty hands on me. So the answer is, that I do *not* systematically destroy my work, only occasionally, and only rampant rubbish; and there is no question, as some have written, I believe, that the idea behind my destruction is to create a scarcity value. That's nonsense. The trouble is, of course, that hundreds of drawings were stolen, or never returned, or appropriated, in the early days and a lot of this has begun to make its appearance in the salerooms over the last few years, often with the most weird attributions, or invented titles. Curiously enough the originals of my Suez pamphlets appeared in the saleroom not too long ago. This was odd, because they were War Office property [see Chapter Five].

Alert readers will notice, possibly with slight irritation, that I do not name the village where the Searles took up residence in 1975. There are moments in the text where use of the name would have made for smoother reading; but if you knew the horror with which Searle views the possibility of casual visitors, calling with books to sign and axes to grind, you would be as content as I am to leave him at work amid the peace for which he has struggled.

As his own books have shown, and various passages quoted in this one will confirm, Ronald Searle writes very good prose. He did not spend all that time with Perelman and Thurber and Beckett without rising to the literary challenge. He would certainly have told his own story far better than I can tell it; but he was too busy drawing. Most questions left unresolved in this book will find an answer in that phrase: 'too busy drawing'. Long may the same excuse apply.

ONE

'I am R. Searle of C.'
(1920–33)

Several times in his life, Ronald Searle has made a new start. He has seldom revisited those parts of his existence he left behind. If one or two of his departures have come more in the nature of escapes, then it was necessarily so, for he has always lived (though not always by choice) in demanding, even clinging, environments, of the kind that can claim a man for life. So far, nowhere has detained him longer than his birthplace. It hung on to him for nineteen years, gaining much more richly from the young man's presence than it had a right to expect, but repaying him with a vivid display of human vanities, set against a background of largely man-made beauty. Even today, when it is changing so fast, Cambridge is not quite as other towns are.

For centuries, two tasks contented the place. As a market town, it served the edge of the fertile Anglian fens. As the seat of an ancient university, it provided an adoptive home – sometimes briefly, sometimes for life – to generations of scholars, eccentrics, holy fools and mere 'young gentlemen'. Even in the Sixties of the present century, some of us arriving in Cambridge as students were forewarned that 'the industrial revolution had passed the region by', leaving its populace with no sense of itself as a mass. Surviving traces of feudal deference, we were invited to believe, were observable in the demeanour of college 'servants' – an outmoded designation which told its own story.

In the event, we observed that while the promised medievalisms were indeed hanging on, they were moribund. We were the last generation of students to be chased through the streets by the University Proctor's 'Bulldogs', a pair of top-hatted heavies employed to impose fines, in multiples of 6s. 8d. (one-third of a pound), upon members of the University caught roaming the streets after dark without an academic gown. That practice, familiar to the young Ronald Searle as a spectator sport, was discontinued; and with it seemed to go the last symbolic dominance of University custom over civic territory. The town had finally begun to assert its own independence. It had new roles to fulfil: as a centre for international tourism, for example, and a focus for the development of new industries in precision engineering, medical research and information technology. Suddenly the most medieval aspect of Cambridge was revealed to be its road system: labyrinthine, unplanned and equipped with too few crossings over the indolent River Cam. As a hasty palliative, one large new bridge was constructed to link the Newmarket and Ely exits from the town. Given the new-age name Elizabeth Way, it was an ugly, ruthless carriageway, one of those urban necessities that skate past some houses at roof-level. Other dwellings were bulldozed aside to make way for a giant roundabout; and among these was Number 107 Newmarket Road, the birthplace of Ronald Searle.

Opposite: 'The Caricaturist', 1974

Thus was lost a prime site for a commemorative plaque, though in other ways, perhaps, Number 107 was no great loss to the cultural heritage. A two-storey terraced house of a type that survives in thousands in Cambridge, it represented in any case only a temporary lodging for the Searle family, who were destined to live their whole lives in rented accommodation. William James Searle, Ronald's father, was never a big earner. At the time of the birth, on 3 March 1920, he was a porter on Cambridge station. Number 107 belonged to Mr Wortley, the milkman. That day in early March, the upper front bedroom, where Nellie Searle lay in labour, was brightly decorated with the first daffodils of the season, and new pink curtains. A girl had been expected, by Nellie at least. It was the first of several important moments in Ronald's life when he confounded expectations.

Some children take their time in achieving a sharply individuated sense of who their parents are, but there was small chance that Ronald Searle would see Mum and Dad as some sort of cuddly composite. Both were strong and stubborn characters. William Searle was locally born, a tough man's man, and quite a Cambridge 'character'. His wife came from 'away' – down in Pewsey, Wiltshire – where she was born on 25 August 1894. Her forebears on her father's side had been watchmakers and jewellers, in a family tradition dating back to the eighteenth century. The Hunts had been a religious family, for the most part Wesleyans and Plymouth Brethren, and those not engaged in the family business tended to be adventurous. There is uncertainty among the family archivists as to the number of siblings Grandfather William Hunt had, but according to the version passed down to Ronald Searle, there were three brothers who all made their way to America. John T. Hunt, who remained faithful to the clock trade, went to Washington and was said to have become an intimate of President Wilson. The shadowy Alfred, a scapegrace by comparison, supposedly decamped to Texas, took up gambling, scored a big win and accepted his takings in oil shares, which made his fortune. Since the Hunts of Texas, to this day, constitute one of the richest dynasties in the world, there are obvious piquant possibilities to the tale. Haroldson Lafayette Hunt, founder of the Hunts' modern business empire, issued a biography detailing a family tree with its roots in America even before the Pilgrim Fathers' landing, but he produced no documentary evidence to support it. What is certain about H. L. Hunt, interestingly enough, is that he started out his career as a professional gambler.

William Hunt, meanwhile, stayed at home and minded the shop, his most notable excursions being marathon bicycle rides, for he was a champion amateur cyclist. On one such trip, to the Cotswolds, he met 'Minnie' (christened Lizzie) Bland, an accomplished milliner from a well-to-do family of tradespeople in Leicestershire. They were married in 1893 and exactly ten months later Nellie Hunt was born, over the shop, in Pewsey High Street. In 1990 she was still living, in a retirement home near Birmingham.

The Searles and Fordhams, on the other side of the family, came of bluffer agricultural stock, the Searles having been settled for at least three generations in the region of Saffron Walden, on the borders of Essex and Cambridgeshire. Great-grandfather Searle lived on one of the fine estates – possibly Audley End itself – near Newport in Essex, where some of his family were in the building trade. Remarkably few members of all these sizeable clans met an early death, but Great-grandfather Searle was an exception: he was labouring in some sand-diggings when they collapsed and buried him alive. His wife, remembered within the family as 'a dear little lady' and 'sweet', was durable as well. She went on to bury two more husbands, if that is not too unfortunate a phrase.

Their son James Searle, just a boy when his father was killed, sought work as soon as he could in Cambridge, and found it at the oldest college, Peterhouse. Perseverance and maturity brought the rank of gate porter, and marriage to Harriet Fordham, a 'bedmaker' (or housekeeper to college inmates) at Trinity College. Harriet's immediate family was settled in the village of Hadstock, near Saffron Walden, but the family name suggests origins planted deeper into the fenlands to the north and east; the village of Fordham lies between Newmarket and Ely, well out into the black earth of the true fen. The whole area, with its intimidating flatness, vast horizons and even vaster skies, tends to be regarded with a kind of superstitious glee by those who have left it behind – and so it is, in a way, with Ronald Searle himself, who is fond of summoning visions of his Searle-Fordham forebears heaving themselves out of the primeval Anglian sludge to populate 'whole villages doped into inarticulateness by poppy tea'.

Once James and Harriet had settled in Cambridge, however, the fens were abandoned. James rose to the rank of head porter (later moving to Emmanuel College), and fathered nine children. William James Searle, one of only two boys, was born in 1896, and proved so keen to join the army that he bluffed his way into uniform at the age of fifteen, and was already a professional soldier, in the Suffolk Regiment, well before the Great War broke out. It was on garrison duty in southern Ireland that he met Nellie Hunt, a girl in service (one of a staff of fourteen tending a family of five) at the castle of Glengarriff, in Bantry Bay. Her employers eventually departed for the Middle East, but Nellie preferred to accept the proposal of the young soldier (he was actually nearly two years younger than she, though perhaps not admitting it at this stage) and return to England. They were married on the second day of 1917, in Cambridge. An outdoor photograph of the family, assembled at James Searle's home in Grafton Street, attests to the un-Cambridge-like clemency of the January weather.

Having fought in several of the worst battles of the war and survived, at the cost of a gassing which permanently damaged his lungs, Sergeant William Searle boasted a longer record of honourable service than most returning men, and might have hoped for the favour of a more comfortable job than the one for which he settled: but at least railway work offered the compensation of concessionary fares, and he stuck at it a few more years,

Left: The wedding day of Nellie and William Searle, Cambridge, 2 January 1917

William Searle wears the uniform of the Suffolk Regiment, with sergeant's stripes. Behind the group stands the outside lavatory of 35 Grafton Street. (Annotations by Ronald Searle.)

while Nellie had the two children. Baby Ronald came first, defying the portent of the pink curtains, but redeeming himself three months later by carrying off a First Class Certificate at the June Baby Show of the parish of St Andrew the Less. If it is true that such awards traditionally disguise a compliment to the mother, then it was not misplaced in this case; for while their photograph confirms that Master Searle was indeed a handsome infant, it chiefly shows that Nellie Searle was quite radiant at this time. Three weeks later, the same church witnessed the baby's christening, his baptismal record bearing the proud family names of Ronald William Fordham Searle. It was the signature 'R. W. F. Searle' that would appear on his first paid graphic work, just fifteen years later.

In April 1922, Ronald's sister, Olive May, was born, completing the family. The round-

Left: Ronald and his parents, undated

The first, apparently spontaneous, signs of a sense of humour are visible.

Far left: Ronald and his mother, Great Yarmouth, 1920

Ronald is aged seven months and well wrapped up against the autumn chills of the East Coast.

Left: Ronald and his father, Great Yarmouth, 10 September 1920

The silent-film Western heroes of the day were William S. Hart and Tom Mix — but the bush-hat has an Australian look.

faced, feline look Ronald presented to the camera as a one-year-old later gave way to something more lugubriously attuned to his experiences, and creations; but Olive has retained it to the present day. The two of them, she believes, shared more of their childhood recreation than is customary for brother and sister, so that they have many memories in common. Just beyond the range of her recall, however, lie the first, strongly sensuous tableaux that registered in her brother's mind. They go back to 1925, or even '24, and a visit, on cheap railway tickets, to their maternal grandparents' home in Pewsey. Grandfather Hunt by now was banned from the road, his Minnie having correctly predicted that in the dawning age of the motor-car, Wiltshire roads would be no place for a veteran cyclist who, besides, was now stone deaf. He made up for the dearth of

*Photograph taken by Ronald Searle in
November 1962. The aspect of the
road remains almost unchanged since
the Twenties, though the locomotives
on the railway tracks opposite the
house are very different today.*

excitement in other ways — like setting fire to his pocket with an ill-extinguished pipe. It is worth recording (without falling helplessly for the theory of comedy as relished misfortune) that this was the first scene of comic misadventure consciously witnessed by Ronald Searle. A more technical kind of visual curiosity was aroused in him when Wiltshire blackberries were mixed with custard, to produce a marbling of nameless colours. And his impressions were, of course, not exclusively visual. No less piercing to the senses was the 'strong, sweet smell of the filled chamber pot' in the Hunts' cottage.

Back in Cambridge, William and Nellie Searle had moved, via a temporary address in Petworth Street, to more settled digs in Devonshire Road, conveniently opposite the railway shunting-yard. The landlady was a Miss Carver, once a reasonably competent amateur artist. Nothing in the way of encouragement passed between her and five-year-old Ronnie, however, as the lady was very old and almost blind. The boy, in any case, needed no coaxing; he had always made drawings. Not even the earliest childhood memory of Ronald Searle went unaccompanied by the certainty that he was drawing at the time. He simply could not recall a time when he did not. Any other necessary stimulus came from St Barnabas' Church School, just round the corner, where he was lettering very creditably at the age of five, and drawing handsomely too, as his first recorded drawing, 'Baa Baa Black Sheep', indicates. What is striking is not just the confidence with which these tricky animals are rendered, but that it has occurred to the boy to present them both in profile *and head-on* — a viewpoint implying a sense of depth and perspective which most young people have to be carefully persuaded to cultivate. 'Ability to draw' is not a phrase used lightly by great professional artists, for whom such an attribute does not begin to come within reach until certain disciplines have been mastered, certain rules understood. But in the realm of instinct, at least, it is clear that by the age of five, Ronald Searle had placed himself emphatically in that category of people who produce a reminiscent outline of reality on the page as if it were a 'natural' thing to do. The process began early whereby he would come to be envied for possessing a pen that was 'an extension of his body'.

What 'Baa Baa Black Sheep' does not show, except to the skilled art-detective, is that

this was a left-handed child, who, had he been forced by misguided disciplinarians into conforming with a right-handed world, might never have developed a fluency in any of the arts of communication, let alone in drawing, where trust between brain and hand cannot bear obstruction. The enlightened Miss Green of St Barnabas' School is to be thanked for taking no more radical role in Ronald Searle's artistic development than this: she left him alone. He naturally was not spared the traditional jibes that used to assail the 'cack-handed'; but the imputation of clumsiness that normally attaches to this unkind term cannot have been endorsed by Ronald's father, who entrusted a vital errand to the tiny child. Every day at lunchtime, he was required to carry William Searle's dinner, between two plates wrapped in a cloth, from the Devonshire Road house to the station – and quickly. William liked his food hotly seasoned, and thermally piping as well. Delay was unthinkable. It was a rather terrible responsibility for one so small.

It is possible that Searle *père* was still on reserve with the army, since Ronald retained vague memories of his going back into uniform during the General Strike of 1926. Changes of uniform certainly did take place around this time, when William Searle left the employ of the London and North-Eastern Railway to join the rapidly expanding corps of Post Office engineers, setting up telephone lines. This was a much more severe physical challenge than had been presented by platform duties, but Mr Searle was ready for it. He had been a regional boxing champion, and his billing, as 'Buller' Searle, still stuck to him among that coterie. He was active in promoting boxing tournaments at the Corn Exchange, along with a punch-drunk sidekick called 'Gammy' Smith, who doubled, in moth-eaten gold braid, as a commissionaire at the Kinema. This was the Saturday-morning haunt of Ronald and Olive, who saw all the silent-cinema serials there, for fourpence, cheering as the projectionist, taking the only available route, climbed the ladder to his box.

At home the memory of a war unknown to the children none the less took time to fade. Certain parts of Sgt Searle's regimental past were ineradicable — most literally his tattoos. Of these he had become ashamed, and he would not voluntarily show them. But since the Searle's bath was a tin tub in front of the fire, it was inevitable that Ronald would glimpse these purchased blemishes, and make an inventory of their strange variety: a Red Indian head with feathers, a sailor with arms folded, a cross with bouquet, an Edwardian dancing girl, a Chinese head with a dagger through it — not the sort of sight likely to diminish the almost occult power which the act of drawing exercised over the young boy's imagination. Of a piece with this private gallery of images were the ritual comradely greetings ('Walla Walla Blacksheep!') Ronald heard his father exchange with old army pals in the street. At home, Sgt Searle had kept his tin helmet and a hat-box full of souvenirs, including daggers, a revolver and clips of .303 ammunition.

With the move to the Post Office, the paternal routine dominated the household in a different way. Now Dad came home for his 'dinner', slept for half an hour, and went out again at 2 p.m. After work, supper was followed by a wash and a shave, whereupon 'Buller' Searle set off for the pub and was not seen again until closing-time. He smoked heavily and drank to match. One night, coming back into a dark house (there being no electric light), he put his head through the glass panel in the kitchen door. Yet it must be said that much of his work was physically miserable. When he was not whipped by the east wind at the top of a telegraph pole, he was waist-deep in a flooded manhole. The whole family dreaded the ring of their own telephone to announce a 'breakdown', which might take the senior Searle away all night, or for days to come. There were no vans to transport him to the work-site in those days, either; he had to cycle, sometimes ten or twelve miles.

Nellie Searle, left at home, would occasionally tire of the children's company and let fly with a Wiltshire curse: 'Damn your eyes on yer!' She was well able to stand up for herself, and not without a certain macabre turn of mind, as Ronald found out when she drew his attention to a minute outcrop of gristle she had discovered inside the lobe of one of his ears. It might come in useful one day, she observed, if ever she had to identify his body — a remark he was probably not meant to remember, though it is hardly surprising that he did. Mrs Searle was also the subject of another domestic mishap, not nearly so amusing as previous ones, perhaps because it occurred at that purposely placid time of day when a mother is settling her children down to sleep. She was adjusting the sash window of the bedroom for the night when the cord broke, slamming the window down on her fingers and jamming them fast against the sill. Her screams, to which pain, shock and helplessness must have contributed, alarmed a passing railwayman, who came in and released her. Both children were terrified by this episode, the memory of which recurred painfully to Ronald for years afterwards.

Miss Carver, the aged landlady, soon died, but the Searles remained at Devonshire Road, paying rent to the heirs of her estate, and standing by while her effects were sold off in an on-the-spot auction remembered by Ronald as 'unseemly'; even the doors were taken off their hinges to accommodate the sale. In later years, Ronald would display a marvellous touch in rendering faintly off-key interiors, and the bric-à-brac of the shabby-genteel. Far from being frightened off by a clutter of *objets*, he revelled in such assemblages – not as outright kitsch, but in a more English way, as failed still lifes: essays in delicately clashing taste. For the moment, though, there was still much to be absorbed in the way of sheer visual information from a wider world, and here the town of Cambridge was notably well stocked. Ronald and Olive became inveterate museum-goers, spending hour after hour traipsing through the hoards of the University's archaeological, anthropological and zoological departments, not to mention the Fitzwilliam with its store of great art. More attractive than Old Masters at this stage, though, were the massed spookiness of Classical Antiquity. Olive remembered Ronald giving her several imaginative frights among the mummies of the Egyptology museum. Anatomy held a particular fascination, for among its exhibits were grotesques which had to be faced as well as seen.

Closer to home, in Mill Road, stood the Free Library where, amid the special odour of the Reading Room – yellowing newsprint and damp customers – Ronald first saw comic art as practised by the elders of *Punch*. At home, the children had *Chips* and *The Rainbow* as their comics; Mum and Dad had the *News of the World*. There were not many books in the house, apart from the odd few William Searle had found on trains and brought home in his portering days. Such pictures as there were on the walls were reproductions of sentimental Victorian favourites, bought with cigarette coupons: 'When Did You Last See Your Father', 'The Boyhood of Raleigh' and the like. Yet behind the door in the entrance hall, in a heavy gilt frame, hung one unusual item which 'dominated the whole of my childhood', Ronald said. It was a black-and-white engraving, entitled 'The Porteous Mob', whose subject was the lynching of Captain John Porteous by the enraged citizens of Edinburgh in 1736. At an earlier, 'legitimate' execution, Porteous had given the order to fire on spectators, several of whom were killed. Himself sentenced to death for this action, he had subsequently been reprieved, but the survivors of his brutality were in no

Left: 'The Porteous Mob' from a painting by James Drummond

In consequence of the lynching of Captain John Porteous in 1736, a fine of £2,000 was levied upon the city of Edinburgh and its Lord Provost removed from office.

mood for mercy: hence the crowded, angry scene which now looked down on Ronald Searle throughout his formative years.

Since children love to superintend their own working replica of the things that fascinate them, it was not long before Ronald was setting up his own museum, in a tiny box-room upstairs. Some exhibits were 'in the family', like the Egyptian beads brought back from the war by Uncle Sid Searle. Others were gathered in by Ronald and Olive themselves, when they walked or cycled out to the far chalk-pits at Cherry Hinton and persuaded the workmen there to hand over such items of geological interest as they might find. Fossils and shells thus formed a durable basis for the collection. Other exhibits came and went. On one occasion, Ronald was given a grapefruit. Never having seen such an item before, he naturally consigned it to his museum. By the time he came to inspect it again, it was a great ball of fluffy grey fungus.

Father, too, made his contributions to the store of wonders. From his telephone excavations he brought clay pipes from the seventeenth and eighteenth centuries, and sometimes birds' eggs, which he would bring him under his cap, on his head. Nothing impressed Ronald so much as 'the unforgettable brilliant blue of the blackbird's egg'. For all the rigours of his work and his assiduous attendance at pubs – he ran a small gymnasium for boxers over one of them – the former 'Buller' Searle was by no means a complete absentee from his children's lives. He taught them to swim, in characteristic style, by taking them to an idle Cambridge stream called 'Snob's', and throwing them in. So enthusiastically did they take to this pastime that Ronald and Olive formed the habit of cycling over to Sheep's Green in Newnham to swim before breakfast, at six or even five o'clock in the morning – and this on schooldays, too. Clearly Ronald had inherited the ex-sergeant's energy and resilience, though not his taste for boxing. A well-timed punch terminated Ronald's one active visit to the boxers' gym, drawing tears which convinced both father and son that here was territory on which they could not meet.

Of the bond between the strong fenman and his sensitive, observing son there was, however, one very eloquent symbol creatively fashioned by the father: not expressly for Ronald, admittedly, though in retrospect it sounds such a very Searle-ish object, both in conception and execution, that one cannot help feeling that his imagination adopted it as intended for his private inspiration. It was a Christmas tree, though quite unlike those stolen from nature (which the Searles, in any case, were unable to afford). At work, William Searle had acquired a two-foot length of main telephone cable, extremely stout and encased in thick lead. Peeling back the lead almost to one end to form a base, he exposed the individual wires, hundreds of them, each one wrapped in coloured paper. These he bent back into the shape of a tree, each of whose branches was a different-coloured wire. It was a marvellous object, rescuing beauty from utility in the most dramatic way, the butterfly sprung from the cocoon. William Searle had demonstrated, indeed, that nature does not have the monopoly of these mad gestures of spontaneous generosity. This improvised decoration, with its fountain of colour and complex, filamented lines, may even have contributed to the formation of Ronald Searle's taste for those very attributes in his own later work. He has always been in demand for celebratory Christmas drawings; but the wiry tree stood not just for festivity, but for the spirit of elaboration in line.

Since dramatic increases in pay were unknown in those years, the Searles' family circumstances changed little. Ronald believed that, even after thirty years' service, his father's wage had crept up to no more than £6 or so per week. They were not poor in the needy sense, but they had no resources. The Micawberish margin of sixpence would make a difference. There were times when the insurance agent would call to collect that very sum on a Saturday and Mrs Searle, unable to pay, would hush the children until he gave up knocking and went away. William Searle had won a silver cup at a boxing tournament, but declined to have it engraved on the grounds that it would be easier to pawn if left unmarked. As with so many Cambridge families, it was lodgers who made up the shortfall in earnings. There were thousands of students to be accommodated, but the Searles at this stage preferred working people like Miss Hammond, a violinist at the Kinema, who lost her job when the talkies came in and made the orchestra redundant. There were always lodgers, and animals too: pet mice and rabbits, and Joey the goldfinch (named after Joseph Grimaldi, the clown) who lived in a cage by the back door. Mr Searle's kit of competitive male-world accoutrements did not lack a racing-hound: it was a lurcher called, with magnificent irrelevance, Doris, and he raced it on Sunday mornings, under the more imposing name of Lemon And White, out on the eastern edge of town, up the Newmarket Road.

Below: 'Mother', 1929

A portrait drawn in Ronald's first set of pastels. Left-handed artists find it more natural to draw a right-facing profile (and, of course, vice versa). Since right-handed artists predominate, the right-facing profile is refreshing in its comparative rarity. Some of Searle's most striking portraits have taken this form. (See Khrushchev and Johnson, p. 134 and Plates.)

For a time there were two grey Persian cats as well; but to catalogue all these pets is to risk spreading the illusion, already too prevalent among British enthusiasts for Searle's work, that he is as smitten by animals as his output of bestialized images might suggest. This has never been the case, except in the sense that the sheer profusion in which they were supplied by an obliging world made them, early on, a familiar and challenging subject for drawing. A representative horse, of a rather lugubrious mien (Searle has specialized in those) was laid on by Mr Wortley, the Searles' former landlord, now just their milkman again. There was also a milkman in the family: Johnnie Alsop, who had married William's sister Beatrice. They lived next to the dairy, in Garlic Row, where Johnnie seldom spoke and Beatrice never stopped talking. She was the nearest to a ready-made comic character in Ronald's life. He remembered her 'fantastic rattling laugh' and her punctiliously barmy habits, like locking the front door, putting the key under the mat outside, and hanging a notice on the doorknob reading 'Key Under Mat'. Contrasting conventionality was to be observed in the Grafton Street home of Beat's sister, Auntie Edie, who would go round dusting the coal left, perennially untouched, in the grate and scuttle. Auntie Edie's front room was used only for Christmas and funerals. Auntie Beat's house smelt reassuringly of warm milk. Family are loved ones, but they are also information. They show startlingly different approaches to the domestication of reality.

Perhaps it was his natural bent, perhaps the autodidactic training of the museum visits, but Ronald had developed quite a sternly categorized consciousness. A revealing note among his family papers records the childhood occasion when he 'saw a policeman sneeze in St Andrew's Street. I didn't think it was possible.' So strong was his system of expectations, his code of appropriateness, that it came as a shock when it broke down. Of course, there are two ways of meeting such a shock: by buttressing those categories, and becoming a moralist; or falling in love with the shock itself, and becoming a humorist — even a fashionable one. At that very time, after all, H. M. Bateman was making a career out of dramatizing the gaffes of 'The Man Who' stepped outside the limits of the social *comme il faut*. The man who never feels he must ultimately decide between humour and moralism is the satirist. By holding the two elements in balance, he shows how the serious man can take in the full horror of the world and still stay sane. This has been one of Ronald Searle's chief tasks in life, second only perhaps to the pursuit — the obsessive pursuit — of line.

A year-ending report from St Barnabas' School in 1929, signed by Miss Green, suggests a period of turbulence overcome. It speaks of 'very much improved' conduct and work done 'much more steadily'. Ronald was sixth in a class of thirty-nine, and his General Knowledge was 'exceptionally good'. The beginnings of studiousness are visible in this, but the most productive of Ronald's studies would always be undertaken on his own initiative. He was now a regular at the library, frequently borrowing five books at a time (anything from *British Butterflies in Colour* to *My Encounters in Zululand*) so that his time was always productively spent. His official education continued to undergo disturbances. After a short period at St Philip's Junior, not far from home in the slightly raffish area called Romsey Town, Ronald progressed in 1930 to the Boys' Central School, a grammar school set at the edge of Parker's Piece, where the Cambridge Rules for sports had been drawn up in the nineteenth century. His first days there brought unwelcome notoriety on account of his baggy shorts, a cut-down pair of his father's working trousers. Such was the ridicule that the Searles had to buy Ronnie his first pair of scarcely affordable 'longs'.

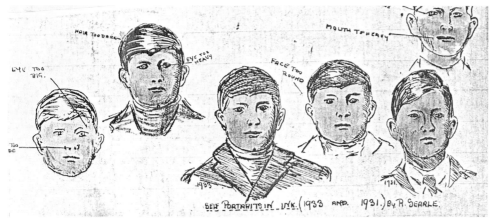

Education thereafter was a more intensive process, but it did not prevent Ronald from adding new extra-curricular activities to his timetable. In particular, it was discovered that he possessed a fine treble voice. Music had never been a major preoccupation in the family, whose listening was restricted to a selection of conventionally jolly records, from military marches to 'The Laughing Policeman' (which might have prepared Ronald for The Sneezing Policeman, come to think of it), played on a Decca gramophone. But Master Searle's soprano timbre found a more celestial repertoire in the choir of St Andrew the Great. Co-opted into that ensemble as an eleven-year-old, Ronald rose dramatically to stardom. In spite of the incurable perplexity that beset him when faced with a sheet of music, his memory for melody was good enough to sustain him in performance, and he came to be much in demand as a soloist, both in Cambridge and in the surrounding villages, where he was sometimes billed as 'The Nightingale of East Anglia'. This talent was almost an embarrassment to Ronald, and in the long run certainly an irrelevance, since by now he was set on becoming either an archaeologist or an artist. Yet he persevered with it, partly for the sake of the pay (7s. 6d. per term, and weddings extra, invaluable for buying art materials), and partly for the fun of the choir outings, which were most ambitiously conceived, involving destinations as far afield as Betws-y-Coed in North Wales, and even Guernsey, which was almost 'abroad'. The Nightingale was sick all the

Above: Olive Searle, 1939

It is the fate of every young lady of Cambridge to be photographed in a punt. 'Not at all artistic', by her own estimation, Olive was shortly to become a calibrator at the Cambridge Instrument Company for the duration of the war.

way over the Channel and all the way back.

There were also hazards attached to the choral life, two of them being the wandering hands of an archetypal paedophile choirmaster, whose weakness ultimately landed him in jail; but Ronald, coming as he did under the more specific protection of the vicar, Rev. Fulford, avoided the worst. For such a staid Victorian conservative, Fulford had some surprisingly 'modern' friends, including Petr Leonidovich Kapitsa, a brilliant physicist who had worked in Cambridge under Rutherford and was currently the deputy head of the Cavendish Magnetic Research Laboratory. Fulford, Kapitsa and Ronald sometimes took tea together, the choirboy deriving tangible benefit from the aquaintanceship in the form of a rich supply of Russian postage stamps – an impressive basis for his new collection. It was none other than Stalin who put an end to this pleasant association. When Kapitsa returned to Moscow on a visit in 1934, he was prevented from returning to England, on the personal orders of the dictator. Both Kapitsa and Searle were destined to spend years of their lives in prison camps, their vicarage tea-party days far behind them.

To his personal collection of collections, Ronald now added books. His library specialized naturally in comic art and the techniques of draughtsmanship. Bookstalls and barrows were plentiful in Cambridge; and though Old David's famous stall was often too heavily besieged by the young academics to whom it chiefly catered, Heffer's Bookshop proved a goldmine. 'Within five years,' Searle has recalled, 'I had accumulated some 500 volumes for a few pennies apiece.' One of his first acquisitions was Spielmann's *History of Punch*, which left its eager young reader with the intention – not merely the ambition – to become a *Punch* cartoonist. Rev. Fulford chipped in with a presentation copy of Arthur Moreland's *Humors of History* (evidently an American edition). The choir money had to go a long way; but then there were other sources of occasional income, such as the long evenings Ronald spent with his mother and Olive, filling cigarette packets, in fives, for slot machines, a labour paid at the rate of one penny per hundred cigarettes. Much better remunerated was the energy Ronald expended in swimming across the Granta river. A senior choir member, one Royston, rewarded him for this feat with a five-shilling piece, the first he had ever seen. Clearly young Ronnie, blue-eyed and earnest, had the knack of appealing to his elders, though it should not be supposed that these were always gentlemen. Among his childhood playmates had been a young plutocrat, Douglas Gillingham, whose family enjoyed the rare luxury of a maid's services. The girl became 'quite attached' to Ronald, and occasionally treated him to a visit to the pictures on her day off. His qualities of seriousness and concentration set him apart from the other boys, and besides – a fact that would never be admitted through the medium of his self-portraits – he was a good-looking fellow.

In some civilizations it is customary to bid farewell to childhood on one's thirteenth birthday. Ronald Searle had an extra reason to do so, because 3 March 1933 was a date which happened to produce one of those once-a-decade conjunctions of identical digits. Ronald used this as the basis of a poem, ten or twelve lines in length, which Rev. Fulford found striking enough to pin to the vestry noticeboard of St Andrew the Great.

> Three Three Thirty-Three
> I am R. Searle of C.

was its opening couplet, marking at least its author's place in the universe. The rest is beyond recall. Perhaps the boy went on to speculate where he might be on 'Four Four Forty-Four'. If he did, he certainly got the wrong answer.

TWO

Co-operation in a University Town
(1933–9)

One square mile of townscape contained most of Ronald Searle's youth. In 1933 his family moved, out of earshot of the railway at least, from Devonshire Road to Number 6 Petersfield, a tall, thin, early-Victorian house facing a small park, the site of a children's recreation ground which still remains. The new address was conveniently close to both Ronald's school and his father's Post Office telephone depot; but the main point of the move was to expand the intake of lodgers. The Searles were suddenly responsible for a much bigger house, while deriving little benefit from it in terms of living-space. Indeed, they were confined mainly to the basement, where the endemic damps of Cambridge bred musty smells, and the windows offered Ronald a view of 'a lot of people's feet'. The profit from 'paying guests' was offset by the laboriously vertical style of living, with Mrs Searle toiling up and down stairs to deliver breakfast trays. Ronald began to feel very sorry for his mother. Petersfield was not a success.

Puberty struck Ronald the same year. His voice survived for a while, but by 1934 the Nightingale of East Anglia had metamorphosed into a corncrake. The soloist himself was delighted by the change. An invitation to join the bass section of the choir was politely declined. Whatever spare time could be reclaimed for drawing was not going to be given away again. Sketching till all hours in the dimly lit interiors of the Petersfield house, Ronald took to supplying his own supplementary desk-top illumination: five candles in a brass candlestick. But not even these sufficed to save his eyes from permanent strain. By the age of fifteen he was wearing spectacles.

His termly reports at the Boys' Central School show a bright beginning (eighth in a class of forty-one) followed by a short slump and a handsome return to form. In reading, he was never less than Very Good, a standard he soon reached consistently in composition, history, drawing – and, as the 'real world' approached, shorthand and book-keeping too. His only Bad grades were registered, early on, in physical exercises. Not even Ronald Searle could be interested in everything. He was hardly inactive, though, for the need to earn money kept him on the move. His life was strictly budgeted, even on a trip to the Central School's summer camp at Looe in Cornwall, as Ronald's 'Camp Book' showed. If a visit to a local tin mine could be afforded, a longer excursion to Land's End could not. He learned very early to look after these matters himself. As the choir income came to an end, he filled in as a butcher's boy (a job his father had briefly done, before his army days), fetching and carrying for old Joe Redfern's shop at half-a-crown for a Saturday morning's work; eight weeks' attendance, in other words, would bring a pound. It was a learning, if not an earning experience. For every congenial sight the butchery business presented, like young Freddie Redfern churning out sausages in the cellar, there were several more chilling ones to take in – like the missing finger of Arthur Prior, the permanent butcher's boy, and the necessary visits to the slaughterhouse, where Ronald would run off and cover his ears while the beef cattle were poleaxed and pigs' throats cut. Such violence, terror and ugliness were themes new to Ronald, but in more collected moments he was engrossed rather than revolted by them. During his habitual prowlings round the Cambridge bookstalls, he had happened on two books, intended for the medical specialist, on surgery and mental deficiency. Both contained pictures which made Ronald feel 'sick and faint', yet he found himself 'horribly transfixed', even by the image of a 'sliced-open face, baring teeth almost to the ear', and he returned to these books again and again. To some personalities, such material might have represented a pornography of distortion; but to Ronald Searle they seem to have come as an inescapable consequence of his innocent liking for all that was grotesque and exaggerated. It was as if he needed to pay his respects to those products of nature which lived beyond the reach of caricature.

In the summer of 1934, the Central School made Ronald a Prefect, and he rose to Head Prefect the following January, just two terms before his formal schooling came to an end. (Further education was financially out of reach.) Suddenly he was facing the Employment Officer, asking her in understandably vague terms to recommend a job where drawing was involved. An architect's office was tried, but the requirements there were far too specialized. Ronald himself, meanwhile, had not the remotest idea of what one did to set up as an independent 'artist'. And so he accepted the job of solicitor's clerk, a virtual office boy, with D. R. W. Stevenson, Squires & Co., of Guildhall Street, Cambridge, at a wage of 7s. 6d. a week. Four years later, at the great age of nineteen, in a local newspaper's readers'-letters feature called 'My First Job', he recalled those beginnings with a vengeful irony – signing his contribution, to spare the feelings of former colleagues, with the name of 'Finklebaum':

Below left: Ronald Searle, early 1935

Photograph taken at the time of Ronald's elevation to Head Prefect of the Central School. Still a fourteen-year-old, he has an unusual gravitas, and a critical blue-eyed gaze.

Below right: St Andrew's Street, Cambridge, summer 1935

A street photographer captures Ronald Searle heading briskly for Peas Hill and his work at the offices of D.R.W. Stevenson, Squires & Co., solicitors. The windowed wall which the horse is passing belongs to Christ's College. Some way further along that side of the street was the shop of Leavis & Co., piano-dealers, run by the family of the Cambridge critic, F. R. Leavis.

So I had succeeded! The job was mine! Another solicitor's clerk was born. Yes, they said, an honourable profession, seeing life in all its aspects — joy, tragedy, the courts. Would I be sent on soul-shattering errands? Would I have revealed to me the intimate secrets of the populace? I ironed my trousers and wondered . . .

The fateful hour approached. Excitedly I hurried off, leaped up the office stairs — and missed! I picked myself up with dignity (was I not a member of the legal profession?), mounted calmly the remainder, entered the hallowed sanctuary and waited . . .

Finklebaum! tie these bundles. Finklebaum! make the tea. Finklebaum! stamp these letters. (It would have to be Jubilee Year — was my tongue sore!)

Yes — I soon departed, too much red tape for me, figuratively and literally — and the times I got tied up in it . . .

The suggestion that this departure was voluntary is misleading, however. In spite of enjoying the kindly protection of the office accountant, later Mrs Vera Piqué (with whom he was still corresponding in 1990), 'Finklebaum' was fired. The immediate cause was his request for an advance on his wages to pay for evening-classes at the Cambridge Art School, though other offences were taken into consideration. It did not count in Searle's favour that he had spent part of his office time 'scribbling', and on fine legal paper, some of it attached to briefs. The job had lasted two months.

The Art School classes were a vital goal. All the tuition Ronald had so far received had come from John Nicholson, art master of the Central School. But the evening course demanded an enrolment fee of 7s. 6d. per term, which the prospective student could not now afford. There were arguments between his parents over what contribution they might see fit to make. Somehow the money was scraped together in time, and Ronald began formal art studies in the still-life class in mid-September 1935. For a few uncomfortable weeks he still had no income to call his own. Then, in October, the problem was suddenly vanquished twice over. Ronald secured a job as a parcel-packer with the Cambridge Co-operative Society, at their large premises in Burleigh Street; this paid 12s. 6d. a week. At the same moment, Sid Moon, cartoonist of the *Cambridge Daily News*, was leaving to join the *Sunday Dispatch* in London. In a moment of wild teenage self-assurance and opportunism, fifteen-year-old Ronald Searle decided that he was the man to replace Moon. He drew a cartoon of the locally topical type Moon had been supplying to the Saturday paper's 'Table Talk' page, and dropped it through the Editor's letterbox — in Searle's recollection, without further proof of his talents. From the Editor's reply, however, it is apparent that some small portfolio of other possibilities had also been tendered.

Dear Mr Searle,

Thanks for your letter and the cartoon, which strikes me as quite promising, though it would need a little alteration.

If you could turn out others of the same sort we might be able to use them from time to time and pay, say, at the rate of half a guinea a time.

Drawing cartoons is, of course, not a whole time job with us. Mr Moon did work of another kind for us and his place was filled immediately he went.

You might come to see me when you are free — early in the week for preference. When you do you can take back the drawings you left.

Yours faithfully,
Morley Stuart.

The jackpot had been resoundingly hit. To begin with, half a guinea, or 10s. 6d., was considerably more than the solicitor's office had been paying for a week's work. Then again, Morley Stuart proved rather better than his word. His offer of more work 'from time to time' was understated. The *Cambridge Daily News* (or *C.D.N.*, as both staff and readers called it) went ahead and printed the cartoon delivered on spec; it appeared on Saturday, 26 October 1935, as cartoon number one in a weekly series which, broken only by holidays, finally expired at number 195. Searle was a 'resident' cartoonist, and under an editor who was as kindly as he was venturesome. At the point of delivery, it was

Left: 'Night Convoy', early spring 1941

Members of the 287th Field Company R.E. snatching a doze on night manoeuvres 'somewhere in Scotland'. Realized in ink, wash and touches of gouache.

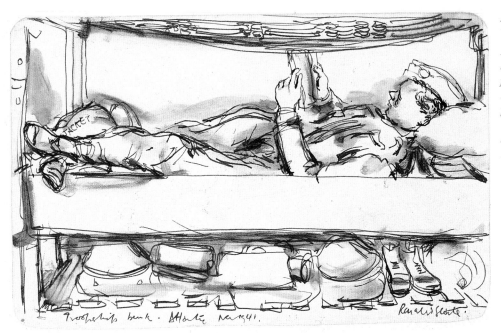

Left: 'Troopship bunk', November 1941

Drawn on board HMT Sobieski. Searle became a specialist in recumbent figures during 1940–1; but a short time after this drawing was made, all personnel were required to set about blancoing every item of equipment aboard. Two days out from Halifax, Nova Scotia, it kept the men busy.

Changi Gaol, Singapore – Ronald Searle 1944

Above: Changi Gaol, Singapore, 1944

A very solid edifice, built by the British in 1936, and dominated by its administration tower. Guard-posts were set into all the corners of the gaol, which could be entered only by the twin-domed gate (at right). In the mid-Fifties, Searle sent a picture to be hung in the chapel there. 'We only wish Mr Searle could make a trip out here to Singapore and visit the chapel,' said a letter of thanks. 'I'm sure he'd be pleased with the setting for his work.'

Right: Exile cartoon, Changi Gaol, Singapore, Christmas 1944

A cartoon from The Exile, *satirizing the continuing officiousness of the British administration. The colours used were probably supplied by Kyohara (Han Do Chin). Used forty-five years later as a Christmas card by the Imperial War Museum.*

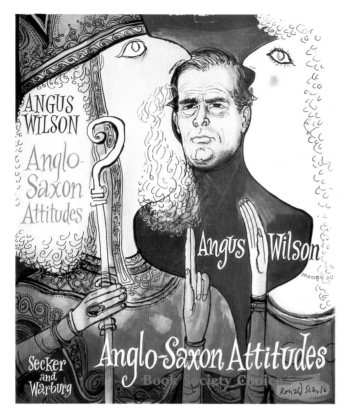

PETER WEST says, 'Watch out for the Aussies.' see p. 14

Above left: Book-jacket for *Anglo-Saxon Attitudes* by Angus Wilson, London 1956

One of Searle's wittiest designs, and a most appropriate setting for the 'medieval' stylized hands he often favoured. No complete record exists of the many jackets — possibly fifty — designed by Searle while in England. This is perhaps the one most commonly found nowadays in second-hand bookshops.

Left: Young Elizabethan. Cover, June 1956

Above right: Merry England, etc. Cover, London, 1956

A drawing developed from 'May I Have the Pleasure?', Punch, 21 December 1955 — a double-page spread on the accommodations of the elderly British bourgeoisie to the unusual demands of dancing.

Right: Cover for Graphis No. 129, 1967

The Swiss-based, trilingual magazine of applied art had regularly appraised Searle's work since 1948. He takes a literal cue here from the Greek graphein, to write. In his exteriors, Searle seldom spurns the chance to include observed graffitti.

Opposite: 'Picasso Birthday Number', *Punch* cover, 24 October 1954

Punch covers were still struggling to free themselves from the old Victorian formula established in the very beginning by Richard Doyle, when Searle, the magazine's resident Picasso expert, produced this interpretation – which still retains, however, the teeth-baring qualities of the old, caustic Mr Punch. This is one of the most exuberant covers *Punch* has ever had, though a learned one in the quality of its parody. Searle produced another Picasso cover for *Punch*, published on 29 June 1960.

Left: Punch cover, 23 October 1957

Featuring Mr Punch as a New York cop. 'I went down to Wall Street– Broadway this afternoon and took some pictures for that possible Royal Visit cover,' wrote Searle to Russell Brockbank on 19 May 1957. 'I'll get back there again next week and see how it looks with some people in it. Perhaps I can even persuade them to throw out some specimen ticker-tape.' In the event, the tape proved more useful to the design than the people.

Left: From *Those Magnificent Men in Their Flying Machines,* 1965

Searle produced the animation sequences from the film, and painted 'stills' which were arranged into an art portfolio. It is interesting that Searle's bird-man, having reached here an ignominious end to his flying career, has acquired the somewhat stupefied gaze Searle commonly applies to birds themselves.

Ronald Searle
Casablanca Jan 1965

actually Olive Searle who saw more of Mr Stuart, for Ronald's habit was to come home from the Co-op, work through Friday night on his cartoon, and go to bed in the morning hours, leaving Olive to carry the finished original to the *C.D.N.* offices. For this she was awarded the odd sixpence in the half-guinea fee. From the remaining 10s., Ronald paid 'a bit for the family' and spent the rest on drawing materials, books and recreation.

During a June heatwave in 1936 — a few weeks after the death of Grandfather James Searle, the college porter, at the age of seventy-three — the signature of 'Ronald W. F. Searle' made its appearance. His style remained strongly Bateman-based, with irruptions from Low when a political caricature of Stanley Baldwin was required, or an explosive 'Gad, Sir!' from a red-faced diehard. Through the summer, when news was short and the 'undergrads' were out of town, the *C.D.N.* ran letter-writing competitions ('If I were Dictator of Cambridge' etc) which Searle was employed to illustrate, his first work of that kind. During this period, the paper also ran advertisements for International Stores, using drawings by W. Heath Robinson, who signed his name in capitals, stacked in three rows. It may have been this that persuaded Searle to make another emendation to his own signature. From late November, he became for the first time simply 'Ronald Searle', in two stacked rows of capitals. The signature still had decades of extraordinary distortions to pass through (finally partaking of Searle's drawing style itself); but at least the rudiments were there, in place — and in time for the Abdication Crisis of December 1936, in case his comments were needed. They were not. As usual, Searle prudently restricted himself to the Christmas preliminaries ('The turkeys have lost all hope'). Still short of his seventeenth birthday, he may even have felt for a moment that the world was passing him by, for in his New Year cartoon, 'Great Expectations', he looked forward to a swelling of his fan-mail ('Two letters, sir — that doubles last year's total!').

Work at the Co-op, all this time, represented no more than a bill-paying continuum. Soon perceived to be worthy of better things than parcel-packing, Ronald was promoted to the Mutuality Department, where Co-op members could arrange a kind of credit. Issued a certificate enabling them to make a major purchase, such as a suit, they were then required to pay off the debt in instalments to the Mutuality men, who toured the district with their registers. One of Searle's jobs was to copy their returns into the main ledger. More disconcerting was the task of manning the discreet counter, screened off from public view, where helpless defaulters would come and explain themselves. Having seen his mother on the wrong end of this process, Ronald found these interviews distressing, particularly when dealing with the rural poor from outlying villages who really had no way out of their difficulty. No very explicit political indignation was attached to these feelings. The elder Searles were politically active in that they supported Labour meetings and functions, where William Searle was a staunch member of the Post Office union. But he was no radical; like many *Daily Mirror* readers of the time, he combined working-class solidarity with the most conservative faith in the nation's traditional institutions. Ronald could add to this a lively awareness of agitations within the town over Italy's annexation of Abyssinia, and the civil war in Spain; he even met one of the young Communist martyrs of that conflict, the poet John Cornford, and saw him address a crowd on Parker's Piece. But Ronald's political self remained ill-defined: 'informed, perhaps, but *unformed*'.

There were rather a lot of other kinds of spectacle to engage a young man's attention. The opening of the new Regal Cinema in April 1937 made available, by cartoonist Searle's mischievous reckoning, 'our 11th place of entertainment (not including the Council Chamber)'. There were weeks when there was too much theatre going on for a single

Opposite: 'Twenty-seven women in one street', Casablanca, January 1965

Captioned 'Vingt-sept femmes dans une rue' in Searle's exhibition at the Bibliothèque Nationale, this scene was painted for Holiday *magazine. It is one of the most brilliant and 'free' of Searle's exteriors, beautiful in spite of the limited appeal of its topographical components.*

enthusiast to see, as another cartoon noted. Special events included Cambridge's first Press Ball ('gay crowd some 300 strong'), where an original cartoon by Sid Moon 'realised more than £1 when offered at auction'. The following week, cartoonist Searle attended a battle of ten dance bands at the Guildhall, where his on-the-spot caricature of Henry Hall's drummer. George Elrick, brought the desired response ('Mr Elrick wants me to send the original of this up to the BBC'). By May, the town's Coronation decorations were in place, and many college buildings, including King's College Chapel, were floodlit. Such was the air of jollity in the town that its Saturday graphic commentator was moved to pay it tribute. 'Although critics are at work on Cambridge,' ran his text, 'for its "number of bicycles and effeminate bicycle baskets", our "self-satisfied attitude" and "depressing" climate and "narrow streets" – it ISN'T SUCH A BAD PLACE AFTER ALL.'

For eight months, the *C.D.N.* cartoons were signed 'R. W. F. Searle'. 'They were dreadful,' he said of them later, in a characteristically accepting tone, 'but they taught me how to draw for reproduction.' It is true that there is nothing of the familiar Searle in them at all, as they are very heavily indebted to the cartoon style of H. M. Bateman (who sometimes appeared in the same paper's pages as the illustrator of advertisements for A.C. Spark Plugs and Kensitas cigarettes). Verbally there was much golly-gosh exclamation-mark humour of the kind perpetrated by Finklebaum in his letter. But these weekly appearances were certainly no less engaging than those of his predecessor, Moon, and there were times when the new man's youth worked positively in his favour. All manner of local topics which might have evoked a jaded response from a veteran were met with ebullience by R. W. F. Searle, to whom much of the town's normal business came as news. In his early weeks, he tackled such subjects of local controversy as Cambridge's new and unlovely Guildhall; the startling new system of electric lights in the streets; automatic vending-machines for postage stamps; and (a hardy annual) the town's preparations for Christmas. Mid-November also saw a General Election, in the aftermath of which Searle produced a House of Commons tableau where a crop of slightly uncertain political caricatures nevertheless show that the artist had made himself familiar with the work of David Low. Generally speaking, Morley Stuart seems to have advised Searle to stick to the local scene. The 'alterations' he had warned about generally concerned spelling, a department in which young Searle's often extensive captions tended to go awry.

The run of Saturday Searles from 1935 to 1939 confirms that Cambridge life in those days moved very much to the rhythms of the University's year. 'The Undergrads are back', in one version or another, recurred as a suitable topic for the beginning of every term, when 'long-suffering landladies begin to long-suffer' (the Searles knew all about that). In spite of his aversion to active participation in games, Ronald kept up with most University sports, particularly rowing, and also town-based events like billiards tournaments and the inevitable boxing. Early in 1936, he began to include in the surveyed scene a figure representing himself – a bearded youth who eventually assumed the classical panoply of The Artist, with sandals, long hair and a battered hat. None of this costume was actually affected by Searle at the time, though the sandals were eventually acquired and the beard, years later, became a permanent feature. Nor were his opinions on art yet as advanced as such an outfit might suggest. When an exhibition of Abstract Art visited the Gordon Fraser Gallery in 1936, the *C.D.N.* reviewer was sceptical about the public's chances of experiencing enjoyment, though the terms of the anonymous complaint – 'scarcely one picture that they can interpret, scarcely one piece of sculpture that conveys a set and easy idea' – do rather condemn themselves. Searle, however, felt similarly baffled.

'Your humble scribe felt something like *this* after visiting the Abstract Art exhibition,' he wrote in his cartoon – 'this' being a Picassoesque rearrangement of the human features. 'Why can't they introduce a bit of fun into it?' the cartoonist concluded. At least he had taken his own advice.

The autumn witnessed an increase in his contributions to the sum of local pleasure. As a member of the newly-formed Students' Sketch Club, he exhibited in a competition show at the Cambridge Technical School, and won Second Prize for a 'Head from Life', one of

Left: Cambridge Anglo-American Society poster, 1938

Recruitment propaganda parodying a durable strain in British advertising, drawn at the invitation of Gershon Ellenbogen, who kindly supplied the original, and who can be seen in the sherry-party frame, carrying a folder marked 'G.E.' The 'Dot' was the Dorothy Tea-room (and ballroom) in central Cambridge.

the 'two strongest sections' according to a *C.D.N.* review. Arts School staff did the judging, 'with the addition of Madame Raverat'. Gwen Raverat, still a familiar name to succeeding Cambridge generations through her autobiographical *Period Piece*, was a granddaughter of Charles Darwin and, Searle found, 'a marvellous teacher'. He had now graduated into the evening life-class, where he 'painfully shaded my way through several years of floppy-breasted nudes with blue toes and purple legs'. The notorious east winds of the fenland, blowing in unobstructed from Russia, made a misery of the models' evening stint.

Ronald himself took on yet more after-hours activity when he co-produced a variety and sketch show in Houghton Hall. Entitled *Charivaria* ('from the familiar *Punch* feature'), the spectacle presented a large cast of previously unknown artistes and included no fewer than five 'short plays'. 'The fact that the producer, Mr Ronald Searle, appeared in all, is sufficient reason for overlooking two or three shortcomings in production,' purred the *C.D.N.* The chosen material was ambitious: one of the playlets, *If Men Played Cards As Women Do*, was a George S. Kaufman piece first performed in one of Irving Berlin's New York revues. The only real blot on the evening seems to have been the audience turn-out, 'appreciative but not very large'.

No such problem was encountered a week before Christmas when Ronald combined his new performing career with his graphic expertise in front of a huge audience of children – the 'Robins Club', organized by the *C.D.N.* A packed and noisy house at the Theatre Cinema saw his debut as a 'lightning artist'. 'His clever portraits, executed in a few seconds, were, in the overheard words of one of his young audience, "jolly good". Favourites such as Mickey and Minnie Mouse and Laurel and Hardy were recognized almost as soon as he put charcoal to paper.' Searle's energy was prodigious. Still not eighteen, he was an evening-class student with a full-time job; a weekly contributor to a newspaper; an amateur theatrical producer, and a performer in two genres. He was also the Hon. Secretary of the Central Old Boys' Dramatic Society, as was revealed the following March when Searle and his close friend Stuart Ludman took to the stage again in *Not What They Seem!*, a one-act play. Ronald took the part of Bishop Morley ('Freezy') Winterbottom, whose 'knowing laugh', it was reported, 'added much to the humour of the play'.

As if all that were not enough, Ronald had also been drawn into University activities through the students' leading magazine, *The Granta*. The respectable literary tradition of this publication had seldom been matched by its graphic embellishments, so it was inevitable that an eager and ambitious local artist would be courted by the student editors. 'After all,' recalled the historian Eric Hobsbawm, who was on the staff at the time, 'most of the undergraduates who *wrote* in *Granta* could have been replaced by a score of others without noticing much difference, but who could have guaranteed another artist as gifted as Ronald?' Socially, *Granta* existed, as Hobsbawm remembered it, 'only in that room above the Market Square, where we brought in our copy, or edited, distributed books for review, cinema passes etc. and, no doubt, hung around chatting and joking and looking down on the market and Great St Mary's. I can't even remember whether we had tea up there. [Ronald recalled Orange Pekoe tea.] Outside we went our own ways, though we did form a network of friendships within our particular colleges, or within (in some cases) the Socialist Club and Communist Party, within the academic faculty. Ronald obviously didn't share these potential overlaps.' But he did see some of the territory on which they occurred, for he remembered Hobsbawm in particular encouraging him to dress up in a

Left: Pseudo-*Punch* cartoon, *Granta*, 8 June 1938

Drawn as part of a parody-extravaganza, 'The Seven Ages of Journalism'. Several of Punch's *stalwart contributors of drawing-room humour in pen-and-ink were much of a muchness in style; Searle here was probably inspired by Lewis Baumer.*

CHILD (who has just come in from the garden): 'What's for tea?'
MOTHER (who dislikes having the little horror ask questions): 'Tea should be
    seen and not heard.'

borrowed gown and sneak into meetings reserved for University members *in statu pupillari* – visits without which Ronald could not have made the sketches on which his caricatures of visiting luminaries depended.

He made his first *Granta* appearances late in 1936, sent in occasional contributions through the following year, and blossomed in 1938 with confident caricatures of touring artistes (e.g. 'Kreisler at the Regal') and guest speakers like Vaughan Williams and Dorothy L. Sayers. Searle's editorial colleagues registered, in print, a certain surprise at his competence ('Vic Oliver looks quite like this'), as well they might, since the rest of the magazine's graphic contributions were painfully clumsy. Soon, Searle was unleashed to produce a bulky parody-feature, 'The Seven Ages of Journalism', which ranged from a full-page spoof of *Tiger Tim's Weekly* to a pen-and-ink version of the etched look of a *Punch* cartoon. The intent of *Granta* was chiefly to amuse: 'lighthearted and, I'm sorry to say, a bit *Punchy*', Eric Hobsbawm called it, 'only we tried to top it up a bit with the Marx Bros and a touch of surrealism – sort of remote anticipations of the Goon Show'. Ronald himself was perfectly in tune with these aims, and quite well equipped to fulfil them in terms of visual reference, since his book-buying programme had greatly intensified. Recent purchases included David Low's *Ye Madde Designer*, an invaluable how-to-do-it for the young caricaturist; Steven Spurrier's *Illustration: Its Practice in Line and Wash*; an *Art Students' Anatomy*; and *Caricatures of Today*, a special edition of *The Studio* expanded to book-length to provide a conspectus of stylistic possibilities, including a good many that were not contemporary at all but historical: Hogarth, Daumier and Phil May; Edward Lear, Rowlandson and Toulouse-Lautrec. For the last two, especially, Ronald developed a profound admiration. His acquisition of Beaumont's *Design for the Ballet* reflected a new interest, nurtured by the Cambridge visits of the Kurt Jooss Ballet Company. Jooss was another caricatural victim; the drawing was one of two Searles exhibited in the 63rd Annual Exhibition of the Cambridge Drawing Society in May 1938. 'Bold and well-executed,' judged the *C.D.N.*, whose reviewers Ronald was still keeping busy. In April he had repeated his lightning-sketch art in a Festival Theatre revue, this time for an adult audience, with 'famous political and screen characters' as his subjects, and 'very "arty" make-up' as his disguise. The chance to present himself as The Artist still came only in fun and fantasy.

At the end of May, the *Cambridge Daily News* celebrated fifty years in business, and Morley Stuart, who as 'Robin Goodfellow' had occupied the 'Table Talk' pages for twenty of those years, devoted a few words to the two draughtsmen who had shared his space: Sid Moon, who had left Cambridge 'for the more exciting life of Fleet St, and our present contributor Ronald Searle, a promising young artist who, I am sure, will make his mark in years to come'. Young Searle, for his own part, was unwilling to wait so long. Already some of his holiday time was being spent at his Aunt Ivy's house in Bromley, Kent, from which base he made repeated sorties into the London newspaper world, touring the editorial offices with his portfolio. The applicant was kindly received everywhere, but there was nothing doing. Two years would pass before these efforts yielded a single opportunity.

The great leap forward that did occur came not in the sphere of professional practice, but of training. On 15 June 1938 Ronald received a letter which justified all the hours put in at evening-classes, and liberated him on the spot from the cares of the Mutuality Department. It came from the Secretary of the Cambridge Education Committee:

Dear Sir,

The Committee have considered the results of your recent examination at the Cambridge Technical School, and I am directed to inform you that it has been decided to award you an Art Scholarship tenable at the School from September 1938. The Scholarship will consist of free tuition, and will, in the first instance, be for a period of one year.

This message represented nothing less than the chance to be a full-time artist. Searle immediately arranged to leave the Co-op in early August. His last weeks there included the annual ritual of the office party, this time to Southend. Some 400 employees would charter a train and disappear for the day – by the end of which, on the return journey, all the young men would be getting very pally with the girls, everyone riotous in paper hats. The following morning at the office, they would all behave as if they had never seen one another before. It was an aspect of the mercantile, corporate temperament that Ronald always found strange. He was not sorry to forgo the chance to study it further.

The exhilaration of departure could be seen in his *C.D.N.* cartoon of 6 August, datelined 'Walton-on-the-Snozzle, many miles away'. 'We have donned our khaki shorts,' his text disclosed, 'and are attempting a little solitude under canvas. Apart from a wretched beast which insists that we are some relation [this was a bearded goat] we haven't a care in the jolly old world – everything is just "OK" and … alright, alright, we know we've got to come back sometime – but until then, happy holidays.' This was not a momentary joy. It persisted throughout Ronald's time at the School of Art: 'Lautrec was more precocious, but he was never as happy as I was then,' he later wrote. Sadly, though, the beginnings of this happiness coincided with the makings of its end. Ronald's studies in General Drawing began on 15 September 1938. It was the day Neville Chamberlain arrived in Germany to meet Hitler at Berchtesgaden and to be told of the Führer's determination to annex the Sudetenland. In Cambridge, Civil Defence exercises were already under way.

That same week, at another exhibition of work by the School of Art Sketch Club, judged as ever by Gwen Raverat, Ronald won a prize with each of his three entries. His performance in Figure Composition, Portrait and Sheet of Studies was rivalled only by Miss Beryl Pickering, one of his new fellow-students, who also took three prizes. This encouragement was welcome, and Ronald already realized that he would be needing it. In point of academic discipline and rigour, the School he had joined was a hard one. Its Head was George Stevenson, whose responsibilities extended from Drawing and Design to Etching and Bookbinding. Miss G. ('Gee') Horsley, still living in Cambridge in 1990, supervised many crafts, like Embroidery and Fabric Printing, but also taught History of Costume, Calligraphy, and Perspective, a discipline whose orthodoxies at first caused Ronald more trouble than he found elsewhere. But the dominant figure in his training was J. G. Hookham, a former Ross Scholar of the Slade School, whose field took in Drawing and Painting from Life, Modelling, and Anatomy. John Hookham, being of the Henry Tonks school, was an extremely tough drawing-master, the more so because he was a man of few words and considerable patience. 'He would sit beside you as you worked for half an hour,' Searle remembered, 'and then *plunge*. Misery!' Yet Ronald's progress was excellent. His first termly report stated him to be 'living fully up to our expectations', with 'a marked improvement in drawing' over the term, and even a recent upturn in the perspective department ('more perception of the difficulties in each problem').

The social mix at the School of Art reversed the statistical pattern then prevailing in Cambridge University. The young men in Hookham's life-class were outnumbered ten to one by the women, some of whom were well-connected in intellectual and artistic life: Peggy Raven, daughter of the Cambridge theologian (and Vice-Chancellor) Canon Raven; Renate Hirsch, whose father owned the Hirsch Collection of music, later acquired by the British Museum; Joan Brock, daughter of the famous illustrator H. M. Brock; Ann Medley, sister of the painter Robert Medley; and Désirée Meyler, who lived at the Observatory because her sister was married to the man who would become the Astronomer Royal. In this large and formidable class, Bernard Lucas, Philip Evett and Ronald Searle were the only representatives of their sex, a position by no means disadvantageous to their social lives, though potentially disruptive of their studies. It was all very well doing daily battle with the problem of drawing the human figure, Searle once wrote, 'but surrounded as we were with delectable student examples, the problem frequently resolved itself in mass desertion of the studio to take the girls on the river'.

Such temptations no doubt presented themselves later, in spring; nobody in his right mind went on the Cam in winter, and Ronald had much else to be getting on with. In December, the Searles moved on again, from the damps and cramps of Petersfield to a much newer house in the almost adjoining Collier Road – the very street where the 'cluttered rooms' of the Art School were. It was Ronald's mother, defeated at last by the Petersfield stairs and her chronic asthma, who precipitated the move. Her son welcomed it. Looking back on the Petersfield years, he realized he had hated the student-lodgers' presence in the house: the way they took the best rooms, cramming the family into the shadows below; the way his mother waited on them; the embarrassing scenes at the beginnings and ends of terms when well-off and over-polite parents would leave or collect their sons, sometimes offering to shower the Searles with compensatory cast-offs as they went. Above all, Ronald hated the students to be taken to his room to see his drawings. If he had to perform, it would be on stage where he controlled the process: but an invasion of his private territory was unbearable to him. 'We never seemed to be private.' These feelings already went deep and, before long, circumstances would ensure that they went deeper still. It was many years before Ronald would be able to arrange his life in such a way as to assuage them. But Collier Road at least brought technological advances, in the form of electric light and a bathroom – the first time the Searles had enjoyed the benefit of either. The days of trooping to the public baths in Gwydir Street were over, as was the danger of falling into a trench outside one's front door. Petersfield, as Searle pointed out in an almost manically jovial letter to his own newspaper, had become very noisy, as it was a favourite site for testing prototype Civil Defence measures. During the Munich crisis of late September 1938, many Cambridge people were reported 'busy digging trenches in their gardens and building dug-outs'. Wholesale distribution of gas-masks had been authorized, and the *C.D.N.* cartoonist suggested some picturesque alternative uses for them.

Searle's career as a stage performer was in abeyance, but new responsibilities rushed in to fill the available moments. A theatrical connection was maintained by his occasional work as a programme-illustrator for the new Arts Theatre. A report on the Christmas Party of the Sketch Club revealed him to have assumed the Treasurership. ('The president of the club is Mrs G. Raverat, a woodcut artiste,' burbled the *C.D.N.*) There were even ventures in sign-writing, that most commercial of arts. Coad's, the drapers, asked Ronald to paint their Christmas sign. Miller's, the town's best-known music shop, engaged him for a much more specialized task, the painting of one of their new vans. Ronald tried hard to extract the necessary trade secrets from a local professional, but found this individual implacably uncommunicative. To release any information at all would be to set up a rival in trade. So Ronald improvised his way through the job, with results that left the client 'furious'. Rarely thereafter did Searle accept a job where individuality of expression could prove an impediment to success.

The New Year of 1939 brought the Golden Jubilee of *Granta*, a new term at the Art School, and in March a *mensis mirabilis* for Ronald, with two exhibitions, a first appearance

Right: Cambridge Daily News
cartoon, 3 December 1938

Number 159 in the series, and a return by Searle to a theme he had first broached eight weeks previously, in the immediate aftermath of the Munich crisis. General distribution of gas masks had begun in Cambridge on 28 September. The habit of partitioning off one cartoon idea in the bottom right-hand corner of a space was a common one with David Low.

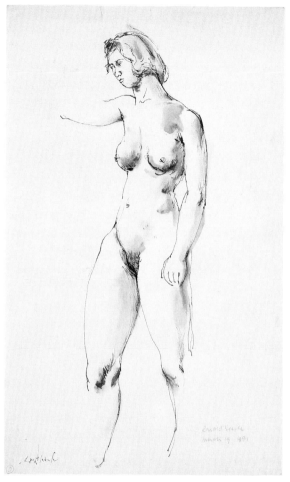 

between hard covers, and a gratifying endorsement from his University friends. *Granta* reprinted a generous selection of previous Searle contributions, with the explanation that 'It is not often that this happens. We do so only when we feel we have a really *good* artist ... we have no hesitation in saying that Ronald Searle ... has been one the most successful of *Granta* draughtsmen since he joined the staff at the beginning of 1937.' No mention was made of the impending publication of a book – but then *Granta* men were hardly likely to number among the most eager readers of *Co-operation in a University Town* by W. Henry Brown. Indeed, the book will never be sought after for its narrative's sake, except by historians of the Co-operative movement, like Brown himself, who had toured the country producing such volumes as *Liverpool's 100 Years of Co-operation* and *The Silken Glow of Macclesfield*. There was little excitement for Ronald in drawing odd rural branches of the organization that had recently employed him, and Morley Stuart sensibly restricted his *C.D.N.* appraisal to the descriptive, e.g. 'the chapters are short and readable'. Nevertheless, it was the first time a reviewer could say that there were 'drawings by Ronald Searle to brighten the pages', and that fact alone has made the book a collector's item.

At the time of its publication, a Cambridge Artists' Exhibition was open at Hensher's Gallery, Peas Hill, within a few yards of the solicitors' office of Stevenson, Squires. The Searles now on view came in a range of styles, though celebrity portraits (George Bernard Shaw, Kurt Jooss, Hannen Swaffer) attracted most attention. For *C.D.N.* readers there was an added incentive to attend: 'Some visitors to the exhibition, by the way, may recognise

Above: Life-class drawings, Cambridge 1939

'At the Cambridge Art School it was drummed into us that we should not move, eat, drink or sleep without a sketchbook in the hand. Consequently the habit of looking and drawing became as natural as breathing.' (Ronald Searle, The Association of Illustrators Newsletter, January/February 1977.)

Above: Winston Churchill, 1939

On-the-spot sketch by Searle at the Guildhall, Cambridge, May 1939, signed by Churchill. The future Prime Minister had addressed a huge meeting of undergraduates at the Corn Exchange on 20 May and returned within days to speak to the townspeople. His curious pose, with hands bunched behind lapels, was as depicted.

themselves pictured among Mr Searle's works, for some of his portraits he has developed from sketches of people he has noticed in Cambridge streets, people who have been all unconscious that they have been used as models.' Ronald's sketchbook now accompanied him everywhere, a habit he recommended in after years to a young audience: 'You've got to give yourself some reserve ... I noted down all the odd little bits I saw – people sitting in buses, sleeves, trees, anything that I wanted to jot down. And though I didn't refer to them, I found they gradually crept into my drawings and gave them a wider basis and a little more personality.' Evidently the practice was already paying off, because at the close of the Hensher's exhibition, many of the Searle items were transferred to Gordon Fraser's Gallery for two more weeks (a future friend in the publishing world, Tony Godwin, was an assistant there). It was virtually a one-man show – his first – apart from three paintings by his friend Janet Curtis, who had just given him Gertrude Stein's *Picasso* for his birthday. Ronald's earlier scepticism in the face of modern art had by now been quite dispelled. Picasso was a particular hero, the foremost among the living ones, and even tantalizingly within reach: a local gallery was offering a pen drawing of Picasso's for a fraction under £10. Ronald could not raise the cash.

His Easter Saturday cartoon that year showed an egg breaking open to reveal a copy of the *C.D.N.* bearing the headline 'Peace in Europe'. As a wish passed on to readers it was considerate, but the political realities now made optimism difficult to sustain. One did not need to be markedly left-wing to see the inevitability, and approve the rightness, of an anti-Hitler war. 'Everybody, I suppose, was against Hitler and Chamberlain and the Spanish Republic,' Eric Hobsbawm has said of his generation, 'but that was the 1937–9 equivalent of reading the *Guardian*.' Measured on that scale, Ronald Searle was certainly the *Guardian*-reading type. He had seen the arrival of the refugee Basque children in Cambridge, and felt their fear. Very soon, the Searles themselves would have a refugee lodger in the house: Dr Gabriele Rabel, a strange and prematurely decrepit philosopher of science, exiled from Austria where she had been attached to the Ministry of Culture. Fat and waddling, with her short grey hair and slightly sour smell, Dr Rabel lived half-blind among a prodigious clutter of papers and domestic overspill, topped off by an ancient typewriter. What she lacked in immediate attractiveness, however, was made up in mystery and a vague sense of importance. She was the European drama literally brought home to the Searles.

Aware as they were of the likelihoods of the coming months, Ronald and his friends determined to secure for themselves as advantageous a start as they could. By volunteering, they had heard, one could choose one's immediate destination, if not one's destiny, in the armed forces. Ronald, Stuart Ludman and their pals decided accordingly to respond to the recruiting appeal that was launched in Cambridge in April 1939. Ronald had evidently researched the matter by 22 April, as he reported the advertised pleasures of joining-up in his cartoon: 'one drill a week ... pay ... 15 days' free camp ... annual bounty ... don't all rush at once!' A specific advantage of the Royal Engineers, he noted, was that they didn't have to walk. So on the following Friday Ronald Searle duly enlisted in the Territorial Army, registering with the Royal Engineers as Architectural Draughtsman AII. He was to carry his number, 2072249, through some of the worst experiences available to Britishers in this century.

Sapper Searle's description on enlistment ran: 'Height: 5'9''. Weight: 133lbs. Max. Chest: 35''. Complexion: Fresh. Eyes: Blue. Hair: Dark Brown.' His father would have classified him as a lightweight, one of many. The recruiting display 'ladders', hung outside the old

Post Office, showed a healthy intake for the Engineers, the Cambridgeshire Regiment and the 2nd General Hospital. Followers of the Saturday cartoon were soon informed of the progress into uniform: 'we have heard of Sergeant-majors, and now we've "had the pleasure" . . . now every time we hear a dog bark, we stand to attention!' Cambridge was too full of young men to be anything but nervous. A few days later, 2500 undergraduates packed into the Corn Exchange to hear Winston Churchill speak. He was back within a week, addressing a town audience at the Guildhall. Searle sketched him, and secured Churchill's signature on the drawing. Ronald's third term at the School of Art was almost halfway through, and it was to be his last. In June, his friend Stuart Ludman, admitted to a sanctum where almost no one was welcome, photographed Ronald at work and at rest in his room, the walls covered with portraits and studies. He had just taken the examination for the Ministry of Education Drawing Diploma. The pass mark was 40%.

Ronald achieved 42%, a figure that probably looked no more likely at the time than it does now. The standards prevailing were, of course, as tough as a student could find; but Ronald blamed a typical 'exam panic . . . I sank without a trace. But at least I got a pass. I remember nothing about it at all.' The time of the century, surely, was not irrelevant to the outcome. By the time the results were released it was August 1939, and Ronald was working up a new vein of 'army humour'. An example appeared as a 'gag' cartoon amid the 'Table Talk' of Morley Stuart on 12 August: '"Pardon me, sergeant," enquired the Camp Hero, "when do you bring round the shaving-water?" ' The *C.D.N.* was also running one of its letter-writing competitions, on 'The Lighter Side of National Service'. The Searle illustrations came easily, but the letters did not. At such a time, readers could not set their minds to the lighter side of anything. The cartoons dried up while a Territorial Camp was convened at Canterbury and Sapper Searle attended for training. The *C.D.N.* for 21 August carried a picture of the 250th Company, Royal Engineers, marching down Station Road after their return. Along the pavement beside them, some fourteen years before, the infant Ronnie had tottered with his father's 'dinner'.

At home, he studied his newest purchases: *The Enjoyment of Laughter* by Max Eastman, and Marcel Ray's monograph on George Grosz. To find inspiration in the German tradition at that moment was unusual but, thanks to the book, Ronald did. 'It cost me

two shillings and changed my artistic direction,' he later considered. Gillray, Rowlandson and George Cruikshank he had learned to revere, and Forain too, in spite of his opinions; but Grosz was something new. 'Grosz exposed the rotting military mind; the filth of war and the stench that lingered after it . . . ' But these were not themes with which to worry the Cambridge populace of a Saturday morning. The last weekly Searle cartoon, number 195, appeared on 26 August. Drawn as 'straight' as any in the series, it carried a chin-up message: 'Your territorials are up to strength. ARP is ready. Evacuation plans are complete. We trust that their services will not be needed – but if they are – it is up to us to behave as the English Channel does when we're not crossing it – REMAIN CALM.' Searle found this piece of work hard to look upon half a century later, but by then he was looking with eyes that had seen every bit as much of the 'filth of war' as Grosz.

The following Monday, Ronald's 'Finklebaum' letter appeared, mocking his first job, now so long ago. The *C.D.N.* was full of forebodings. On the Wednesday, a Mill Road draper advertised '1058 Yards Heavy Black Italian Cloth' for the black-out. The following day it was announced that 'Evacuation starts tomorrow – official'. Germany invaded Poland on Friday 1 September. Urgent Mobilization was ordered, and 2072249 Spr R. W. F. Searle received his 'Notice to Join'.

THREE
The Exile
(1939–45)

Whereas the Army Council, in pursuance of His Majesty's Proclamation, have directed that the 250th Field Co. R.E. be embodied on the day of 2 Sep 1939. You are hereby required to attend at 43 Parkside not later than 9 o'clock that day. Should you not present yourself as ordered you will be liable to be proceeded against.

The mustering took in the heart of Ronald Searle's home territory, between the Central School and Petersfield, just a minute's march from Collier Road. Sapper Searle was issued with rifle No. ERA 214667, and armed himself privately with a new sketchbook, the twelfth in a numbered series. For a few weeks, army training was simply superimposed on an intermittent version of his old civilian life. He continued a sporadic attendance at the Art School life-class. The *C.D.N.* had the benefit of a few more drawings on 'The Lighter Side of National Service' ('Battle dress is the blinkin' right name for it – I always have to fight to get the thing on!'). A month into the war, these contributions ceased. By the time the newspaper received further drawings from Searle, his work had utterly changed, and so had he.

His sketching was halted for the briefest moment by a corrective operation to the index finger of his left hand. With extreme objectivity, he recorded the horrific peeling-back of flesh in his sketchbook. The surgery, performed at Addenbrooke's Hospital, was bungled; the finger remained bandaged for months and still gave Searle discomfort fifty years later. Yet two days after it, he was back in the life-class. By 2 November, sketchbook No.12 was full. Ronald and Stuart Ludman, who had been billeted on the Searles, had made their farewells to their chums; they were about to be dispersed. The following day, Ronald's unit departed for Dereham in Norfolk, where his billet was a pub, the Crown, in Church Street. For some bureaucratic reason, he had been transferred from the 250th to the 287th Field Company. Ten days later, they moved north again, up to Sheringham on the North Sea coast. It was there, billeted at 'Marsden' in Cliff Road, that Ronald first saw a drawing of his in the national press. The latest of his tours of Fleet Street, in July, had paid off; St John Wood, Art Editor of the *Daily Express*, had commissioned an illustration for a Zoë Farmar short story called 'The Refugee'. Obedient to the text, the drawing showed a plump, nervous lady chewing the flowers off her hat; slightly Thurberesque in its wonkiness, it may have taken Dr Rabel as its real-life inspiration. Ronald had supplied Rabel with some illustrations, too – or rather, pictorial tabulations, which accompanied her article 'A Decimal System for Organisms' in the January 1940 edition of the Cambridge magazine *Discovery*, edited by C. P. Snow. No further work could be expected to arise

Above: Self-portrait, November 1939

A pencil drawing from the same sketchbook as the life-class material (p. 41). The war was two months old, and Army Sketchbook No. 1 was about to be opened. Of all Searle's self-portraits, this is perhaps one that gives the strongest impression of the 'East Anglian cunning' with which he got through the war.

from that, but the *Express* was a different matter – or might have been, if the page-designers had not, in the process of printing Ronald's hard-won illustration, chopped off his signature.

Non-war in Norfolk was a lulling experience. Waiting, guarding, strengthening coastal defences – perhaps this was all that was going to happen. Years before, when a 10s. ticket would buy you as many trips as you cared to make in a week from Cambridge to King's Lynn or Hunstanton, Ronald had learned to love the wild east coast, and now he rediscovered it – bitterly raw in winter, but sprinkled with elegant surprises to which the forces had unexpected access. Stuart Ludman was lucky enough to be billeted in Beeston Hall (at Beeston St Laurence), its splendours unmistakable in spite of shrouded chandeliers

THE REFUGEE

IF Florence Tarley's house had not been just the kind I feel in heart with I should probably have stopped visiting her years before. For Florence since her husband, Ben, was killed in an airplane crash in 1927, and she had moved down to Kent, had become more and more trying. She suffered from servants.

Considering that her little cottage had only three tiny bedrooms, a kitchen, sitting-room, and a small dining-room, and that she could anyway only employ one general, the dramatic quality of her domestic experiences was surprising, at least. I often wondered why, since she was strong, capable, a young thirty-nine, she did not give up and look after herself. But she said that she must have time for her garden.

I remember the incident of Queenie. It was a steaming damp week-end last autumn, and I had walked from the station to find Florence sitting crouched over the log fire, scribbling hard. To look at her you could not have believed that she had been an exceptionally beautiful girl, was in fact an extremely handsome woman.

She began at once: "Hello, my dear. I'm desperate. What do you think the creature did?" There was no query use. "Last night I said she could out (she had been so trying all day glad to be rid of her), and of waited up for her (I let her

"And suddenly, my dear, she started to eat the flowers off her hat ..."

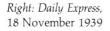

by ZOË FARMAR

pink and white clouds of fruit blossom drifted over the meadows, the flippant little lambs, the close-hooded clusters of oasts, the banks of wild violets, everything we came upon seemed to strike Hepper as a personal welcome.

She and Florence chattered all day while I, sun-happy and vague, wondered. Was it really safe to leave Florence, so far away from help, in charge of a lunatic? Had Hepper done anything more drastic than Florence had told me? But I could not get down to any serious consideration of the problem in the sunshine. Tomorrow morning, on the train journey to work, I would think again. . . .

I had to catch the 8.15 train, and when, at seven o'clock, Florence brought me a cup of tea, I inquired after Hepper. Had the sun been too much for her?

"Oh, no, she is dressing now. She says she wants to see you off at the station, but I'm to stay at home and spray the roses before it gets too hot." Slightly irritated and early-morningish, I said, "Since when does she give you orders, Florence?"

But in Kentish homes the walls have no need of ears, a remark in one room echoes clearly throughout the house, so Florence gave no answer, only pressed two fingers to her lips.

I was still feeling surly as Hepper and I set off for the station. "But I will carry your case," she said, an I let h   ently
har

and boarded-over panelling. Ronald always kept a sketchbook in the knee-pocket of his battledress trousers. Before long, War Sketchbook No.1 was full.

Passed A.1 by the regimental M.O. on 14 April, Ronald departed the following day for Tilshead Lodge on Salisbury Plain, where, in War Sketchbook No.2, he captured the sheeplike submission of a soldier undergoing the Company haircut; another writing a letter home; many others giving way variously to boredom. Then it was back to Norfolk – Cawston, near Norwich – and another rare thrill from the publishing world. *London Opinion*, one of the leading pocket magazines of the day, offering a few laughs, some light reading and the occasional discreet nude, had taken two Searle cartoons for the same issue. They were army gags, but the heaviness of Bateman had now gone, to be replaced by a speedier, spontaneous look more suited to the rhythm of a quick laugh. He had cut loose, in search of a style.

Above: 'I think it's a dud –', London Opinion, July 1940

The first Ronald Searle cartoon published in a journal for national consumption. The hard-working style of the Cambridge years has been replaced by a minimalist outline, bringing him closer in feel to more 'modern' draughtsmen like 'Paul Crum' (Roger Pettiward, 1906–42).

Elsewhere, the Blitz roared and the Battle of Britain clattered over the Garden of England, but the 287th Field Company stayed stolidly in Norfolk, moving only from Cawston a few miles north to the resort of Cromer, where they served out the year. Headquarters Theatre put on *The Man With A Load of Mischief* in Sprowston Village Hall, with designs by Ronald Searle. At his billet, the Newhaven Court Hotel, he decorated a panel in oils. It was an almost pleasant life, especially when camouflage work began. There had been no fun in mining bridges to thwart a possible landing, but the notion of coating strategic emplacements with improvised disguises looked a lot more attractive. A small group went around together, with John Wiggins as carpenter and Searle as painter. The sight of a naked grey pillbox was anathema to them. At the very least, they would convert it into a shaggy haystack, though seaside locations required a more elaborately jaunty beach-hut treatment, with those rickety balustrades and verandahs typical of the battered shoreline. An officer nominally supervised several such gangs of operational chameleons, but the work by its nature was scattered and the men were motorized. To Searle, at times, it all seemed 'like school days again, really'.

The New Year of 1941 brought a chance to exhibit in the galleries of Norwich Castle, where the material on view consisted exclusively of wartime artwork by members of H.M. Forces stationed in East Anglia. Inevitably the show was enjoyed on many levels ('The paintings by A. D. Chinnery are medieval in their bursting vitality and complete absence of technique'), but all were agreed that the excellence of Sapper Searle dominated it. Even *The Studio*, the high-toned art magazine, said so. The *Eastern Daily Press* nominated his 'Cookhouse Fatigue' as 'probably the picture of the exhibition, a real gem, full of character and real humorous observation'. When the show transferred to Heffer's Gallery in Cambridge, a *C.D.N.* reviewer, more familiar with the standards now expected from Searle, noted an over-emphatic Epstein influence here, a touch of Picasso there, and presciently described 'Restaurant' as 'an English subject well treated in Continental fashion'. He might even have spoken of a 'European' style, had there not been a war on.

The artist did not pursue his drawings to his home town. On 8 January he had entrained for Carlisle, *en route* for Scotland with War Sketchbook No.4 at the ready. The little town of Kirkcudbright, in an inlet of the northern coast of the Solway Firth, did not sound an obviously enticing destination; yet the visit proved warmly pleasurable. What Ronald could not have foreseen was that Kirkcudbright sustained a thriving and extremely hospitable artistic community. From the moment they stepped in at the front door of 'The Crafts' on 6 February, at the invitation of Dorothy and Bill Johnston, Ronald and his new friend Matt Kerr (a native of the Isle of Arran) were assured of a lively social life. With

the Johnstons' young daughters, Cécilé and Pat, they would play chaotic games of billiards or talk art and artists late into the night; and the soldiers shared in the luxury of rural civilian food. The family had entertained soldiers before, but to Cécilé, 'Ron and Matt were different. They seemed to pop in and out more often and although they were in Kirkcudbright for only a few months made many friends ... Ron was gentle, shy, modest and humorous and had an enormous energy [in] pursuing his dedication to art. He spent a lot of time drawing, mostly his army colleagues in the barracks, and some of these were sent to the Ministry of Information.' The town's forum was the Paul Jones tea-room, where Ronald met more of the town's artists, but it was to the Johnstons that he was most attached, even if he could not be entirely relied upon to appear when expected. Cécilé surmised that neither he nor Matt Kerr was a very good military man, 'because they got into quite a few scrapes. There was the time when Matt came alone because Ron was on a charge. He had fastened the poppers on his gauntlets on opposite sides, clamping his wrists together – he was on guard duty and couldn't salute a passing officer. And another time he went left while the whole 287th Field Coy. R.E. went right on the

Right: At the Paul Jones Restaurant, Kirkcudbright, February 1941

'Molly', Ronald Searle and Matt Kerr in Kirkcudbright's noted meeting-place. Molly was their favourite waitress, who 'always gave us extra helpings of everything, when we could afford to go there, instead of the NAAFI'.

Sunday morning church parade through the town.'

He could not help endearing himself, sometimes quite seriously, to the Kirkcudbright girls. 'Most of my girl friends fell in love with Ron a little,' Cécilé remembered, 'or a lot. I can remember the feeling of one-upmanship when I heard from him, or Matt, and was so pleased to look after some of his drawings after he left Kirkcudbright ...' The drawings, as always, covered the widest range of genres. One landscape, 'River Dee at Kirkcudbright', was accepted by the Royal Scottish Academy for exhibition in April. More domestically, there was a new line in off-the-cuff cartoons, produced in the first instance specifically to amuse Cécilé and Pat. The girls were pupils of a progressive academy, evacuated from Edinburgh to the west coast for the duration, that boasted the fine (if obscure) old Gaelic name of St Trinnean's. To their great delight, Ronald made free with the traditions of this institution, not only Anglicizing its spelling but representing it as a forcing-house for juvenile delinquency of a positively Sohoid raffishness. These inventions would eventually bring their creator great notoriety, and a certain amount of guilt as well; for though 'the real St Trinnean's' was closed in 1946, on the retirement of its founder and Head, Miss C. Fraser Lee, the reputation of 'St Trinian's' continued to plague both her and her former pupils. For the time being, however, the prototype drawings remained with the Johnstons.

The 287th, meanwhile, had become more pressingly engaged. There was a to-and-fro between Kirkcudbright and Stanley in Perthshire – Ronald's twenty-first birthday passing without much pause for reflection – followed by a week's privilege leave in Cambridge, where Ronald did not fail to put in what attendance he could at the Art School. Then it was back to Kirkcudbright, sketching in the Paul Jones and trying to keep in step with the army. After ten more days in that delightful community, it was time to go. Middlewich in Cheshire was the site of the next convocation of Engineers. It provided a base for working excursions northwards into Lancashire and westward into Wales: pontoon-bridge exercises in Lancaster, manoeuvres in Tenby; a brief stay in West Derby, Liverpool, repairing bomb damage; and even bloodshed in the Welsh borders, where, during a stopover at a Royal Artillery barracks at Newtown, Searle saw, and drew, the consequences of a shooting accident – a stricken sergeant, head lolling back to expose the throat, slung between the shoulders of two brothers-in-arms. He was learning, in Sketchbook No.6, to capture not just the individual at rest, or the tableau group, but moments of urgent activity, 'photographed' by the mind and filled out by memory – the beginnings of reportage.

The movements of the 287th became even more agitated. July 1941 brought manoeuvres on Ilkley Moor and work on the Manchester Ship Canal; back at Middlewich, Ronald drilled holes for explosives with a rock-drill compressor, an item which, later in the war, Sapper Searle might have dreamed of possessing. At the end of August, they departed again for the agreeable coasts of Wales, at Barmouth in Merioneth and Holyhead in Anglesey. The men were not to know it, but their lives were about to suffer a drastic reduction in elements both agreeable and western. Ronald wrote off to Cécilé Johnston in Kirkcudbright, asking her to send his remaining drawings to Cambridge. Of those he had kept with him, he sent a few likely-looking cartoons from Middlewich to appropriate magazines. One bunch went off by registered post, on 13 July, to 'Miss Kaye Webb, Assistant Editor, *Lilliput*, 43, Shoe Lane, E.C.4.' Here was another thing Ronald didn't know: he was writing to his future wife.

Embarkation leave was announced. It began on 21 September, when Ronald returned at once to Cambridge and presented himself yet again at the Art School for life-class.

Opposite top left: Somewhere in Norfolk, 1940

John Wiggins, carpenter, and Ronald Searle, draughtsman, relax atop one of their own pieces of pillbox camouflage. Now a Northamptonshire farmer, John Wiggins writes: 'Ron spent most of his off-duty time sketching – anything – anywhere! Miss Anderson's café in Cromer, and the tearoom behind a woolshop [were] favourite haunts, possibly because of a weakness for waffles and cream cakes. Ron's duty to survey the camouflage worksites resulted in him having to ride a motorcycle, not having had much experience on same ... The army life was not for Ron, but he made the best of it.'

Opposite top right: John Wiggins reading *Stolen Death*, Cromer, November 1940

Wiggins appears to have fallen asleep over his thriller, Stolen Death *by Leo Grex (Hutchinson, 1936). A drawing from War Sketchbook No. 2.*

Opposite centre: 'Ginger' Lewis, March 1941

Drawn during the Kirkcudbright period: a left-facing profile deriving great authority from economy. One feels that the head is unquestionably 'right'.

Two years had passed since the start of war, but absence from formal study had only intensified his determination to draw. Comic art was a sideline, but a promising one, for there was good news from Miss Webb; she had taken three cartoons, 'including the one about the schoolgirls'. It showed a fairly dishevelled bunch of pupils (bare flesh visible above the stocking-tops was the perennial give-away) scrutinizing the school noticeboard, over the caption: 'Owing to the international situation the match with St Trinian's has been postponed.' Strictly speaking, the girls must belong to another foundation if St Trinian's are their expected opponents, but the drawing has understandably always been called the first St Trinian's cartoon. What it does with ironically perfect appropriateness is to announce the existence of the genre, while suspending its actual onset *sine die*.

'Owing to the international situation, the match with St Trinian's has been postponed.'

Above: Cécilé Johnston, April 1941

The original St Trinian's, or St Trinnean's, girl at the time of the founding of the fantasy academy. She writes: 'I remember a group of artists – Lena Alexander, Jessie King, my parents, Anna Hotchkiss and others talking about Ron in the Paul Jones one day and they were all sure he was a young man of great exception whose talents were rare …'

Right: Lilliput, October 1941

The first 'St Trinian's' cartoon. One of the two Searle cartoons published in the October 1941 edition of Lilliput, *and first seen by Searle under bombardment on a street in Singapore. The girls of this unnamed rival establishment are stockier than their counterparts at St Trinian's, but afflicted with the same difficulties in the stocking-top area.*

Just before departure, it seems to have dawned on the army that Sapper Searle's pursuit of graphic line was a good deal more dedicated than his performance of army duties. As the draughtsman himself saw it, 'the military authorities took a closer look at the available material they were going to war with, and decided that I wasn't good value for money in a case of life and death. So they took no chances, took me down to what they considered was my proper ceiling – and paid me less to do the same thing.' He was removed from Trade Group 'A' and remustered as Pioneer Draughtsman (Arch) E III. This chiefly entailed a drop in pay from 4s. 9d. to 3s. 3d. per day, but was not otherwise greatly displeasing to Searle, whose campaign to keep his head down and maintain a humble sapper-ship right through the conflict required, he later stated, 'a great deal of East Anglian cunning'.

The 18th Division made its way to Scotland in late October, where it sailed from Gourock on the 29th, destination unknown. Searle's Engineers were packed into H.M.T. *Sobieski*, a 12,000-ton Polish vessel of corroded and ramshackle aspect, along with the

2nd Battalion, the Cambridgeshire Regiment, and a contingent from the Royal Artillery. The overwhelming probability, at this stage in the war, was that these men were intended for North Africa, though their route at first might have suggested Greenland. A prudent policy of U-boat avoidance sent the *Sobieski* first north towards Iceland, whence it plunged in a squiggling route across the north Atlantic towards Nova Scotia. Reveille came at 6 a.m., and mornings passed in a round of disciplinary drills; physical training came at four in the afternoon. There was seldom enough activity to fill the day, except in the case of Ronald Searle, the man with the sketchbook.

Some way short of the North American coast, U.S. vessels took over escort duties from the Royal Navy, and herded the troopships into Halifax. Fishy as it was, the town smelt 'like an exotic spice island' after the seasick days below deck. Then the men were transferred – by no means 'legally', since America had not yet joined the war – to a much larger troop-carrier, the 40,000-ton U.S.S. *Mount Vernon*. On this vessel was concentrated a sizeable fraction of the youth of East Anglia, with two battalions of the Royal Norfolk Regiment added to the Cambridgeshires, the Artillery, the Engineers and many other units. There were more than 5000 men in the convoy that sailed from Halifax on 9 November – the first time in the Second World War that British troops had been carried by United States transports.

Their route took them directly south, to Port of Spain in Trinidad for fuel and water, then onward down the coast of Brazil to the Equator, which was crossed on 23 November. Somewhere off Argentina, the *Mount Vernon* made a loop to port; sailing eastward now, the men were at last facing Africa. But it was at this moment, on an even greater ocean, that the Japanese chose to attack Pearl Harbor, on 7 December. The news transformed the *Mount Vernon* overnight into a declared 'Allied' possession and a legitimate target. The convoy made all speed for South Africa, its British passengers less certain then ever of their ultimate destination, though calmed by their mighty intake of American food and the smoking of hundreds of freely distributed Camels. Searle was broadening his repertoire of physiognomies by sketching, among others, the black American sailors who were about to see the continent of their ancestors.

Three days' shore leave were allowed in Cape Town. Sapper Searle found the experience overwhelming and frustrating by turns. The hospitality of the British South Africans was so hearty as to be almost inescapable. When he did fight free and took his sketchbook into the streets, he was left drooling by the visual richness of the scene. Excited and rushed, he 'forgot about the necessity to seek the human being behind the material and scribbled on regardless'. Some of his scribbles, none the less, look beautiful now in their slightly fading inks. One caricatural portrait, of a white South African formally dressed with a riding crop, carries for the first time a spicy flavouring of George Grosz. It must have been the brush-cut hair that set the association off.

The fortunes of Ronald Searle's war now took a cruel turn, disguised as a treat. As the convoy headed up into the Indian Ocean, crossing the Equator again on 21 December, the *Mount Vernon* abruptly split off and turned back, putting in at Mombasa. Speculation as to the ship's new orders was drowned in the considerable partying. But Searle, unburdened this time with invitations, took to the streets and feasted his eyes instead, revelling in the same African forms that had inspired Picasso. It was to be his last moment of working solitude for three years. By New Year's Day, the ship was three days out into the Indian Ocean again: another eternity of empty horizons, rising and falling. The difference now was that the sun set astern of the ship, which was therefore heading due

east. The 53rd Brigade had been ordered to Singapore.

Having passed the Chagos Islands, the *Mount Vernon* was most of the way there when, on 9 January 1942, Brigadier C. L. B. Duke issued an Order of the Day to All Ranks, British Troops. 'We have been selected,' it revealed, 'for the task of assisting the forces now in Malaya who have been putting up such a splendid resistance against superior numbers to a treacherous invasion.' Brigadier Duke's opinions were more forthright than his syntax. He praised 'the conduct and spirit shown during the voyage and at ports', and gave it as his view that 'no finer troops could have been sent'. Thanks were offered to the captain and crew of the *Mount Vernon*, and the Order concluded by wishing its recipients the best of luck. 'Remember that however far away you may be you are fighting for our King and Country at home. Pray for God's help in achieving success to our arms in the just cause we have taken up.'

To judge by the propaganda that was now fed to the men by army lecturers, the deity would not need to be badgered too hard for his help. The slant-eyed Japanese, according to this rigmarole (which was being simultaneously recited to Australians approaching the problem from the other side), were a helplessly myopic people, and could not have shot straight even if they had been permitted to do so by nature – which, as a matter of fact, they were not, being incapable of closing one eye in order to aim. They were a superstitious race, moreover, and foolishly imagined others to be just as jittery; that was why they had a habit of setting off fire-crackers in the night, in hopes of panicking opponents. Many who heard this sort of thing strongly sensed that it was rubbish, but of course had no first-hand knowledge with which to oppose it. The best impressions Searle himself had formed of the Orient came from ancient artefacts in museums and Fu Manchu at the Kinema.

'I am beginning to doubt that we shall ever get off this boat again!' Ronald wrote to Cécilé Johnston, well into the third month of voyaging. But at last, on 13 January 1942, the island of Singapore was reached. The transition from boredom to fear was instantaneous. For many who had come so far, the expedition could have ended then and there, for even before disembarkation they could hear the sound of Japanese planes attacking. Only a combination of dank mist and driving rain kept the secret of their arrival, so that no bombs fell. The 53rd Brigade, roused from its plump leisure, was rushed on to

Left: Mombasa, Kenya, just after Christmas 1941

Searle's feeling for exuberance in architecture begins to come through. 'What Searle can do better than anybody is straight topography. His sense of place and feeling for the personality of architecture is absolutely convincing.' (George Melly, New Statesman, 27 November, 1964.)

the mainland of Johore, its route obstructed by the masses of villagers fleeing southward before the advance of the Imperial Japanese Army. Dressed for the desert war they had first thought of, the newly-arrived British kept to the roads; the Japanese had command of the jungle paths, and their infiltrators passed easily among Malays and Chinese. Their efficient foot-soldiers were backed by tanks and a relentless airborne strike-force that went virtually unopposed. It was not long before the 53rd Brigade collided with the British retreat that was happening in front of it and joined in – except for the Engineers, who were required to carry on advancing into no man's land, where they would put to the torch any matter that might prove useful to the enemy. Such few drawings as survive from those days show wrecked landscapes, confusion, carnage.

By the end of January, British forces had abandoned the Malayan mainland to the Japanese and to history. Blowing up the Johore Causeway, they fell back, 80,000 strong, on to Singapore Island, together with five or six times as many Chinese refugees. 'I look to you all,' said General Wavell's Order of the Day, 'to fight this battle without further thought of retreat.' But there was no effective defence to be put up against Japanese bombing, which, Searle recalled, sent 'massive waves of human misery' running from one area to another. On 9 February, Japanese forces established themselves on the edge of the island. A hideous battle ensued. Searle made a drawing of an emaciated corpse draped over barbed wire at Bukit Timah, the high hill that was most fiercely defended of all. There was nothing to be done. By 13 February, the Japanese were shelling the packed town and closing in. Under fire, in the debris of a Singapore street, Ronald Searle spotted a ragged copy of a little magazine: October's *Lilliput*, with its St Trinian's cartoon. It was the first time he had seen it – a moment of sublime irrelevance. Somewhere else on the island, Japanese forces were seizing the water-supply. On 15 February, General Percival, commanding Singapore's defences, recognized that there was nothing for it but to surrender unconditionally. He met General Yamashita that afternoon and signed the documents.

There followed two days of confusion while the Japanese, the inferior force numerically, gauged the size of the problem and assigned numbers to their prisoners of war. Ronald Searle's was 1/5594. At length, Changi, the area occupying the eastern end of the island, was decided upon as a good site for herding men, and more than 50,000 of them were marched the fourteen miles to get there. As Singapore lies almost exactly on the Equator, this was a highly unpleasant experience in itself. Even as he marched, an exhibition of Searle's work was opening at Heffer's Gallery back in freezing Cambridge. Proudly pre-sold by the *C.D.N.*, it contained army sketches and some 'quick studies of men aboard his ship "with convoy somewhere on the Atlantic". They were mailed home especially for the exhibition, despite the difficulties he was labouring under.' How much harder those conditions were now no one in Cambridge could know, as 'Robin Goodfellow' reminded his readers: 'It is a hard thing to have to say, but there is nobody to whom you can apply for information. It is just a case of waiting until news arrives, as it assuredly will do from one source or another.' A little more than a month later, 'official' sources did bring Cambridge families not the worst news of all, perhaps, but bad enough. Under the heading 'Malaya Postings', the *C.D.N.* gave lists of 'Cambridge men serving in Malaya whose relatives have been informed that for the present they must be listed as "missing".' Among these: 'Sapper Ronald Searle, R.E., only son of Mr and Mrs W. J. Searle, 29, Collier Road, Cambridge. An old Central School boy and art student at the Technical School. Formerly *Cambridge Daily News* cartoonist, he has had considerable success as an artist ...'

In rapidly deteriorating circumstances, he was still having it. In a remarkable burst of reportage immediately after the capitulation he recorded the triumph of the Japanese. Then, as defeat sank in, he set himself to document the collapsed postures and glazed-over faces of the prisoners housed alongside him in the wooden huts of the 'India Lines'; the queue for the skimpy rice ration; the triumphalism of collaborationist guards, notably the Sikhs. The Japanese themselves, at this stage, virtually ignored the POWs; having failed to live up to the code which stipulates that defeat without death equals dishonour, they were beneath contempt. The Allied troops were simply left, mouldering and malnourished, in their prisons, where they began to learn to live with the gradual decay of their bodies. To be a captive was bad enough; to be confined in the self-obsession of one's

Ronald Searle.
Bukit-Timah Singapore 1942

Left: Corpse at Bukit Timah, Singapore, January–February 1942

Bukit Timah was a village in the western half of Singapore island, and the site of the island's highest point — lower than 600 feet, but an obvious focus for defence. The Norfolks and Cambridgeshires were called in from the north-east to try to relieve the Argylls, and an unavailing battle raged for several days. The Ford Works building near Bukit Timah was finally chosen by Yamashita as the site for the ceremony of surrender.

own physical wretchedness was far worse.

But within a few months their captors had begun to see a new possibility in the ragged horde behind the wire: forced labour. Active co-operation in this was unlikely to be forthcoming, but Major-General Fukuye set about creating some sort of appearance of assent by distributing a printed form on which prisoners were 'invited' to swear, on their honour, that they would not under any circumstances attempt to escape. Far though they were from Geneva, the Allied administration held out for its rights under the Convention, and recommended refusal. The first furious response of the Japanese was to shoot four men. Then every prisoner capable of movement was concentrated in the Selarang Barracks square: more than 15,000 men in a confined yard, where serious disease soon broke out. The Japanese insisted that no man would leave Selarang until the escape forms were signed. Only when the Allied commanders persuaded the Japanese to upgrade the instruction to an official order was the situation resolved. The men signed their papers under protest and returned to their quarters. From a barrack roof on 3 September, the third anniversary of the outbreak of war, Ronald Searle had sketched the whole vividly teeming scene, a vital piece of reportage. If before the Selarang incident some of his drawings were made as studies – a matter of broad human interest and technical exploration – they were seldom so disinterested thereafter. As conditions worsened, his sense of mission grew in strength. Health, opportunity and materials permitting, he would bring back from this experience a pictorial record of scenes which, he already knew, would otherwise scarcely be believed. It was important work – unique, as it turned out – and it was an objective reason to survive, which every man would come to need. To adopt an

Below: The no-escape form, Singapore, 1942

Returned to the signatory by an expert pilferer, it became just another piece of drawing-paper. Later in their captivity there would be no question of the men's attempting to escape, diseased and starved as they were, into the surrounding hostile territory.

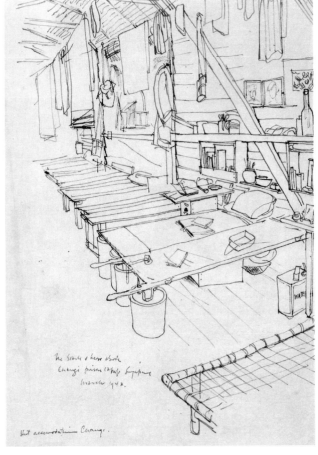

Right: Hut accommodation, India Lines, Changi prison camp, Singapore, March 1942

The second of the improvised beds, the one with books lying on it, was Searle's; the one beyond it belonged to Matt Kerr, who slept on bare boards. They shared a 'table' between them, and Searle's pencils and brushes were kept in a ginger jar at the head of the bed. It was much the most comfortable accommodation the prisoners ever had. Looking at this drawing in 1990, Miss Gee Horsley, Searle's one-time teacher of perspective, remarked how correctly he had observed that effect in this case.

extreme 'attitude' toward one's own confinement might give one a point of view, but there was no moral nourishment in it. Doctrinaire reticence of a Christian kind could hold men back from engaging in the sordid but vital bartering processes that might keep them in touch with life. Many went under. Nor did the converse policy of ruthless self-interest often survive its first fury. As one ex-captive, John Stewart (then John Ullmann) had expressed it: 'When all efforts were directed to the acquisition of food and the avoidance of strenuous work assignments, even if they were successful, the time came when there was no more point in pursuing the aim. The rewards were found wanting, and solace non-existent. The struggle was then abandoned.' Proof now against either tendency, Ronald Searle set about scrounging the wherewithal to draw. Eventually the network of pilferage returned to him the form on which he had 'promised' not to escape. He drew a pair of marble-featured Japanese guards on it.

Life had come to a kind of halt, but far away it still went on. Three days before the Selarang crisis, Ronald's sister Olive was married in Cambridge, to Sgt John Fenn. Five months had passed since Ronald had been posted missing. No news of him would come for nearly eighteen months more. Olive would write to every neutral or humanitarian authority she could think of – even the Pope in Rome – to ask for help in tracing him, but nothing came back. It was perhaps a merciful silence.

Grim as these months had been, they were actually much the most pleasant that Ronald passed in Japanese hands. He still produced portraits of his friends, including Matt Kerr (Stuart Ludman was a prisoner too), and entertained a wider audience by rediscovering his flair for theatre. As the first Christmas in captivity approached, festive shows were

Above: The Selarang Incident, Singapore, 3 September 1942

Sketched by Searle from the roof of a barrack block. This panorama, uniquely, was 'corroborated' by a photograph, taken by an Australian called Aspinall using X-ray film which he also managed to process (see To the River Kwai *by John Stewart, Bloomsbury 1988). Searle's version, inevitably, captures much more of the life of the scene. General Fukuye, whose orders made the Selarang protest necessary, was executed in April 1946.*

devised for the rudimentary theatre they called the 'Changi Palladium'. Ronald designed some sets for both *Dancing Years* and a raucous revue called *Gentlemen Only*, presented by the '18th Divisional Concert Party'. The performance was later adapted for the amusement of the Dutch contingent within the camp, as *Alleen voor Heeren*. December, as Ronald was to find out in following years, would always keep him busy, so heavy was the demand not just for theatre designs but for Christmas cards and calendars.

A more adventurous form of publication was now in the offing. The theatre store-room, formerly the projection-room of a wrecked cinema, was adopted as the editorial office of *The Survivor*, a new magazine designed for circulation within the camp. Five copies of each edition were produced (they were carbons: the fifth was almost illegible), and Ronald had to draw all the 'plates' and hand-colour them in each copy. Apart from him, the driving forces behind this publication were Jack Wood (later to be Mayor of York), and above all Hilton Tranchell, a vividly eccentric physiotherapist from Ceylon, who at various stages in his career had obtained a degree in Divinity from Yale, fought in Spain and told fortunes on the sea-front at Margate. Having been incarcerated by the French after his escape from Spain, Tranchell knew something of prison psychology and was convinced that a good dose of radical opinion would get the men healthily talking. He favoured texts that were unruly and, to put it gently, anti-conservative. A contrasting serenity was generated by the beauties of Searle's artwork, most of it done in borrowed styles excavated wholesale from memory. The production-line method of working was not easy to operate, Searle found:

> Trouble came when a valued contributor flogged his watch to a Tamil for a supplementary tin of pilchards and, after eating them, wrote nostalgic poems about his 'beautiful homeland' which had to be beautifully decorated. It was difficult making five copies of an E. H. Shepard, in aniline dye and brown crayon, with the Editor waiting to type a slashing indictment of the Immaculate Conception on the back of them.

That very indictment brought the downfall of *The Survivor*. If all church personnel within the compound had been as convivial and impartially humane as the celebrated Padre (later Canon) Noel Duckworth, a hero to every survivor who knew him, nothing would have happened. But there were other clerics, army chaplains clinging to their little authority, who took offence and brought the matter to the attention of the British Commandant – who might have deflected the complaint had there not been something in *The Survivor* to annoy him too. Searle had perpetrated a cartoon that was mildly deflationary at the expense of generals. A closer inspection of the *Survivor* file followed, with the result that it was pronounced too dangerously bolshie to continue. *The Survivor* was formally banned on 3 March 1943, Ronald Searle's twenty-third birthday. A drawing of the editorial office after the edict shows Tranchell and friends sitting despondently around a chess-board amid the store-room clutter – which had disguised, throughout the life of the magazine, a wall-cavity where a secret wireless was housed, keeping the POWs surprisingly well informed of the progress of the war. Now the radio had to be removed, in a latrine basket, to a halfway house in the infectious diseases hut.

A more serious disciplinary consequence of *The Survivor*'s non-survival came next. Searle and his partners had unwisely attracted attention to themselves, and were considered trouble-makers. For some time, the Japanese had been drafting large parties of men out of the camp and putting them to work on building, landscaping and transportation projects, locally at first, but now increasingly far afield. The next time such groups were

Room in which wireless was operated for nine months.

recruited, the British authorities ensured that the unruly element departed with them. Hilton Tranchell was put aboard one of the infamous 'hell-ships' and transported to Borneo. Ronald Searle went north, to the Siam–Burma railway and a life of horror.

It is questionable whether the supply-route from Siam (or Thailand) to Burma was utterly essential to the Japanese war effort. Certainly there were experimental features in the way they went about driving it through – as there had to be, given the extreme difficulty of the terrain and the debilitating tropical weather. Indeed, previous theorists had accepted that a railway line from Ban Pong up to the Burmese border at Three Pagoda Pass would be impossible to build. But with limitless supplies of slave labour the Japanese could afford to defy such scepticism, since the limits of the possible would be physically explored not by them, but by their coolies. It was all to be finished by the end of the year. The fact that the last spike was actually driven in ahead of schedule is rather sickening to absorb. It is more appropriately memorialized in one of the most famous sayings of the war: that one man died for every sleeper laid. The word 'sleeper' has never borne a more poetic burden.

Very large numbers of labourers were needed. Searle's contingent, 'H' Force ('G' Force had gone to Japan), was moved out in open trucks during the night of 8 May. Transferred to a train, thirty men to a steel goods wagon, they took five desperate days to roll north to the Siamese rail junction of Ban Pong. While his comrades dozed, Searle drew them, rescuing something strangely stirring from their horrible discomfort. Scrounged paper was in short supply; the remains of an earlier drawing can be seen in the heavily shaded thigh of one of the figures. It looks rather like a death's head.

To lie down at Ban Pong amid the filthy detritus of previous 'transit' passengers was hardly a relief. But it was better than what followed – a hundred-mile march up to the

Below left: By train to Siam, May 1943

Something of the steeliness of the goods wagons in which they were transported seems to have transferred itself to Searle's rendering of his comrades. In the dark shadows of the upper thighs of the nearest figure, the beginnings of a head from an earlier drawing can be seen — a hollow-eyed, skull-like apparition.

Below right: Self-portrait at Konyu, Siam, July 1943

Searle's really serious medical troubles had just begun, with malaria, a poisoned hand and beri-beri in the legs; a swelling of the belly is also apparent, since his shorts will not close at the front. The top left-hand corner of this movingly direct self-appraisal has been smoked.

section of track where 'H' Force would work. Most of the progress was made at night. Some men died of fevers, some of exhaustion. Searle, who had suffered enteritis and gastritis back in camp, together with tropical ulcers and manges brought on by malnutrition, was still comparatively viable, though beginning to hallucinate. The route plunged suddenly into jungle — mud, slime, insects and rain. The path itself seemed to be trying to suck the men down. Even on this punishing slog, Searle had made drawings: including a portrait, of a young Thai girl at Tamuang. Pretty and impassive, she was the last embodiment of human attractiveness he was to see for eight months.

The expected camp existed in name only. It had to be built first, then lived in. The monsoon had come and nothing was ever dry. Searle continued, remarkably, to record the routine of the day. What he could not draw from life he 'drew up' later. Portraits of the Japanese guards, which had been somewhat generic in the early days, now took on an angry specificity. Individual crimes were graphically itemized: a bamboo-stick beating administered for failing to number off in Japanese at roll-call; a sadistic game played with a prisoner forced to hold a large rock above his head until, one way or another, he collapsed and earned a further beating. Watching such scenes was part of the day's work, which the slave-labourers were obliged to dedicate each dawn to the Emperor in a chanted Japanese oath. Astonishingly, Searle sometimes made drawings at first light before

beginning the eighteen-hour labour on the railway. Sometimes he found that the man he had sketched that morning, left behind to wrestle with sickness, had died during the day.

Sear' .s drawing entitled 'Fit Parade For Work' — which was indeed how the Japanese regarded it — shows the swift decline in the physical condition of the men. Several have legs of the same swollen thickness all the way down, the classic symptom of fluid-retention associated with the vitamin-B deficiency disease, beri-beri. By July 1943, Searle had moved a couple of camps further up the line and contracted beri-beri himself. A famous self-portrait, drawn that month in the jungle, shows his army-issue spectacles almost intact, but otherwise it is a severely battered figure that faces the viewer. All his medical troubles had come at once. First, malaria, one of the quick and vicious kinds (it recurred within the month); then a poisoned hand, which had to be submitted to a makeshift operation performed by the tireless M.O., Major Kevin Fagan. The bandage that appears on Searle's left arm in the self-portrait is apparently unconnected with this episode, or with the tenosynovitis that attacked his left wrist the same month, causing his fingers to curl towards the palm of his drawing hand. The beri-beri is out of sight.

The thrust of the railway had reached full speed, and every man remotely capable of bearing a burden was dragged into service, battering a path through jungle and rock. If he was not chipping a hole in a mountain with hand-tools, he was ferrying endless baskets of debris from a rock-blasting site up ahead. Men were dying on the job in full view of their friends, but there could be no pause to mourn or protest their passing. After the war, Searle was more than once called upon to describe this period in broadcasts, and one incident he always recounted: 'In one particular case I know, a man was tipping his basket

Below left: Cutting into the mountain, near Konyu, Siam, June 1943

'The body just went backwards and forwards, backwards and forwards, day after day.'

Below right: 'Fit parade for work', Siam–Burma railway, 1943

Sufferers from malaria, ulcers, beri-beri and dysentery are lined up for the day's labour. The most visible symptoms are the hugely swollen legs of the beri-beri sufferers.

over the edge of the cutting, and he fell with it; and we weren't allowed to go near him, we weren't allowed to touch him. They had to go on tipping their rocks over the edge of this cutting, until the man was buried by his fellows.'

Searle himself, never the likeliest of chain-gang labourers, was severely treated by his overseers. He was beaten many times with the flat of a pick-axe or with a bamboo stick, though such blows as landed on his slouch hat were softened just a little by a protective layer of jungle grass. When no more immediate reason presented itself, guards would beat men out of boredom or resentment at their own discomfort, for they too were living in the jungle on shorter supplies than usual. They made a spitefully punitive attack on one of Searle's hands, putting him in the camp hospital, though they chose the wrong hand if they intended to stop him drawing. That drawing was going on they knew, since it was Searle's practice to coax paper out of them by promising to concoct pornographic pictures for their private pleasure. In a famous post-war book, Searle's friend and fellow-slave Russell Braddon loyally maintained that Searle never handed over the desired orgiastic visions, but in fact he sometimes did, and it is hard to see how the ruse could have worked for long if he had not.

In August, Searle's condition took several turns for the worse. Malaria struck twice more that month, in severe forms that left him hallucinating again. Gravely weakened men were now facing a new danger: fly-borne cholera, which had spread straight down the railway line from the north. Men in agonies of hunger would throw their rice away because they saw a fly land on it. What they did not see, they could not guard against (although the Dutch prisoners, with their previous experience of Java and Sumatra, knew enough about cholera to keep their mortality figures comparatively low). To survive the disease was rare, and desperate anyway in its consequences, since in the first crisis of fever half one's meagre body weight could be lost. Searle made a dreadfully moving drawing of a man dying in this condition. 'I desperately wanted to put down on paper,' he later explained, 'the unbelieving horror that this man felt when he knew that the fly had settled on his rice and not on someone else's.' The man died the next day and was immediately cremated on a pyre kept permanently burning for the purpose. The fact that Searle drew them makes these scenes possible to imagine. It was at this time that he reached what he judged to be his personal rock-bottom: 'Between bouts of fever I came to one morning to find that men on each side of me were dead, and as I tried to prop myself up to get away from them, I saw that there was a snake coiled under the bundle on which I had been resting my head.' He had also heard, from up the line in Burma, that his friend Matt Kerr was dead, of cardiac beri-beri.

Searle spent three more months in Siam. That he avoided cholera is the best that can be said for his experience. Such labour as he was able to do was accomplished in a daze which it was helpful to encourage. 'Your mind worked on a fantasy level. Everyone went through their head recounting every fairy story, every nursery rhyme, anything idiotic that would fill up a corner of the head. But the body just went backwards and forwards, backwards and forwards, day after day.' Beri-beri had spread to his feet and a skin disease (tropical perfligas) was rapidly colonizing his entire skin. Like all the men, he had suffered throughout from tropical ulcers, where the skin would go bad like a fruit, the rottenness eating inward towards the bone with the help of maggots. A particularly severe one now attacked his right ankle; his drawing hand was succumbing to ulcers, too. On top of these 'natural' ills came a vicious blow from a guard's pick-axe, the spiked end this time, which actually penetrated Searle's back as far as the spine. His legs paralysed, he was carried off

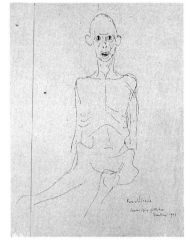

Above: Prisoner dying of cholera, Siam, 1943

'I desperately wanted to put down on paper the unbelieving horror that this man felt when he knew that the fly had settled on his rice and not on someone else's.' Since the Japanese were terrified of cholera, the victims of the disease offered Searle the safest hiding-place for his drawings; his testimony could be slid under them where they lay.

to the sick lines again – not a heavy task by Death Railway standards, since he now weighed around seven stone.

During October and November he was seldom in charge of his own consciousness, let alone his destiny. The Siam–Burma railway was completed on 25 October. A celebrated feature film, *The Bridge on the River Kwai*, later gave it to be understood that British personnel might have drawn some mad sense of achievement from their forced collaboration on this project. As will be seen from a number of survivors' accounts, there was no question of wasting moral energy on the formation of an attitude to the railway. A man's own survival became his full-time task. Whatever fragments of concern were left over, he might donate to his fellows and the goal of getting as many out of the jungle alive as could make it. Ronald Searle himself did not consciously enjoy the small relief of that return. No memory of the journey back down the line to the Kanchanaburi basecamp remained to him. Once there, he was assailed by two types of malaria simultaneously, one of them the appalling 'Malignant Tertiary'. Wild fevers were punctuated by hyperactive outbursts of misleading 'lucidity', in one of which Searle went rushing through the camp shouting that he 'had water'. Those capable of movement were more than interested, but when they got to Searle, they saw it was a malarial mirage. 'Mad as a cut snake' was the phrase Russell Braddon used to describe such a condition – though, as it happened, cut snakes were otherwise not unwelcome. The men ate them. From the intermittent restoration of his faculties, Searle did recall the kindness of some Australians who tended him at this time, and spared him part of their tiny hoard of sulphonamide drugs. Braddon was among the group, and remembered the Englishman's condition:

> When the line was finished he was a sick boy. I remember that there was nothing much of him, that he was like a baby or a monkey or something. We thought he was dying and we – some of his remaining friends – used to put him out on a groundsheet in the sun. I don't know why, but we felt that the sun would do something. He could barely move, and we had no food, he had dysentery, malaria and was covered in running sores, and each day we expected him to die. He was a tough little one, though; he wasn't going to. His mad Heath Robinson mentality got to work and he had us make a bamboo pipe so that when he had to urinate, he didn't soil himself. No one else in those camps had managed to devise their own sewage system. If you can imagine something that weighs six stone or so, is on the point of death and has no qualities of the human condition that aren't revolting, calmly lying there with a pencil and a scrap of paper, *drawing*, you have some idea of the difference of temperament that this man had from the ordinary human being.

While the remains of 'H' Force were moved back down to Singapore, the remains of Searle had to stay behind, still dangerously near to death when malaria returned. Should the central nervous system overreact to the challenge of the parasite *Plasmodium falciparum*, the result can be cerebral malaria, a condition no less liable than cholera to take the patient's life. What saved Searle, perhaps, was that he no longer had the strength to overreact to anything.

In December he was transported from Kanchanaburi to the Sime Road Camp near Singapore racecourse, a journey he did not subsequently recall. Somehow he had retained his drawings, in flat folders in a bag, and his battered army specs. Malaria returned on Christmas Eve. It would have speeded his recovery to know that on 29 December the Red Cross had let the family at Collier Road know that he was a prisoner – almost two

Below: Twenty-fourth birthday card from George Sprod, Singapore, 3 March 1944

Drawn by the Australian cartoonist in Sime Road Camp and presented to Searle in the middle of a malaria bout. Sprod later became a Punch *contributor and now lives in Sydney.*

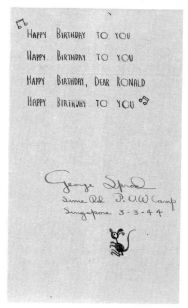

years after his capture. That they knew nothing of his condition was a blessing, however. A new and undiagnosed fever struck in the first days of 1944; and even in their sounder periods of health all the railway survivors were suffering from shock. But Searle knew the cure – his drawing, for which materials were not quite so desperately difficult to obtain within a populous camp. And Searle had a new ally in the graphic business – one of the Australians, George Sprod, who had made similar beginnings in the cartoon world before the war had interrupted him. Searle and Sprod together set about designing decor for the Barn Theatre (of Hut 16), which had a whole spring programme of shows mapped out. Searle scrounged a squared-paper exercise book from somewhere and made it his 'Theatre Notes and Stage Designs' notebook. It cannot be said that he carried on as if nothing had happened; but it was an astounding resurgence of the creative spirit.

The Spring Season was to open with *Cinderella and the Magic Soya Bean*. At Sime Road's 'Flying Dutchman Snack Bar' (gooey balls of sago rolled in grated coconut a speciality), an exhibition of the relevant designs was mounted, offering 'a preview in drawings by Ronald Searle (of *Lilliput*) and George Sprod (of *Smith's Weekly*)'. The drawings, with the exception of costume designs, were offered for sale at $1 or $1.50 each. Flattened by malaria, Searle wasn't there to see them go, but in his absence he made $18.25 and Sprod $7.50. A quarter of the money went to the Concert Party, a good deal of the rest towards replacement materials for the artists.

Such was the general eagerness to entertain and be entertained at the Barn Theatre that shows ran for five nights each, followed by a two-night pause while the next production accomplished its get-in for the next five-night season. Searle's delightful designs for both drama and revue survive in his notebooks, along with some posters of the time – all work necessarily done in advance, which was just as well, since recurrences of malaria were unpredictable. He passed his twenty-fourth birthday emerging from a bout, comforted by a birthday card from Sprod. Feeling stronger, he allowed himself to be cast in the forthcoming *Rag Bag Revue*, as the Ghost in a sketch called 'Hamlet Goes Hollywood', Item 9 on the programme. Sure enough, when opening night came round, Ronald was back in the grip of malaria, but he went on anyway; authentic trembling and a sepulchrally hoarse voice did wonders for the role, and he held out for five days. He was back on the boards in April, playing in John Drinkwater's 1927 comedy *Bird in Hand* (typical line: 'Father, you know I've never wanted to marry anyone but Joan. You've known it for a long time'). These parts had to be written out by hand from a master copy.

Much appreciated though the theatre season was by all, it must have convinced the Japanese that their prisoners were sufficiently revived to face further work. On 4 May a procession of trucks arrived to make a wholesale transfer of men to Changi Gaol – not the camp in which they had first languished, but a modern prison built by the British themselves only eight years before. The Gaol had been intended to house 600 prisoners. By the time the Japanese had finished emptying their other Singapore camps into it, more than 10,000 men were concentrated inside. Half of them were accommodated in stifling, clangorous cells, the other half in huts and courtyards within the high perimeter wall. On arrival, Searle was placed in Cell C.1B, a 'mass' cell containing 200 men. In case this was a staging-post on the way to some new jungle horror, Searle sketched his new environment at once. He was actually to remain in C.1B for some months to come.

On a good day, life in the Changi courtyards resembled some enormous medieval fair, with all manner of strange crafts being practised and tiny transactions made. Any number of unofficial miniature kitchens might be boiling up some fragments of greenery, or even

Above: Ikada, Changi Gaol, Singapore, July 1944

The friendly guard sketched in unmistakably friendly fashion. A matter of months after the atrocities of the railway, Searle was already discarding any 'global' hatred of the oppressors.

an illicitly bartered egg. Red Cross parcels did reach Singapore from time to time, but on all but one occasion were simply intercepted by the Japanese, on whom the possible advantage in feeding their labourers seems to have been lost. Their new tectonic aim was the shaping of the Changi area into a military airfield. Essentially this meant removing all the hills, again with hand-tools only, the kind of task over which the Egyptians had presided 4000 years before. The alternatives to airport slavery were 'P' Party – which performed stevedore work at the docks and the railway station, and was favoured by the virtuoso pilferers – or heavy haulage duties close to the Gaol. Sick men were reckoned suitable for pulling tree-trunks, as they could be harnessed to trailers in groups of sixteen or more. A prisoner not engaged on any of these work-details received half rations.

Searle had scarcely accustomed himself to these new conditions, and sketched them, when he was smitten by a further item from the medical lexicon: dengue fever, which offers as its chief attraction a week's intense pain in the joints and limbs. Recovery brought nothing to celebrate, merely another sharp attack of malaria – the fifteenth by the sufferer's own count, and the eleventh officially diagnosed by the M.O. This one lasted eight days. Searle was left in wistful mood. In the occasional diary he kept he noted that he had been a 'prisoner $2\frac{1}{2}$ years = 911 days'. The cease-fire was a year away, less one day.

The very next day, however, a rare private pleasure was added to the pains of 1944, when Searle was assigned to work in the prison gardens. Within twenty-four hours he had reached an accommodation with an unusually benevolent guard, Ikada, who, gently bribed with a portrait of himself (perhaps the most sympathetic of all Searle's Japanese studies), allowed the artist to roam with his sketchbook a little further than duty strictly required – mainly to nearby beaches, where the large freedom of the sea could be contemplated. For years, his subjects had been all too festeringly human. The chance to draw trees and village huts (*kampongs*) was a healing in itself.

By contrast, Searle's supposed hours of rest had become dramatically busier, since his old Sime Road colleague, George Sprod, had suggested the reintroduction of a camp magazine. 'Printed and Published at the Office of "The Exile", Cell 21 – C3 Floor, Japanese Prisoner of War Camp, Changi Gaol, Singapore', *The Exile* was announced as a fortnightly, and for a while succeeded in keeping to this amazing timetable. Ten editions were produced, the first five in two months. Stoutly bound (by 'The Changi Bookbindery'), they had a print-run of just one: a single copy had to circulate among 10,000 potential readers. Searle was naturally Art Editor, Sgt Jack Wood the Business Manager and the Editor was Bernard Campion, who had survived the sinking of the *Prince of Wales* and now operated *The Exile*'s miraculously scrounged typewriter. Articles gathered in from all over the camp ranged from Searle's pleasant expositions of modern-art movements to quite risky pieces of 'creative writing' like the poem that began 'My Lady Cholera, Death headed ...' For fear of a *Survivor*-style débâcle, religion and politics were generally avoided, though some polemical forecasts were advanced on the state of Britain after the war. Performances by Changi's leading female impersonator, 'Judy Garland' (an Australian never designated by another name), were always enthusiastically received; but some shows, even those with stunning sets by Searle, earned ungrateful reviews which angered those readers who felt that excessively high standards were being demanded. There were even calls for the suppression of *The Exile* on these grounds, but Campion skilfully diverted the controversy into a debate about standards themselves.

The Exile's Art Editor was ransacking his brain for every conceivable illustrative style he could think of, from Dali to the women's magazines. It seemed that with crayons,

Above: Australian prisoner, Singapore, 1942

An unusual combination of comradely portraiture, showing the glazed-over look of a man beginning to realize what he's in for, and formal experimentation with the techniques of cubism: the full-face portrait includes strong elements of a left-facing profile, and the line mixes naturalism with stylization.

pencils and a few concocted inks and stains, he could call up any shade or shape that 'magazine elegance' had taken when last the POWs had had magazines to look at. His gag cartoons often hit upon a rueful aptness for imprisoned men (goldfish to goldfish in a bowl: 'Maybe it would be better, darling, if we didn't see each other again ...'); others recycled old *Granta* jokes, or caricatures from the 'lightning-sketch' days (lady to Groucho: 'Oh Mr Marx, I think your *Das Kapital* is wonderful'). The whole production of *The Exile* had the mark of friendly teamwork upon it – Searle's old pal Stuart Ludman had joined the editorial board by edition No. 3 – and it is a shame that copyright problems, and the natural reluctance of subsequently better-informed, better-fed writers and artists, have prevented any sort of post-war reprint of its very distinguished improvisations.

Tempting fate, Searle opened *Exile* No. 5 with a frontispiece entitled 'Me and My Malaria', a relationship which was resumed a week later. His system was no longer dangerously surprised by these attacks, but recovery was made arduous by a serious reduction in the food ration. This time, the convalescent Searle shared gratefully in a meal of boiled cat – an ordinary semi-domestic feline taken unawares by one of the group and converted, by the addition of scrubby local spices, coconut and seaweed, into one of the most delicious meals the brethren could remember enjoying. Whatever resources of strength Searle acquired from this dish were immediately expended again in the production of a gala Christmas edition of *The Exile*, followed by renewed exploration of the medical textbook. Jaundice was observed late in November and blossomed in mid-December into the genuine saffron-hued hepatic syndrome, lasting five weeks. If this setback was in any way traceable to the ingestion of cat-flesh, however, Searle seemed undeterred by the possibility, as his next substantial meal – not nearly so palatable because of the strength of the taste – consisted of boiled dog. Rations were now too low to permit any inhibitions. Three kittens which had been delighting Searle's eye for a fortnight, as his drawings show, delighted his palate, and those of his starving friends, on Christmas Day. They were fried.

The periodic visits of the Kempei-Tai, the Japanese Gestapo, still put anyone at grave risk who was found to be harbouring 'subversive' materials like Searle's drawings; but luck and ingenuity kept him out of trouble. In direst need, a pouch of drawings could be slipped under the body of a mortally sick man. Prisoners who had acquired Searle drawings for themselves often buried them in bamboo tubes for later retrieval. The artist himself was actually expanding his technical range at this time, having found a new source of materials in a Korean guard. Kyohara – the Japanese name he was obliged to use – was not trusted by everyone. There were some prisoners who saw in him a typically far-sighted collaborator who prepares for the change of military fortunes well in advance, presenting himself in a flattering light to his future masters; but his subsequent career, so far as it is known, does tend to confirm the story Kyohara gave. A guard commander and a versatile linguist, he had a certain freedom of movement which allowed him to make contact with a Chinese Communist sabotage organization in Singapore. He also initiated certain 'underplots', as he called them, of his own, including the clandestine preparation of an aeroplane in which several Britons, including Searle, might escape along with himself. The plane certainly existed but, fortunately for all, this rather too buccaneering scheme foundered well short of the attempt. The mutually advantageous alliance with Searle in particular continued to develop; from the Chinese, Kyohara obtained some stimulating supplies, including paper of long-forgotten quality and watercolours, which were in use by January 1945.

Otherwise, it was hard going in those early months of the year. The tide of war had

Above: 'Jap front-line soldier', Singapore, 1944

Captioned thus in Forty Drawings, *though later generations would no doubt prefer 'Japanese'. Whatever the cultural differences between the Japanese and their prisoners, it still took men of unusually limited human sympathy to inflict the casual brutality that they did. This face might stand for all that was most formidable in their determination and ruthlessness.*

turned against the Japanese and was swamping their European ally, as Changi was well aware from its hidden radios. A further drastic drop in rations occurred in February. Another cat disappeared into the stewpot. Searle's weight had recovered to nine stone; but in March, the day before his twenty-fifth birthday, he suffered an awful loss. Just after ten o'clock that night, Stuart Ludman, who had come through the railway horrors better than most, died in the Changi Gaol Hospital of cerebral malaria. The two had been friends half their lives.

Such losses only emphasized the meaningless of this life, now entering its fourth year. Developments in Europe were followed with interest, but they failed to inspire any direct sense of involvement. It was dangerous to encourage the thought that the war, the imprisonment, the meaningless toil out on the scorching Changi airfield, might soon be coming to an end. *The Exile* came out strongly against over-optimism. Yet cheerfulness still broke through, particularly at show-time in the 'Coconut Grove' theatre, where the pianist Bill Williams and his lyricists regularly gave their countrymen something to sing about. Their latest revue, staged in the first week of April 1945, featured a large mock-up of an ocean liner — Searle's design, as ever — which nudged its way on to the stage and 'docked', with the implicit intention of picking up the Changi-ites to take them home. This *coup de théâtre* was accompanied by one of Williams' most singable songs, 'On Our Return', a number both optimistic and nostalgic — and, in the event, uproariously received. To the Japanese contingent in the audience, which included General Saito, Commander-in-Chief of all Southern Prison Camps, this stage picture caused immediate and disastrous

Left: Kittens, Changi Gaol, Singapore, 10–25 December 1944

Sketched over a period of a fortnight, and then eaten. 'Like rabbit, but more delicate,' Searle reports.

Overleaf left: Cartoon ideas notebook, Changi Gaol, Singapore, 1942–5

Several of these numbered notions made it into print in the post-war years. No.100, the fly-in-the-soup joke, was published in Lilliput *in August 1946, for example. No.88 became part of the St Trinian's canon; and 'Haven't we met before somewhere?' became the title of a book, in 1966.*

Overleaf right: Easy-to-swallow notebook (actual size), Changi Gaol, Singapore, 1944–5

Made for Searle in Changi by fellow-prisoner F. G. Mann. Searle used it for diary notes which he could literally swallow if challenged. 'Dec 44' notes include: 'Fried kitten . . . quite filling, good meal.' 'May 45': 'Planning systematically for future. Seems vital now.'

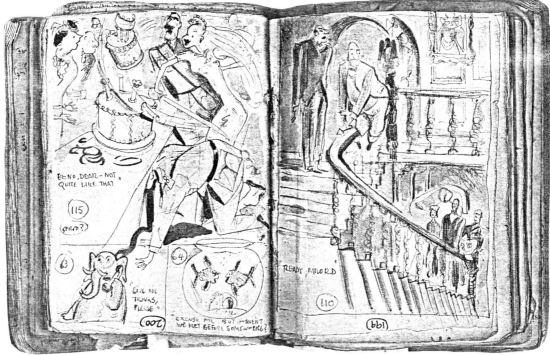

offence. Not only did they terminate the show on the spot, but went on to close down the theatre and reduce rations yet again. Allied bombing-raids on the Singapore docks had already written off one of the best sources of unofficial scraps and scrounges. Of the eleven ounces of food the Japanese now allowed per man per day, two-thirds of the quantity was made up of rice, a limited nutrient; even the extra portion distributed on 29 April, the Emperor's birthday, was no help in keeping beri-beri at bay. Epidemics now sprang up quickly. Even those men presently free of malaria or dysentery were despondent. The production rhythms of *The Exile* had slowed: first monthly, then two-monthly. For many, the only solace was a smoke – dismal smouldering grasses or papaya leaves, rolled in paper from a book or, in Searle's case, from the corner of a drawing. Some of his most evocative sketches of gaol and jungle were docked at the corners for the sake of a roll-up.

Memories like these were understandably much dwelt upon, in the post-war years, by ex-POW organizations which fuelled themselves emotionally on a continuing hatred of the Japanese. Ronald Searle never associated himself with such feelings. He came to the view that if only the Allied prisoners had possessed a better understanding of the historical and cultural premises upon which Japanese policies were based, the notoriously unpredictable and 'inscrutable' aspects of their behaviour could have been explained and some general amelioration of conditions possibly negotiated. That some common ground might have been discovered was proved to him personally in April 1945 by the behaviour of Captain Takahashi, the prison administrator directly responsible to General Saito. Some months before, Takahashi had peremptorily sent word from his concrete tower overlooking the gaol that a consignment of Searle's drawings was to be sent up for inspection. It was known, from Searle's theatre designs, posters and programmes, that he was engaged in this kind of work, but it was with considerable trepidation that he made up his portfolio, naturally omitting any incriminating 'action' drawings, or even portraits, of the Japanese. The response from Takahashi on that occasion had been a polite note and a complimentary packet of fine paper for Searle's use.

Now, in the immediate aftermath of the 'Coconut Grove' disaster, came a further instruction from the administrator, ordering Searle and three colleagues to report to the nearby Beach Club, where officers of the Imperial Japanese Army took their ease. These premises were to be redecorated and embellished to the highest standards starving men could attain, with Searle murals on several specified walls. There did not seem to be any deadline attached to the work, and the men were generally left unsupervised. The explanation for this most preferential of treatment was two months in coming. One day, privately, Takahashi declared himself an artist – a former Paris student, he said. In proof of his claim, he borrowed Searle's sketchbook and dashed off a by no means inelegant outline of a mother and child. Terminating the interview with a gift of pencils and crayons, he politely withdrew, and the matter was not mentioned again. Desultory work on the beach villa continued for a further dreamlike month, until Takahashi was abruptly transferred away from Changi altogether. It seems likely that his distribution of favours had been officially noted and punished. Decorative work at the Officers' Club ceased at the same time and the erstwhile muralist found himself on 'P' Party, unloading artillery shells at the docks.

The war in Europe had ceased two months before, but conditions in Changi had only deteriorated. The men felt abandoned and depressed. Searle was soon back in the hospital huts, waiting for treatment on an abscess in his left calf. It grew into a huge ulcerated crater in his leg, which was surgically excavated under anaesthetic on 10 August. By the time Searle was ready to take notice again, the news was in: two atomic bombs dropped and surrender negotiations under way. On 15 August the cease-fire was ordered and the war officially ended; but many Japanese commanders in theatres of war distant from the atom-blasted homeland found it impossible to comply with this instruction. The Japanese command in Singapore was one such. Some prisoners were told by guards that they would be shot *en masse* the following day, in compliance with a mad order issued by Count Terauchi, Commander-in-Chief of all Southern Armies. It failed to happen – nobody knows by what margin.

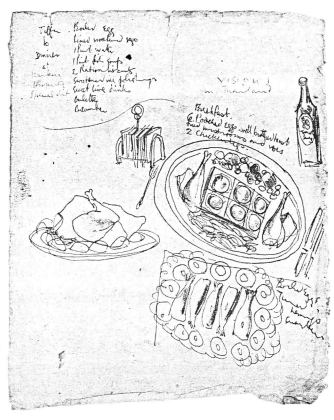

Above: 'Visions in Thailand', Siam, 1943

Brought back from the railway by Searle in 1943, an A to Z of remembered food. On another page, the seductive shape of a roast turkey is recalled, along with a vast breakfast consisting of six poached eggs, two chicken legs, well buttered toast, fried mushrooms etc. That Searle could take pleasure in the visual *memory of food does much to make plain the special character of his imagination.*

On 20 August Ronald was allowed to send a brief message home, the merest confirmation of his existence. The Japanese, still, weirdly, in charge but bowing politely now, produced Red Cross parcels, cigarettes and food, which they had somehow overlooked. The Union Flag was openly on display. Searle remained in the hospital, recuperating slowly. Another week passed without developments until, at last, B-24 planes suddenly appeared over the camp, dropping leaflets confirming that the war was really over. Searle emerged from the hospital to draw the scene, then staggered back again. The following day, medical and supervisory staff were dropped in advance of supplies, lest the prisoners fall upon unfamiliar foods too recklessly and harm themselves. The nourishment was parachuted in twenty-four hours later, on the day when the Japanese vanished, all at once, from Changi. Singapore was formally surrendered on 24 September in a signing ceremony aboard H.M.S. *Sussex*, the ship which sent ashore the first white bread Searle had tasted for three and a half years.

A different order of reality had taken over. Admiral Mountbatten arrived to preside over a suitably public re-observance of the surrender ritual in Singapore on 12 September. Two days later, he made a tour of inspection of Changi Gaol where, in terms of accommodation, disgracefully little had changed. Searle was back in Cell C.1A, along with his friends Jack Wood and Paul Miller (later a Canon of Derby Cathedral). Accompanying Mountbatten was his press attaché, Tom Driberg M.P., who knew Miller from pre-war days and whose attention was drawn to the *Exile* office, where edition No.10 (the last) had just been produced. Impressed by the enterprise, Driberg mentioned it at once to the Supremo who, with a characteristic mixture of real curiosity and flair for public relations, responded with an impromptu invitation. Within minutes, Searle found himself beside the Mountbattens' driver in an open limousine, with Lord Louis and his wife in the back seat, and Wood and Miller following behind in a jeep, a vehicle Searle had never seen before. The convoy skimmed along through cheering crowds and arrived at Government House. Here drinks were taken in some quantity while the Exilists told their story, after which Mountbatten returned the compliment with an hour's briefing on the shape of the Burma campaign and the military prelude to Japan's defeat.

Then, still in their prison rags, the men took their places for dinner, amid a blaze of medals, pips and braid. Searle sat between Major Sherman R.M. and the Supremo himself, opposite the Mountbattens' secretary, Elizabeth Ward. Lady Edwina was flanked by Miller and Wood. 'The conversation was quite intimate,' wrote Ronald in a 'privilege' air-mail letter to his sister Olive, 'as though we were friends of the family. Port followed and there were more long talks and drinks ... Generals were small fry, in fact when we came back to Gaol at midnight the Army Chief-of-Staff Major-General Kimmins gave me a chit signed by him to show the sergeant-major in case they wanted to know why we were out late! The A.C.O.S. was just like a father. It was so fantastic ...' Mountbatten, for his part, had been attentive to the prisoners' stories, some of which he reproduced that night in his personal diary, closing with Searle's pick-axe-in-the-back story.

Below: The beach near Changi Gaol, Singapore, 21 July 1944

One of the views Searle was allowed to sketch by the tolerant Ikada (see p. 64). Such a scene must have represented not just the possibility of sailing away some day, but the actual and visible marvel of a virtually unpopulated landscape, after Searle's years of oppressive proximity to hundreds of other bodies.

Ronald Searle. July 1944. Singapore

Beach near the prison

Above: Drawing by Takahashi, Singapore, June 1945

Lightning sketch of mother and child by Lieutenant Takahashi, offered to Searle in proof that the Japanese administrator had trained as an artist in Paris. It is touching that he chose to depict at such a moment what is universally the symbol of the most trusting kind of love.

Right: Planes dropping pamphlets, Changi Gaol, Singapore, 28 August 1945

Searle struggled out of the camp hospital for long enough to witness the dropping of leaflets by a B-24 Liberator, about whose mission an unusual amount is known, since the captain of the plane, Eric William Myers, wrote to Searle after his appearance on BBC-TV's Panorama ten years later. It was, said Mr Myers, a white Liberator numbered KH 270 bearing the letter B on either side of the fuselage and a black cross on rudders and fins. He had taken off at dawn from the Cocos Islands and his total flying time was fourteen and a half hours. As many cigarettes as possible were dropped on the camp, but the main objective was to give instructions, by leaflet, to the Japanese guards. The aeroplane, for once, was aptly named.

Ronald Searle

'Planes dropping pamphlets' announcing end of war, over Changi gaol camp Singapore August 28 1945

Ronald Searle was confined to Changi an infuriating fortnight longer, 'smoking (Player's) like a chimney — 20 a day' and eating 'good and adequate' food. He was buoyant, but deeply exhausted: 'I feel like an old, old man.' He had come through on his own terms and with respect. His fellows had looked to him for solace on many occasions and in many forms. In the words of a fellow Changi artist, Philip Meninsky, 'they would have been concerned if he stopped drawing'. Rightly so, for it would have been an unmistakable sign that he had stopped living.

On 27 September 1945 the remnants of the 18th Division set out on the journey home. Arriving at the harbour, they found their transport had a familiar look. It was H.M.T. *Sobieski,* the very same old tub in which these men, and so many others never to be seen again, had sailed from Gourock, four years before.

FOUR

Girls will be Searles
(1945–53)

'"C.D.N." Man Announces Safety With A Cartoon' ran the headline in the Cambridge paper of 22 September 1945. Before his departure from the East, Sapper Searle had taken the opportunity of sending off a 'hurried note' to his former colleagues by special plane. 'How impossibly wonderful it is to be free again, just to enjoy the minor pleasures of life again – a piece of bread, a tailor-made cigarette, and being able to walk freely without fear of a Samurai sword snicking one's head off!' he wrote. The phrase 'minor pleasures of life' came to him ready-made, since a book of that name, by Rose Macaulay, had been one of his Changi possessions. It had been printed on a kind of India paper, all too suitable for conversion into cigarettes. Years afterwards, when Searle met Miss Macaulay at a party and told her that her book had contributed in this odd fashion to the history of its own subject, she took mortal offence and stalked away. The incident disappointed Searle, even though he had become used to failures of imagination on the part of Britons who had never been prisoners. It was impossible, from the start, to get people into the way of comprehending what had happened in Singapore and Siam. The tradition of misunderstanding was indeed inaugurated by the *C.D.N.*, for the 'cartoon' to which it jovially referred was in reality a montage of vicious portrait heads of Japanese, explicitly captioned by Searle as 'the type of men who were responsible for the death of over 13,000 of our prisoners on the Thai–Burma Railway'.

For the moment, however, Searle was crossing the Indian Ocean and taking a rest from sketching. There were debriefings to be undergone on board the *Sobieski*, and many letters to write, some of them very delicate and sad. With contrasting gusto, he tried to ease his own family into imagining the otherness of his life for the past four years:

> You'd never imagine the mixture of peoples we've lived with since 1942 – Dutch, Javanese, Ambonese, French, Italians, Chinese, Malay, Sikh, Tamil, Gurkha, Japanese, Korean, Danish, Swedish, Russian, West Indian, American, Canadian, South African, Australian, New Zealanders, Spanish, Mexican, Eurasian, Anglo-Indian, Siamese, Indonesian, Burmese, Belgian, Czechoslovakian, Estonian and dozens more ... It will be a change not to hear broken English, tho' I don't know when that will be, for the crew on this ship is Polish!

A half-day's shore leave at Colombo had brought out the sketchbook again: 'There are some beautiful faces among the Indian women, rather like those serene, enigmatical faces you see in early Indian painting or 4th Dynasty Egyptian papyrus portraits.' Writing to Olive, he was perhaps revisiting museums in his mind, but also looking forward:

Above: Self-portrait on a cannibalized page, Siam, 1943

Typical example of a book half smoked, half drawn upon, in Changi. Vision and Design was a collection of essays by the art critic and painter Roger Fry (1866–1934), published in 1920.

Oh dear — I am impatient. Anxious to get home and get things started again — I wonder how difficult it will be to recapture these last, lost years? ... I don't know what my plans are yet, things have been rather a mess but I rather fancy I shall get married quickly and settle down to my work.

From the middle of the Red Sea he confessed a craving for apples, as yet unsatisfied; he had tasted his last one in Cape Town in 1941. Cox's Orange Pippins had been available at Colombo, but not to personnel lacking the relevant ration book. Whatever else the war had done, it had not neutralized bureaucracy.

Pumped full of vitamin B and quinine, Searle was well and putting on weight. In two months, he would gain two stone. At Port Suez, seven letters from his sister and parents were waiting. From these he learned that he had not been completely forgotten in London. The little magazines, notably *Lilliput* and *London Opinion*, had continued to print such gag-cartoons as he had left with them, and at one point he had even been named among the Twelve Best Cartoonists of the Year. Tom Driberg, he was told, had given his story full prominence in *Reynolds' News*. Ronald hoped, in his answering letter, that Driberg 'didn't put too many gory details in his bit ... it was a long time ago and I'm not suffering from the effects now. It was horrible while it lasted but it seems a dream now.' Olive's husband Jack Fenn had just been sent off East as part of an occupying force. In the last of his seaborne letters, written in the Mediterranean, Ronald fancied he had passed Jack's ship in the Suez Canal: 'A big trooper packed with soldiers and A.T.S. and all the rest passed us in the middle lakes — quite close it was — and they shouted to us "We're going to Singapore!" We told them "You can have it!"' By now, Ronald had caught a 'bea—utiful cold' and was wrapped up against the European chills in a new issue of clothes. He had already re-established a chatty mode of discourse with his sister:

> You know you were lucky to have had that job [Olive had been a calibrator with the Cambridge Instrument Company] otherwise I suppose you would have been a WAAF or something. I must say though that the nicest service girls I've come across since Singapore have been Wrens. Very charming they are — and they looked after us well. I was rather embarrassed at first meeting women again — but I soon got over it.

On 24 October 1945, five days short of four years after its departure from Gourock, the *Sobieski* deposited its round-trip passengers at Liverpool. Their home for two grim, anticlimactic nights was 79(E) Transit Camp, Poverty Lane, Maghull. Housed in Hut 37, Group 8, Sapper Searle was informed that his weight now amounted to 11 stone 1lb, and that his army back-pay for the last three and a half years came out at a round £210. Dragging two kitbags of assorted accoutrements, he took the train to Cambridge on 26 October and was met by the family at the station. No civic welcome was laid on for the surviving soldiery; any wholehearted celebration would have been inappropriate. For every family who put bunting out to welcome a son home there was another to whom nobody would be returning. One of Ronald's first melancholy tasks was to call on Mrs Ludman, Stuart's mother, and tell her what he could of the last years of her boy. To Matt Kerr's family on the Isle of Arran were forwarded those few belongings that had been taken from his body and sent back down the Burma railway line.

The embrace of family life in Cambridge could not be borne for long. Within a fortnight, Searle was lodging in Chelsea with his old art-school colleagues Pamela and Bernard Lucas, trying to find an address of his own and reintroduce himself to London's editors.

Above: Portrait photograph, Cambridge, December 1945

A portrait made at the celebrated Cambridge studio of Ramsey and Muspratt shortly after Searle's return from Singapore. 'Strangely enough he didn't seem any different,' his sister Olive recalls, though the pencil moustache was a novelty. It had already appeared in George Sprod's birthday card (see p. 63). Many prisoners were very scrupulous about shaving, in spite of the practical difficulties. Searle's Dutch friend Klaas Kooy maintained the same razor-blade throughout his years of confinement.

His best potential contact was Miss Webb of *Lilliput*, whose by-line he had also seen over a 'London Letter' published in an armed-forces magazine called *Gen*. She had been delighted to see her erstwhile contributor, long believed killed, resurfacing in Tom Driberg's article: but their meeting was somewhat delayed, first by an over-efficient secretary who turned Ronald away because he had no appointment, and then by Kaye Webb's burst appendix. She and Ronald were corresponding well before they did meet; she had already fallen for his handwriting.

Quick to appreciate the drama of its former pupil's confinement, and his traceable development of a fluent, economical line, the Cambridge School of Art mounted a well-publicized exhibition in December: 'Life As A Prisoner In ﾃapanese Hands Recorded By A Cambridge Artist'. Arranged in six narrative groups, the exhibits gave an impression, said the Technical School administrator John Scupham in his catalogue note, 'not of diversity but of unity; of horror, and boredom, and beauty flowering in strange places, held in the compelling unity of one man's vision'. Clearly this body of work was considerable enough to make Searle eligible for retrospective nomination as a War Artist, a status he had made some attempt to secure for himself in mid-1941 by sending material to the Ministry of Information. Curiously enough, his case had just been considered again, a week before his Cambridge exhibition, at a meeting of the Artists' Advisory Committee of the same Ministry, held in the National Gallery; but again, no action was taken. As Ronald was not informed of this procedure, one wonders what work of his the Committee considered. It may even have been the 1941 submissions, no longer relevant to his case. Proper recognition of Searle's wartime drawings would not arrive for another forty years.

Ronald stayed in Cambridge for Christmas. One of his gifts was an attack of malaria. Life restarted in earnest in the New Year. Chelsea Town Council, according a returning POW the preferential treatment that was his due, allotted him a room at 34 Tite Street. Only later did it emerge that this was the renumbered 16 Tite Street, sometime home of Oscar Wilde. Searle's first-floor back room had been the great man's library. Now it was converted, with sister Olive's help, into 'a gleaming white cube of a room', where his work as a professional artist began, and new friends got to know him. The notion of girlfriends was rediscovered; Ronald had courted no very serious sweetheart before the war, and his sexual experimentation had been circumscribed by the 'working-class-proper' ethos of his home. Now he had a fierce appetite for beauty in all its forms, including the more distant and idealized. With the most companionable of his new male friends, the journalist David Arkell, he took to frequenting the ballet again. Arkell, who remained a lifelong friend, had been a prisoner himself, interned at the St Denis camp in Paris, an experience that failed to extinguish his genial Francophilia. Ronald, in his company, found himself exposed to happily novel continental tastes, revelling particularly in the Roland Petit Ballet des Champs-Elysées, which visited the Adelphi Theatre with *Les Forains* – an experience so delightful that Arkell felt it marked the point from which Ronald's destiny would somehow be linked with France. They followed ballet both as paying customers and backstage observers. Ronald took his sketchbook to the ballet classes of Vera Volkova. He was amazed at the 'enormous meals' the ballerinas ate, but then enormous meals were still a novelty wherever they occurred. Getting back into the discipline of conventional drawing, Ronald even attended briefly at the Central School of Arts, until malaria returned to put an end to such pleasures. This time, the army put him in the Princess Beatrice Hospital, where new treatments ensured that he would not be troubled by the disease again.

Below: Newspaper advertisement, Cambridge, December 1945

Including Searle's portrait of General Masatochi Saito, drawn from life earlier the same year.

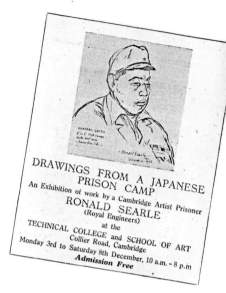

Above: 'Yes, Fido is just like one of the family', Changi Gaol, Singapore, c. 1944–5

Searle's first cartoon for Punch, *published 20 March 1946 and reproduced in the* Punch Digest *eleven years later (Corgi edition, 1957). The magazine liked to get value for its copyrights.*

Above: 'Hand up the girl who burnt down the East Wing last night', Changi Gaol, Singapore, c. 1944–5

The second St Trinian's cartoon, and the first to explore life at the school itself. Published in Lilliput, *April 1946.*

The groundwork he had already put in began to bring returns. On 20 March 1946, a childhood ambition was realized when *Punch* first printed a Searle cartoon. 'Fido is just like one of the family' inaugurated a productive strain in Searle's broader comic output, where language is seen to speak the literal truth. Another tradition commenced, or recommenced, almost at once, when the second St Trinian's cartoon – the first to explore the horrors of the foundation itself – was published by *Lilliput*. The full catalogue of schoolgirl Guignol was revealed only very gradually over a period of years; the public's enthusiasm for the genre easily outlasted its creator's. It is interesting that Searle initiated a series starring an appalling boy ('Orrible Albert) in *London Opinion* a month before the re-emergence of St Trinian's, but Albert was not 'orrible enough to catch on.

It was certainly to Searle's advantage that his signature on a drawing came with a journalistic 'story' attached. The magazines which were interested in his work tended to want to recount his dramatic history. *Illustrated*, *London Opinion* and *Strand* (with a piece by David Arkell under the pseudonym 'Ray Garson') all told the tale in 1946, as did forces' magazines, concentrating understandably on *The Exile* and its artist. Much of the Searle material that was now appearing had been originally conceived and drawn in Changi. The *Illustrated* article, which reprinted a wide selection of the wartime work, including one of the most ravishing of the 'escapist' theatre designs, very soon travelled as far as Singapore itself, where it was read with interest by 14608544 Cpl Sunnucks S.A., of 2 Company, A.L.F. Signals. Learning from the article that a Korean called Kyohara had been of service to Searle, Alan Sunnucks made some researches in the nearby Korean POW camp, where he found Kyohara himself recovering from an appendix operation and facing a miserable future among certified pro-Japanese collaborators. Sunnocks wrote to Searle describing the situation, and so did Kyohara, now reverting proudly to his Korean name of Han Do Chin. Searle, in turn, taking advantage of his recent acquaintance with the Supreme Allied Commander, South-East Asia, wrote directly to Mountbatten, who again was admirably prompt in his response. Within days, he had had Han Do Chin 'discreetly contacted' and removed to a civilian internment camp; he also arranged for the Korean to be brought to headquarters to be thanked in person by Colonel Wild, 'who you may remember was the officer who concealed the Union Jack in Changi'. The next ship to Korea took Han Do Chin home. After a couple of letters of thanks, he disappeared into the thickets of local politics, as an associate of the 'Left Wing Labouring People's Party'; and then this brave and talented individual was heard of no more. Searle, in gratitude for his help, sent Mountbatten a portrait of a Kempei-Tai man which, Lord Louis said, did much to 'brighten' his gloomy government office. He concluded the correspondence by hoping Searle was fit again, and 'fully recovered' from his experience as a prisoner of war – a hope worth expressing, but not likely of fulfilment, then or later.

Sapper Searle was discharged from the army on 10 June 1946 and transferred to the Reserve the following day. Campaign medals had been awarded, and one taken back: the authorities decided that since Searle had technically not set foot in Burma he was not entitled to the Burma Star, a decision in which all the vast administrative clumsiness of the previous seven years could be seen pithily summarized. Searle was furnished with a minor pension, and some time later, a bizarrely arbitrary sum in 'reparation' from the Japanese. This amounted to £60 per prisoner; and it so happened that on the morning the cheque arrived, Ronald had heard from a dealer that a fairly important drawing by Annibale Carracci, one of the fathers of *caricatura*, had become available – at a price of £60. Searle endorsed the cheque, handed it over, and took the Carracci – a piece of art

Left: 'Life in a Studio, No. 2',
Lilliput, March 1946

The miscreant boy is more or less
identical with 'Orrible Albert, who
made his first appearance in London
Opinion that same month. Well
before Searle had offspring of his own,
children are identified as the natural
enemies of the artist's creative
environment.

history seemingly willed into his possession by a belatedly generous fate.

Friends, too, were doing their best for him. He attended the 1946 Labour Party Conference at Bournemouth not in a fiery burst of conviction – though like most returning servicemen he was pro-Labour in a disgusted, enough-of-all-that way – but as illustrator to Tom Driberg, who was reporting on the proceedings for *Reynolds' News*. The resulting sketch of Herbert Morrison was obtained at the cost of some unease, since the paper had booked Driberg and Searle into a double room. The sexual tendencies of the older man were not known to Ronald, who, indeed, had gone through the war experience without witnessing any homosexual behaviour; in the general desperation of life, sex had been an irrelevance even to men who subsequently identified themselves as homosexual in civilian life. But for Searle there could be little doubt of Driberg's orientation when, sitting up in his single bed, he enquired brightly, 'Ronnie, are you a masochist?' Since Ronald had just endured, without protest, the spectacle of the Member of Parliament peeing into the washbasin, there was perhaps a case to be made for an affirmative reply; but Searle favoured a decisive 'No', which terminated the discussion. Future collaborations between the two were innocent of any such proposals and Ronald, while unsurprised by the eventual disclosure of Driberg's duplicitous career, continued to harbour 'fond memories of the greedy old villain as a splendidly stimulating companion'.

In July, Searle's identity-card registered a change of address to Studio Two, 77 Bedford Gardens, off Kensington Church Street, an address which has since acquired a composite history of its own as an artists' colony. The painter Jankel Adler lived upstairs and the two combative Roberts, Colquhoun and Macbryde, on the floor below. Eddie Wolfe had a room right at the top; John Minton was also in residence; and Keith Vaughan frequently called by. Each man made a different accommodation to the need to earn a living, with Minton coming closest to Searle's territory as a magazine illustrator and book-jacket artist, though he also taught at the Central School. Searle himself could not yet afford to turn down any offers of work. It was a question of learning on the job, and if necessary of inhabiting alien styles in order to meet the expectations of employers and their settled readerships. Sometimes he had to produce, with a straight face, the sort of illustration he would have sent up rotten elsewhere. This applied especially to *John Bull*, a magazine which, inside a cover usually bearing a soupily painted, out-of-focus version of the kind of genre scene Norman Rockwell used to do for the *Saturday Evening Post*, purveyed stories which were illustrated in a style borrowing equally from women's fiction and boys' adventure comics. These were, however, colour illustrations and represented invaluable experience for Searle; and he soon earned another little residency on the magazine, decorating the weekly effusion of a 'philosophising taxi-driver' called Herbert Hodge. The stolid Hodge and his stolid readership were at one, but Searle disturbed the peace; in fact, some readers felt positively threatened by him. A Mrs E. Sharples of Lower Ince, Wigan, wrote in to announce that she got 'a nauseous feeling just glancing at Ronald Searle's ridiculous illustrations. Who on earth ever saw people with such large bodies, thin legs, tiny feet and elongated shoulders as those he depicts each week?' A man from Sheffield added that some drawings were 'more suggestive than humorous' (there had been a scene of seduction, on a couch); while a south London reader opined, uniquely, that the drawings 'resemble the scribblings of young children'. An end was put to the argument by an effective intervention from Herbert Hodge himself. He confessed himself enormously tickled by Searle, who, he said, 'besides bringing out ideally the substance of what I write ... manages at the same time to poke subtle fun at me', which was certainly true. 'He is doing with his exaggerated and grotesque style,' Hodge explained to the Sharplesites, 'what the satirist does with words: telling people "look what funny creatures you are".' This was well put, particularly in its choice of the word 'creatures': because it is clear that what disturbed these readers most of all was the animality Searle revealed in man.

Ronald's *Sobieski*-borne prophesy (or was it a resolution?) concerning early marriage and a settling-down had by now moved swiftly towards fulfilment. As the messenger-gods of the Royal Mail seemed to have been urging all along, Ronald and Miss Webb of *Lilliput* had fallen for each other. He had come to the *Lilliput* office in his 'awful oversized

Left: Ronald Searle and Kaye Webb in the studio, Bedford Gardens, London, c. 1950

Searle's 'Crucifixion of a Thief' hangs on the wall above his head (see Plate facing p. 32). (Photograph by Tom Blau.)

army clothes and little moustache', she had shown off by taking him to the Gargoyle for drinks, and soon a serious affair was under way. Since theirs was a partnership destined to be sundered, it is tempting to search (as they both did in maturer years) for reasons why they should have known better; but amid the glooms of 1946, what better things were there to trust in than the happy instinct of love and the urgency of physical affection? It is true that Ronald was still very close to the pains of his captivity; but in the eyes of Kaye Webb this made him the more cherishable – even noble. His suffering had sanctified him a little. She, a strongly built woman with a charming tinkly voice (later much in demand for broadcasting), represented the very principle of vivacity and gregariousness, not to mention experience. Six years Ronald's senior, she had been married twice already, was the daughter of journalists, and had come up to *Lilliput* through *Picturegoer* and *Picture Post*, at a time when few female journalists reached positions of responsibility outside the particular world of women's magazines. She had 'lived', where Ronald had avoided death; in her, perhaps, he could embrace his 'lost years'. It has often been unthinkingly said that Kaye 'discovered' and promoted Ronald, and made him famous, as if such feats of hyperbolic 'packaging' had been possible in the scuffle of the Forties. She was certainly an early enthusiast for his work; and he had been careful to present her with a portfolio emphasizing his versatility ('I can draw like this, and *this* . . .'). But beyond providing a network of contacts which would have built up more slowly without her help, there was not a great deal that she could have done by way of management of his reputation. Clearly, he had discovered himself.

Right: 'Corps de Ballet in the wings at Covent Garden', *Le Nouveau Ballet Anglais,* Paris, 1946

Searle's contact with the dancers' world was maintained in his contributions to Richard Buckle's magazine Ballet.

His first album of drawings, a monument to that process, was published in November 1946 by the Cambridge University Press, where an old *Granta* friend, Colin Eccleshare, was now working. *Forty Drawings* was the title of the volume, and its presentation, between plainly printed yellow-buff boards, was soberly academic. Frank Kendon, poet and C.U.P. staff man, supplied a brief introduction which spoke of 'a balance of objectivity and sympathy which is not so common a virtue as to be casually passed by ... It is notable that, in prison or out of it, he always naturally looked to his fellows as human beings, and to all as in some sense his companions.' In spite of a selection process that had minimized scenes of forced labour or torture, the book remained powerful enough to cause distress. There was a great deal in it that the public was now anxious to forget, and devotees of pure draughtsmanship were not numerous enough to make the publication a commercial success. The Searles later bought up a large number of copies to be distributed as they wished. In the early Fifties, Ronald's mother made a present of one of these, a signed copy, to a young neighbour who was moving away from Cambridge. He found it so distressing that, much to his subsequent chagrin, he threw it away. It was an austere and truth-telling book — just what the times found hard to bear.

Frank Kendon also wrote to Searle privately, urging him in a fatherly tone to 'take care of your gifts' and continue to 'go about open-minded making notes'. In raising the possibility that 'you do not yourself know how seriously valuable to humanity drawings like some of these are', Kendon was in error, since this was the very conviction that had kept Searle going; but his appreciation of 'the direct statement' made by the drawings was profoundly felt. 'You must forgive me,' he concluded, 'if I say that a greatness lies within your reach in that direction, and I do deeply hope that you will make yourself have time and leisure somehow to continue moving that way.' But it was hard to reconcile these high-flown affirmations with the necessity, which Kendon acknowledges, of making a living. Searle did not wish to linger in that zone of indecision where an agonized choice has to be made between 'pure' starving-in-a-garret creation and 'commercial art'. For one thing, he had had enough of starving. And he was in demand. The one foot he had placed only half-willingly in the cartoon world had been securely shackled there by eager editors. The confident breadth of his repertoire in illustration has been noted. The path to greatness, at least for the time being, would have to be the road to work. It was no longer only his personal need that dictated this. By the end of the year, it was certain that Kaye Webb was pregnant.

Ronald had every right to be astonished by this news. Post-war doctors, continuing the deliberate tradition of misinformation that had marked the Singapore experience from the start, had advised returning POWs that they would probably remain sterile for at least three years after their repatriation. It now became evident that Ronald Searle had fathered twins, a feat paralleled at much the same time by his Changi colleague and fellow-artist, Philip Meninsky. They compared notes on the subject, Searle in a telegram intimating that he would 'appreciate a few words with those b—y doctors'. At this late date, it all sounds a rather charming and bohemian episode, but it was very much more awkward at the time. Divorce was a laborious process, and Kaye Webb had not secured her freedom from her previous husband; nor was it certain that senior administrators of the publishing business, Victorians by birth and upbringing, would look tolerantly upon this irregular behaviour. It was therefore decided that Kaye should escape one of Britain's coldest winters and travel to America, where her father was Washington Correspondent of the *Daily Herald*, and have the babies well away from London's gossips, and its rationing too.

Ronald himself was still tied to England, though his work was not: he had begun to find a new market in France, where reprints of cartoons had been appearing for some months. It was the French who published Searle's second book, a little selection of sketches from theatre-land called *Le Nouveau Ballet Anglais*. The French publishers, it must be said, displayed a more spirited sense of occasion than had the phlegmatic Cantabrigians. 'Et voici,' ran the Editor's Note, '*la juste récompense de son courage et son endurance; pour son deuxième Noël d'homme libre, deux recueils de ses oeuvres paraissent simultanément . . . En France, nous sommes heureux de publier le premier livre de Ronald Searle redevenu homme libre.*' At that particular moment, he may not have felt particularly *libre*, however. His prospective family life having disappeared to the land of plenty, Searle set to work as though attempting the all-time record for sundriness of freelance contributions. The *Daily Herald* provided a sort of continuum with the illustrations it commissioned for its 'Country Diary'. The column, signed 'Suffolk Farmer', was genuinely supplied by a Stowmarket man, B. A. Steward, whose premises at Greenlane Farm, Stonham, Searle visited in August to take sketched notes of landscape, livestock and implements. But since the *Herald* was then only a four-page (single-sheet) paper, the resulting illustrations had to be squeezed down virtually to postage-stamp size; Searle had chosen a woodcuttish, updated-Bewick style, and considerable ingenuity was required if any sort of statement was to be made within these dimensions. Still, it was work – like the regular illustrations required by *Lilliput* to accompany the prose ramblings of Patrick Campbell, and the cartoons taken by *London Opinion*, *Men Only*, *Pie* and *The Tatler*. Driberg collaborations were also accepted: their best-remembered outing for *Reynolds' News* was a visit to Edgington's rope-works in the Old Kent Road, where specially ordered hangman's ropes were being made in anticipation of the outcome of the Nuremberg Trials. Searle's growing reputation for the macabre was not always consciously sought.

Punch took another drawing in March, a talking-animal joke; the Art Editor, Kenneth Bird ('Fougasse'), was a keen animal-welfare man, which is why, Ronald surmised, he had approved a cartoon of a circus horse complaining 'Careful – that stung!' to a whip-wielding ringmaster. A better source of earnings, and a fine shop-window in view of its vast circulation, was *Radio Times*, but Searle did not find the work congenial. The magazine's timetable was oppressive – collect the script on Friday, read it and produce the drawing by Monday morning – and he found himself too often with a doomy Third Programme play to illustrate. *Radio Times*, moreover, seemed almost unconsciously to promote a graphic orthodoxy among its contributors. The heraldic styles of Eric Fraser and Sherriffs had been very dominant, encouraging heavy bodies of black ink and etched-looking textures. Scraper-board and woodcuts were much used in the creation of a restrained 'English' presence. One can see why the charms of this regularized cameo format, superbly filled though it almost always was, would cease to appeal to Ronald Searle, who none the less continued to contribute occasionally until well into the Fifties. Once, during 1947, he was called upon to illustrate a programme in which he himself was involved: *The Enigma of the Japanese*, extracts from which were preserved as historical testimony in the BBC Sound Archive. The format again (a scripted discussion) was unsatisfactory; but to hear Searle telling of the Japanese atrocities, in his almost too smoothly reasonable voice, is still an eerie experience.

By the time that programme was broadcast, the twins, Kate and John, were three weeks old. They had been born in Doctors' Hospital, Washington D.C., on 17 July, and would stay in America three more months before sailing home with their mother on the *Queen Elizabeth*. Their father, in the meantime, had managed to fit in some journeying of his own – the first time he had travelled with a group of fellow-artists. Paul Hogarth, at that time an art editor, Communist Party member and political activist, was in touch with several Communist-front 'friendship' organizations, among them the British Yugoslav Association, under whose auspices he was invited to put together a group of artists who might like to visit Yugoslavia and testify to its national reconstruction. The centrepiece of this work was the 'Youth Railway' in Bosnia, then under construction by international teams of young volunteers. Hogarth had been impressed by *Forty Drawings* and, in the certainty that no form of railway-building could be as unpleasant to contemplate as the one organized by the Japanese, he invited Searle along. Ronald seized the opportunity eagerly, as he had reached the age of twenty-seven without knowing anything of continental Europe. He left from Victoria by train in mid-August, in a company which included Hogarth; Francis Klingender, the Marxist art-historian; Laurence Scarfe, from the Central School of Arts and Crafts; and Percy Horton, a portrait specialist. The others

Below: 'By God – if I had a horsewhip I'd horsewhip 'im', *Tribune*, 21 October 1949

Tory diehards at the Conservative Party conference regard the blithe invader with brimming hostility. During his brief period as an openly political cartoonist, Searle, like most practitioners of the craft, enjoys the drama of his public position.

found the journey arduous, but Searle, having known far worse discomfort, made light of it while taking in his first glimpses of Paris and Venice.

It took a good five days to get down to the Nemila Camp on the railway site, but Searle's appetite for sketching was undiminished by fatigue. Hogarth, later a specialist in graphic reportage, had never seen such speed and decisiveness.

> He was more equipped than any of us to cope with it. It was the first time I was involved with a working artist of my own age ...The work I did was pretty awful. In fact it was watching Ronald at work that convinced me I'd just been messing about, and needed to get my act together. There was never a day without sketching as far as Ronald was concerned, he was used to it; and then at night he impressed everybody by sitting down and keeping a diary.

While Horton made portraits of political leaders and engineers, and Scarfe wandered into the countryside alone, Hogarth and Searle sketched side by side. Eventually they took off on their own, to isolated villages in the mountains of the south, where the culture was strongly Muslim, a sector which Searle found much the most interesting. Returning via Sarajevo, they spent five days in Belgrade before taking the train home. Sixty drawings by the group were exhibited at the Leicester Galleries the following February, but the best upshot of the Yugoslav trip was a follow-up excursion which Hogarth now began to organize.

Above: 'The Ruins of Warsaw', 11 August 1948

To Searle's characteristic feel for public places is added a technique for dealing attractively with the chaotic texture of rubble – slightly reminiscent of the shaly feel favoured by Graham Sutherland. (Original in the possession of Paul Hogarth.)

First, Ronald Searle had the unsettling experience of meeting his own three-month-old twins and deciding what could possibly be done with them. Both parents were working flat out, and in any case there was no room for them in London; so it was decided that they should be looked after, almost in the manner of a wartime evacuation, by Kaye's mother in Westgate-on-Sea, on the north coast of Kent. This arrangement actually worked rather well. The twins in their earliest years saw less of both parents than they might have, but whenever Ronald was able to come, his time was completely their own – a luxury which disappeared later on. They retained happy memories of Westgate, while their parents spent far from restful times in the Bedford Gardens studio. The neighbours on one side were given to making clusters of morose-sounding bumps on the party wall, which turned out to betoken darts practice; while from the domain of Colquhoun and Macbryde below came whoops and hollers and the occasional crash, unmistakable symptoms of orgiastic ecstasy. One night, Ronald went out to post some drawings and did not come back, leaving Kaye convinced that he had been drawn into the saturnalia, as indeed he had. 'Do you know what they were doing?' he said wonderingly on his return. '*Scottish dancing!*'

It took the best part of a year to find a suitable flat. During that time, Ronald Searle married Kaye Webb at Kensington Register Office on 12 March 1948 and got down to some serious breadwinning. The *Daily Herald* work had come to an end, but there was quite challenging colour stuff to be done for the *Strand*, where Art Editor Robin Jacques allowed some of the *Radio Times* group to have a bit more fun. Minton, Ardizzone and Anthony Gross were all regulars here, along with the young Walter Fawkes (later 'Trog') and Pearl Falconer, who in her uninsistent line (and the small extremities of her figures) was of all the illustrators perhaps closest to Searle's own 'feel' at this time, and certainly admired by him. In spite of paper shortages, and travel and currency restrictions, it was a boom time for pen-and-ink. Overloaded with unpleasantly factual images during the war years, the British public had a great appetite for visual information mediated by the artist's graceful touch. Even industrial corporations were beginning to be aware of this, hence Searle's involvement in a book called *Tanker Fleet*, first in a series entitled 'Shell War Achievements' telling 'The War Story of the Shell Tankers and the men who manned them.' The artist was invited to join the tanker *Theliconus* on Tyneside in early February and sail down with her to the port of London. This was a deeply uncomfortable voyage, spent for the most part on a freezing deck recording the ins and outs of pipework and superstructure; but the finished book, designed by Paul Hogarth and reproducing Searle's drawings in a sympathetic russet-brown, emerged as unexpectedly handsome and definitive. The chapter 'Singapore Whirlwind' had required little or no research, though that period was always harrowing to revisit, even in imagination. Kaye Webb remembered being half-strangled more than once as her husband wrestled with a nightmare.

His first cartoon album was now on sale. Its title, *Hurrah for St Trinian's*, expressed a sentiment with which he would never concur. Even though scarcely more than a dozen St Trinian's drawings had yet appeared, the invention of new horrors for the girls to wreak already looked likely to become a chore. The new volume, as well as co-opting the inaugural 1941 drawing into the St Trinian's corpus with a neat change of caption ('... the match with St Helen's has been postponed'), gathered together the best of his published cartoon work so far in a package dedicated to Morley Stuart, '30 Years Editor of the *Cambridge Daily News*'. Almost as heavily featured as the schoolgirls was the since-forgotten figure of 'Orrible Albert. The drawing styles vary in a way which a more

Sig and Russ during their book reading in the Interpreter's Office
Changi Gaol, Singapore.

Ronald Searle 4

Left: Sydney Piddington's telepathy act, Changi Gaol, Singapore, 1944/5

A scene recorded in the Changi Interpreters' Office. Piddington, at the blackboard, successfully transmits a message to the blindfolded Russell Braddon. Major Osmond Daltry is the foreground figure with the eyepatch; Searle himself (with pencil moustache) is the uppermost of the background figures. The Piddingtons, Sydney and his wife Lesley, were a sensation (much played upon by cartoonists) in London during the summer of 1949.

exacting public might have found puzzling, but Searle had now got beyond the point where he could carry on explaining in what grotesquely different circumstances some of these ideas had come to him, how the idioms of Anton or Osbert Lancaster had been used to give imprisoned readers the comfort of a familiar style, and so on. The book created little immediate interest anyway, selling 1493 copies in its first year.

The offer of another trip to Eastern Europe came as a most welcome interruption. Czechoslovakia and Poland were the destinations this time. To Searle it was a revelation just to get as far as Nuremberg and form, in the ruins of the city, some idea of the European conflict he had missed. Czechoslovakia proved frustrating. Searle did meet the sculptor Franta Belsky there, and made another great friend, but the queues for Polish visas in Prague were impossibly long. Searle and Hogarth might have spent their whole time waiting had they not met a film-maker called Ludwik Perski – a friend of their common acquaintance, Feliks Topolski – who happened to be shooting some footage inside the Polish Embassy. He inventively proposed to the bureaucrats a flattering scene wherein the visas of some distinguished visiting artists would be stamped; and so Searle made his European film debut in the act of 'being offered a cigarette, being shaken warmly by the hand, and miming the reception of a visa from the hand of the Vice-Consul'. The real visa came two days later, and Searle and Hogarth continued on their way. They both worked very hard on this journey. Hogarth had an assignment from *Coal* magazine, so they went down the mines in Silesia. They toured Krakow and Gdansk, and witnessed a Warsaw that 'didn't exist'; and they were sneaked in, along with a small army of sketchers, to witness the Intellectuals' Congress at Wroclaw, an event attended by an odd troupe of international talents, from Picasso to Ehrenburg, Fadeyev to A. J. P. Taylor. Since the Soviet Union was at that moment breaking off relations with the United States over an

Above: Title page detail, *The Inconstant Moon* by Noel Langley, London, 1949

Part of the deliberate attempt by Searle and Langley to fashion an instant 'collector's item'. The cameo style of Searle's is a beautified version of the kind of miniature supplied by illustrators of the post-war years to Radio Times. Noel Langley (1911–80) was a South African-born novelist and playwright, who died in California.

Top left: Lilliput *cover, September 1950*

Originally drawn in pen-and-ink in 1949 and republished in Ronald Searle's Golden Oldies *(1985). An understandably rare example of a Searle joke on the deprivations of desert-island life.*

Top right: 'Old man, Zenica', The Studio *cover, January 1949*

One of the drawings brought back by Searle from his visit to Yugoslavia in August–September 1947. 'It is apparent to even the most unpractised eye,' wrote Bernard Denvir, in the June 1949 edition of the magazine, 'that his work must have a deeper foundation than the more technical sleight-of-hand facility which makes successful the ordinary commercial artist.' Zenica (or Sjenica) lies about one hundred miles inland from Dubrovnik.

extradition matter, the proceedings were more notable for controversy than enlightenment, but the sensation of standing on a political and philosophical borderline was exciting. Searle returned to England feeling that the journey had been the most important thing to happen to him intellectually since his imprisonment, an experience he could now place in a fuller cultural context. Having visited Auschwitz and seen what intelligent, cultured members of the European tradition were capable of, he came to distinguish in his own mind between excusable and inexcusable barbarity. 'Scientific elimination,' he decided, 'is quite different from someone beating a thousand people to death because they can't communicate. It's not the same attitude. And so the preference was there: I'd rather have Japanese fascists than Nazis.'

Back to domestic concerns Searle came, and he and Kaye moved into a Bayswater flat. The Bedford Gardens premises were kept on as Ronald's studio and as a halfway house for a succession of visiting Australian Changi-ites, among them Russell Braddon. The sensation of BBC Radio, that summer of 1949, was a mind-reading act called The Piddingtons, and Braddon was their manager. In Changi, he had been half the act, on the receiving end of Syd Piddington's 'telepathic' messages; Searle had sketched the prototype routine in performance. Now he helped Braddon introduce the finished article to London's press. Such was the sudden fame of the man-and-wife duo that Braddon was invited to write a book detailing their history. When *The Piddingtons* appeared in 1950, its narrative was dominated by Braddon's dramatic account of life among the allied POWs, which he was then encouraged to develop into an autobiographical work of his own. This became

The Naked Island, perhaps the most widely read of all eye-witness treatments of the Japanese tyranny. That this book's fame eclipsed that of *The Piddingtons* was no bad thing from the point of view of the supplier of drawings, since in the earlier book his work had been embarrassingly credited on the title-page to 'Robert Searle'.

30 Burnham Court, the Searles' new address, was in Moscow Road, a fact that was probably noted with undue interest by such government departments as maintained a Searle file. Ronald had consorted with a good many Communist Party members since the war, had travelled to Eastern Europe, and was identified with left-wing causes (not always voluntarily: on at least one occasion, his name was appended to a far-left manifesto without his permission). That he was regarded as politically suspect became clear when his friend Jankel Adler cited him as a referee in an application for British citizenship, which was turned down on the grounds that the company he kept did him insufficient credit. These official suspicions were naturally quite groundless. It was true only that Searle had joined the Labour Party, a gesture he later regretted as an avoidable loss of the artist's independent neutrality. He undertook to draw for the Labour Party Press Service, which ran a weekly page in *Tribune*, from which it was the shortest of steps to the job of contributing a weekly cartoon to *Tribune* itself. This residency, which ran on until the summer of 1951, is remarkable for the anti-Tory venom sustained by Searle while he was simultaneously contributing funnies to the right-wing *Sunday Express* – a 'double' worthy of the cartoonist Vicky, who was employed for most of his life by managements who detested his opinions.

Above left: At the drawing-board, Bedford Gardens, c. 1949

Searle in the act of drawing a St Trinian's girl in the late Forties. There were no more than a few dozen such drawings in all, Searle protests, yet the British public has behaved as though they represented a major part of his output. (Photograph by Kaye Webb.)

Above right: At the drawing-board, as seen by himself, c. 1949

A self-portrait evidently belonging to the same period as the photograph. At this stage in his career, Searle was not as hard on himself as he later became in his self-depictions.

During his short period of practice as a political cartoonist, Ronald Searle comparatively seldom went in for derisive *ad hominem* attacks in the style of Vicky or Low. Much as he hallowed the tradition in which they worked, reaching back to Rowlandson and Gillray, he failed to fit the pattern of the required temperament. As he wrote a few years later,

> It is not sufficient for a good cartoonist to be a competent artist with a sense of humour. He must enjoy a political prejudice that is narrow and strong enough for him to take a positive attitude. He must be a man with a wholehearted conviction of his own 'rightness' (I almost said 'righteousness'), and must have clear enough vision and be sufficiently well-informed to comment authoritatively on almost any political eventuality within a few hours. He must laugh public opinion into what he believes it should be, and must good-humouredly destroy with their own weaknesses any who are distasteful to his purpose.

Searle was certainly capable of carrying out this programme on occasion, but for the daily grind of political comment he lacked the essential fascination with the political process, and (emphatically) an appetite for the company of politicians themselves. In *Tribune* he took an obstinately 'civilian' viewpoint, concentrating most effectively on the fatuities of what one might call the poodled rich. Very much as cartoonists of an earlier day had paraded capitalists in top hats, Searle deployed snooty ladies in jewels and furs as a hyperbolic symbol of what really exasperated him: the mentality of people who simply hadn't 'moved on', who were in effect still living in the pre-war era. He made much of their inability to come to terms with Austerity ('I'm utterly unable to understand the Socialist mind, darling. Pike in aspic the price it is – and they cut the cost of utility stuff'); and of course they were also fun to draw, in all their ornate wrinkliness. The role of the Tory lady in crystallizing Searle's comic style should not be underestimated.

That crystallization occurred just too late to show up in *The Female Approach*, Searle's second cartoon collection, published just in time for Christmas, 1949. This was another rather motley assembly, some items still dating back to the army era, but it was very funny even when immaturely drawn. Sales figures reflected an increased public relish of St Trinian's: *The Female Approach* sold 16,000 copies in its first year. It came with the distinguished endorsement of 'A Letter from Sir Max Beerbohm', who expressed pleasure in 'finding myself back in the slaughter-house of St Trinian's' (a Johnsonian reference that would later come in useful to Searle and his publishers), and took the opportunity of commending *Forty Drawings*: 'the main impression made on me by the book was just one of beauty'. In October, the Searles visited Italy and stayed with their friend Jennie Nicholson in Portofino, and she had taken them along the coast to Rapallo to meet the venerable Max. 'I have a *little* talent,' he explained to Ronald, 'but I have used it well.' Ronald was hardly neglecting his own; in Portofino he completed no fewer than ten paintings that were exhibited at Wolf Mankowitz's Little Gallery immediately on his return.

Absences abroad could no longer be undertaken without negotiation. It was *Punch* that had made the difference. On All Fools' Day 1949, Kenneth Bird (the cartoonist 'Fougasse') had taken over the editorship. While change was in the air, G. L. Stampa, who had served *Punch*, amazingly, since 1894, took the opportunity of resigning from the post of illustrator to the theatre column. Bird, who had been looking for a way to use Searle, gladly nominated him as the replacement. Searle knew that stamina and loyalty would be required; the theatre critic, Eric Keown, had been in place since 1932. But *Punch* was not

Above: Eric Keown, 1952

The Punch *theatre critic in snuff-taking pose, as depicted in* An Experience of Critics.

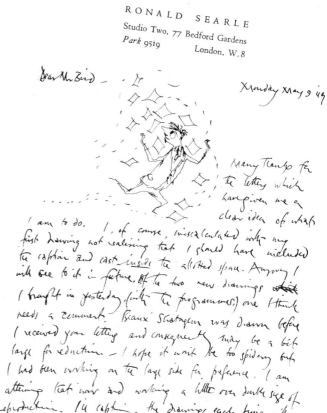

RONALD SEARLE
Studio Two, 77 Bedford Gardens
Park 9519
London, W.8

disappointed in its choice. Searle stayed in the job for twelve years, intermitting only on account of illness or foreign assignments. This could not have happened, clearly, if Searle and Keown had not been content in each other's company. In fact, it went much further than that. In different ways, the two men actually kept each other in the job. A few years later, when Malcolm Muggeridge took over the *Punch* Editor's chair, he had the not unreasonable idea of drafting in Kenneth Tynan to write the theatre reviews; but Searle, arguing that this would be the quickest way of ushering Keown into an early grave, talked him out of it – a sound instinct, since the unruly Tynan would surely not have stayed long in Mr Punch's slightly self-satisfied confraternity.

Searle, for his part, did not really enjoy drawing for the theatre column at all. It was an uncomfortable job: the sketchbook on the knees in the stalls, the spy-glass at the ready, the notes on costumes and poses and tableaux – and the need to master the facial eccentricities of all the leading players. After a first night, Searle took these elements home and wrestled them into shape immediately, working into the small hours. It was very often a miserable labour. Stampa had not attempted caricature, which for Searle (and his employers, once they saw what he could do) was the point of the exercise; yet he didn't consider himself a 'natural' caricaturist, in love with the business of marrying a likeness to the extravagances of his pen. In the opinion of *Punch*'s official historian, Searle's 'magnified, pointed jaws and spindly extremities ... sometimes ... masked a likeness', but in view of the fact that Searle was 'the first *Punch* contributor for many years to produce real caricatures', he gladly overlooked this – and so he should. What did cause Searle trouble at first were the dimensions of his drawing, and an anxious correspondence passed

Above left: Max and Florence Beerbohm with Ronald Searle, Rapallo, October 1949

Max and Florence (née Kahn) are appraising the pictures Searle has just been painting in Portofino. In the preface to Searle's The Female Approach, *Beerbohm wrote: 'There seem to be no bounds to your strangely inventive faculty, and to your power of converting the macabre into the most pleasurable of frolics.' The meeting was arranged by the Searles' friend Jennie Nicholson, daughter of the poet Robert Graves. (Photograph by Kaye Webb.)*

Above right: Letter to Kenneth Bird, 9 May 1949

Searle writes to the Editor of Punch *to say that he now understands the rules of the theatre-column drawing, whose size had been misinterpreted. 'I am glad you like the results and the way I am treating the jobs,' Searle added. 'I am enjoying it very much despite the slight "teething troubles" I am causing!'*

Right: Dinner for cartoonists offering their services to the *Inky Way Annual*, London, 29 April 1947

The Inky Way Annual *was a book-format venture published during the Forties to help explain Fleet Street to its public, and raise money for the charitable Newspaper Press Fund. In this remarkable convocation of cartoonists, David Low is naturally accorded the Captain's chair. The full line-up is (back row, left to right): Vicky, Ronald Searle, David Langdon, Joe Lee, Gabriel, Frank Joss, Norman Pett, Trog (Wally Fawkes), Arthur Potts, Tim (William Timym), Ian Gall. Front row, left to right: Sid Moon (Searle's predecessor at the C.D.N.), Arthur Ferrier, Leslie Illingworth, David Low, E. H. Shepard, Neb, and J. C. Walker.*

Below: Sir Ralph Richardson as Volpone, unpublished, 1954

Above: Eric Keown interviews Fernandel, Paris, November 1958

The great French film comedian Fernandel (Fernand Contandin, 1903–71) was filming at the Boulogne Studios in Paris. Photograph by Ronald Searle, giving some idea of the foldaway Keown limbs.

between himself and Bird, the forms of address on both sides ('Dear Searle', 'Dear Mr Bird') testifying to the survival of the ancient Victorian civilities at *Punch*, where Round Table members were revered as repositories of the old tradition. But the drawings themselves were welcomed as 'just what's wanted'; and so Searle settled down for his long stint in the stalls – quite a process in itself, for Eric Keown was six feet seven and a half inches tall: the moment when he took his seat was invariably marked by a loud groan from the playgoer sitting behind. The ever-courteous Keown, however, had a way of collapsing in upon himself, folding like a giant pair of hinged scissors to minimize the obstruction. A snuff-taking Francophile and an unsnobbish gourmet, Keown constituted one of the two reasons why Searle stuck at the job so long. The other was what Keown himself described as 'the feeling of innocent excitement as the curtain rises, in whatever theatre, on whatever play'.

Nobody who visited the Bedford Gardens studio could fail to be impressed by Ronald's 'Deadlines' chart, a thing of terrible and complex beauty involving the interests of *Punch*, *Tribune* and the *Sunday Express*; *Lilliput*, where the Patrick Campbell series continued (there were Campbell books, too); a sequence of ephemeral magazines of the Left (*Circus*, *Seven*, *Our Time*), in which Paul Hogarth was involved; and any number of more or less specialist publications, from *The Bookseller* to W. H. Smith's trade circular. Kaye Webb had moved on from *Lilliput* to *The Leader*, an interesting but doomed general-interest magazine where her husband also became a contributor. In 1950 he attended the Old Bailey trial of the 'atom spy' Klaus Fuchs on the *Leader*'s behalf, bringing back drawings of Fuchs' pale figure in the dock; sketching within courts was illegal, but Searle's visual memory was already trained to reproduce scenes after the event. His talent for reportage was to be exploited only very patchily by British publications. It was in America that the extra dimension of comment implied by the pen-stroke came to be prized.

It would seem a tough time to be taking on a new book – and not a compilation either,

Above left: Punch *theatre caricature, 18 May 1960*

Alec Guinness as Lawrence of Arabia and Aircraftman Ross, in the Terence Rattigan play, Ross, *about T. E. Lawrence, writer and adventurer, who joined the RAF in 1922 under the name of J. H. Ross.*

Above right: Punch *theatre caricature, 7 May 1958*

Stanley Holloway as Alfred P. Doolittle, Julie Andrews as Eliza Doolittle, Rex Harrison as Henry Higgins in My Fair Lady, *Drury Lane. 'Queer as it may sound from a critic,' wrote Keown in his review, 'I cannot wait to see it again.' Searle was the first theatre-column illustrator to provide proper caricatures of artistes, and his exhaustive notes enabled him to show them in attitudes which playgoers would recognize in the production itself.*

Ronald Searle in Paris
?. Peynet

Above: Searle by Raymond Peynet, 20 May 1950

The Searles' Perpetua Books published Peynet's popular series on the 'Lovers' theme during the late Fifties. In the introduction to a Penguin selection (The Lovers, 1962) Searle wrote: 'Far from being a clumsy adventurer, Peynet approaches his dedicated field with the delicacy of a poet.' The lyrical impulse is uppermost in this sketch.

but an original album done from scratch; but Searle was now so completely in the grip of his work that the most appealing relaxation he could contemplate was more work, of a different kind. An alert publisher, sensing this, had got Ronald and Kaye together over lunch and let fall the suggestion that 'the most successful and exciting books are those made purely for pleasure'. Invited to suggest the project that would personally please them most, the couple simultaneously nominated Paris — with the consequence that in May 1950 Ronald went missing from his usual publications and made his first proper visit to France, bearing the publisher's instruction to 'have a good holiday and bring back whatever you please'. The Searles returned with the makings of *A Paris Sketchbook*, which was published in time for Christmas with a dedication 'For Kate and John who were left behind'. Kaye Webb's text took a deliberate second place to the drawings — 'the subjects were decided by whatever Ronald felt he wanted to draw' — but gave a lively impression of a city that for most Britons was still romantically out of reach. There are interesting glimpses of Ronald gulping the city down into the digestive system of his sketchbooks. In one place where he merged two shops into one for the sake of a composition, a crowd of literal-minded onlookers insisted on explaining to him where he had gone wrong. Twice in Montmartre he was knocked off his stool by crocodiles of sight-seeing schoolgirls, in a fine example of poetic justice. The authors started assembling a graffiti collection, which in the first edition of their book they quoted in such wildly approximate French that schoolmasters used it to exemplify what not to put. (One grammatically unexceptionable item — '*Coca Cola donne le cancer*' — was tactfully euphemized in a later edition to '*Coca Cola donne la douleur*'.) In a bar in Clignancourt, Ronald had his fortune told by a Russian-French gypsy girl, who correctly prophesied success for the book and advised the artist, for the sake of his future *bonheur*, to place in his breast-pocket, at ten o'clock that night, a pinch of salt, a piece of bread and a hair from his head. To Ronald, such a prescription came as no great novelty. In Cambridge, until his early teens, he had always carried, and in the same pocket, a fenland amulet consisting of a dried rabbit's foot, a piece of coal and a sprinkling of salt, all knotted in a handkerchief. It was not the first time, either, that his fortune had been told. He had been warned by a resident soothsayer in Changi that he would find his life changing completely at the age of forty. There is always the possibility that the recipient of such information will subconsciously act upon it, as though it were a piece of advice rather than a prediction. Still, one way or another, it turned out to be true.

Best of all, Paris brought Ronald first-hand knowledge of artworks he had been reading about for twenty years — and, in the quaint person of Kiki de Montparnasse, a surviving link with the likes of Modigliani and Derain, whose model she had been many years before. By the time Searle met Kiki, she was 'singing and dancing for odd francs'; yet in the act of sketching her, he felt himself joined to the dream-world Paris of early modernist art. Back in the present, he became a victim of his own craft; lunching with a platoon of French cartoonists at the Père Jean restaurant, he was caricatured by all. With André François (a *Punch* contributor) he was already friendly, but to be welcomed with such warmth by Peynet, Grambert, Jean Effel and the others was surprising and gratifying. And it was not an isolated gesture: ten days later, the entire staff of *Le Canard enchaîné* stopped work to throw a party for the visitors, and then went back to work overtime — as did Ronald, forty-eight hours later. In October, the Leicester Galleries held an exhibition of his Paris drawings, thirty-five of which were sold for £327 12s., ready-framed. The frames, as the artist ruefully noted, cost £116. St Trinian's could not be abolished yet.

The new aspect of Searle which the Paris book put on show was his relish for architecture and sculptural extravagance. Where many graphic reporters were content to suggest enough of the cityscape to lend the foreground subject a credible habitation, Searle gave fullest value to buildings, delighting in the personality they independently generated. So, far from simplifying ornamental styles, he entered happily into their complexities, and the more agitated their lines, the better it seemed to suit him; and yet the focal topic of a drawing still detached itself without effort from the attractive tumult of ribbed and billowing detail behind. It remained to be seen whether this relatively serious style of drawing could be amalgamated with the comic to produce a single graphic personality, impartially available for all subjects.

In architectural terms, it was to the Moorish that Searle turned next, though his journey was intended more as a convalescence than an assignment. Ronald had plainly been overworking and had contracted stubborn bronchitis, which only a burst of winter warmth looked likely to cure. Morocco was recommended, so with an assurance from the *News Chronicle* that the paper would look favourably upon any material they brought back, Ronald and Kaye (by now a feature writer with the *Chronicle*) left for Tangier late in February 1951, moving on later to Fez and Marrakesh. In normal times, this would have been a standard tourist itinerary; but the times were unusually fraught, with the French making a late assertion of colonialist will against a number of Moroccan nationalist factions. Searle, with his useful knack of getting drawn closer to the centre of events than he intended, saw something of both sides of the argument. He could attest that the French had not, as was hysterically claimed, dropped bombs on Fez; but on the other hand he did receive a very full account of nationalist grievances from the outlawed leader of the Istiqlal Independence Party, Allal al Fassi, whom he drew while Kaye conducted an interview largely consisting, on her side, of exclamations of shock and dismay ('*C'est vrai? C'est* affreux!'). The couple returned to England as proprietors of some fine drawings, a face-to-face 'exclusive' with a wanted man, and an unexpected reputation for skill in the

Below: Kiki de Montparnasse, Paris, May 1950

The one-time model of Modigliani and Derain sketched in right-facing (left-hander's) profile. Somewhat inebriated at the start of the encounter, and more so as it progressed, Kiki retaliated with a self-portrait of her own, heavily influenced by the nose Searle had so challengingly outlined.

intrigues of the casbah. The *News Chronicle* was delighted with what it received, and began actively considering what further assignments it could find for the team of Webb and Searle. Up to now, Ronald had been known in the *Chronicle*'s pages chiefly as an illustrator of advertisements, currently for BP petrol and Smith's Alarm Clocks, while at the same time appearing as one of the famous faces used by the Basildon Bond notepaper company in their series 'The Choice of Distinguished People'. E. H. Shepard, delineator of Winnie-the-Pooh, had drawn a portrait of Searle for this purpose. It was by no means Shepard's best, but there was honour in the salute from an older generation.

An avowedly Distinguished Person, though, could hardly go on living in the disjunct style to which the Searles had become accustomed, with the twins now crammed into the Moscow Road flat under the supervision of a Norland nanny, and Ronald hiking over to Bedford Gardens to work. The needs had evaporated that dictated such a piecemeal arrangement. In the autumn of 1951, therefore, the family was at last gathered together under one impressive roof, at 32 Newton Road, W.2, just off Westbourne Grove. Designed by the young Denys Lasdun and built in 1938, it was 'one of the first houses carried out in an absolutely uncompromising contemporary manner'. Built in the first instance for a pair of bachelor artists, it was topped by a splendid studio favoured by north light, as the estate agents say, and a fine terrace overlooking half of Paddington. As Searle remarked to his friend David Arkell, 'If one *had* to overlook half of Paddington, this was the way to do it.'

Another old friend, George Sprod the cartoonist, remembered Ronald resolving, as they plodded round the walls of Changi, that when he got home he was going to have a pound a day set aside, just for luxuries. The Changi-ites thought this was a pretty stiff expectation at the time, but by 1951 they would have had to concede that the vision of opulence was within Ronald's grasp. Those with a taste for delicate ironies might also have been interested in the history of the site whereon Searle now stood contemplating the rooftops of West London. The previous dwelling on that land had been the home of Sir Henry Ridley. He was the man who introduced Brazilian rubber seedlings into Malaya, and thus brought prosperity, and strategic importance, to Singapore.

Below: 'Every Letter Tells A Story', July 1951

Newspaper and magazine advert-isement, with a portrait of Searle by E. H. Shepard (1879–1972), Punch artist and illustrator of A. A. Milne's children's stories and poems. A later 'Basildon Bond' advertisement ('Letters of Consequence') featured a mock-up of a 1941 letter to Kaye Webb in which Searle accepted the fee for cartoons submitted (including St Trinian's No. 1) and promised to send more. Searle looks back on his involvement in this campaign with a healthy playfulness, an aversion from over-seriousness and unusually amiable sarcasm.

FIVE
Back in the Jug Agane
(1951–61)

The young comic artists of Europe, looking for guidance in the styles of the fashionable masters of the early Fifties, faced a choice between three men: two Romanians and Ronald Searle. André François (born André Farkas) seemed to offer a tempting short-cut. People said he drew like a child, which was not true, but did tempt a lot of orthodox draughtsmen into trying to forget their training. Saul Steinberg was superficially easier to emulate, since his approach involved spareness and reduction, a handy disguise for the immature artist afraid of his own stylelessness. Steinberg made available something dangerously like a formula, a way of making an average idea look special. At the sight of such a possibility, Searle himself remarked (evoking a tableau that sounded very like one of his own drawings), 'the vultures put on their hobnail boots and gallop down the newly opened roads of another man's labours'. Down Searle's own road it was harder to follow. Within even the craziest of his drawings, the beautiful correctness of observed reality still ruled. He was not making the world look funny, but experiencing it as funny; it was less a style than a psychological condition.

Above: Self-portrait, early 1950s
One of Searle's last 'serious' views of himself, it combines the sleekness of his post-war success with the wary scepticism of the ex-prisoner.

Abandoning both political extremes at once, he left *Tribune* and the *Sunday Express* in 1951 and followed his wife to the *News Chronicle*, a six-page broadsheet costing a penny. The *Chronicle* was something of a haven for stylists of the pen. Its political cartoonist, staunchly Leftist and impatient with the paper's gentlemanly Liberalism, was Vicky (Victor Weisz). The Australian Arthur Horner contributed spot drawings and, before long, his 'Colonel Pewter' strip. Richard Winnington illustrated his own film reviews with caricatures that in their dashed-off way displayed exactly what Searle meant by 'natural' instinct for a likeness. Eventually George Sprod would be drafted in to do pocket cartoons. Where none of these men was at home was in reportage, which is where Searle came in; he and Kaye Webb became the newspaper equivalent of an outside-broadcast unit, making a brilliant start in late October with their coverage of Dr Edith Summerskill's electioneering in Fulham. Searle's masterly drawing of the street scene attracted an immediate bid from the Nottingham Castle Museum; he gave it to them for nothing.

A week later, Searle and Webb were back with the first of a new series, *Looking at London*, which grew into a book of the same name. In those years between the Festival of Britain and the Coronation there was a great upsurge in Britain's affection for its surviving signs of 'character'. The Searles went looking for it, taking a participatory approach where possible. Instead of merely interviewing Portobello Road stall-holders, they applied for a licence themselves, learnt to say 'flogging' instead of 'selling', and

Above: News Chronicle, 24 October 1951

Dr Edith Summerskill, with microphone and cockaded hat, addresses the voters at the General Election on behalf of the Labour Party in West Fulham, London. She was returned, but the Conservatives won the Election with 321 seats to Labour's 295. The original was given by the artist to Nottingham Castle Museum after they had offered to buy it.

Opposite: 'The Greedy Carpet', Paris, 1972

Used as the cover to the catalogue of Searle's Bibliothèque Nationale exhibition, January–March 1973, this was exhibit No. 110 (as 'Le Tapis Gourmand') in that show. It was stolen on 16 March (along with No. 103, 'Mad Monkey'), and never recovered. The original is still officially 'owned' by the Bibliothèque Nationale. (See p. 162.)

disposed of a wide variety of bric-à-brac, including 'an ostrich-feather fan, named Maud'. From their researches into barrel-organs, they returned with a barrel-organ themselves, playing it at suitable points on the way home to Newton Road, where it was parked for many years outside the door. Needing a rest from London, they later took in the Rolls-Royce factory in Derby; the Loughborough Bell Foundry; and the cheese and pie industries of Melton Mowbray, whence a fine Stilton was dispatched to Ronald on his thirty-second birthday. (No Rolls-Royce, though: Ronald never did drive a car.)

On the comic side of the ledger, the St Trinian's industry was reporting distressingly healthy results. Even The Founder himself was pleased when a *Times* leader mentioned his creation, after disturbances in 'a Persian girls' school' had to be calmed by troops, firemen and police. But in a 1951 BBC radio interview for young people, by way of emphasizing to his teenage questioner (it was the illustrator Quentin Blake) the desirability of a good technical grounding and a versatile approach, he prophesied the demise of 'these awful St Trinian's schoolgirls that I do', which were 'quite fun while they last' but would shortly need to be replaced. Searle's personal timetable was several years ahead of that of the public, who had only just realized how much they liked the girls. With *The Female Approach* now in its seventh impression, a third cartoon selection was published in November 1951. Its first print-run of 20,000 had virtually sold out by New Year's Day. *Back To The Slaughterhouse* (Max Beerbohm's title, quoted from Dr Johnson) pulled together drawings from more sources than ever, now including the *Sketch*, *Leader*, *The Saturday Book* and *World Horizon*. Perhaps the most forward-looking joke was the one

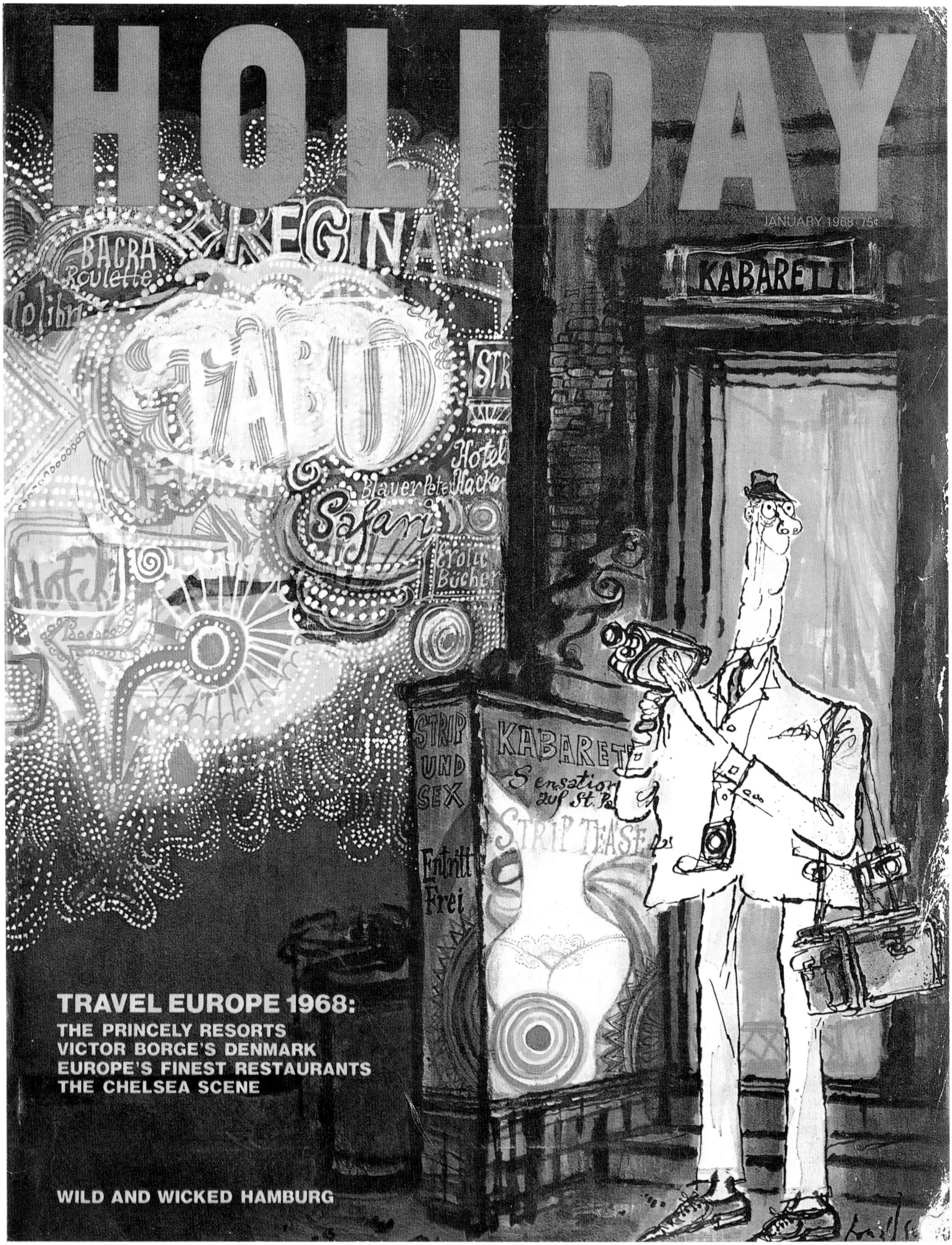
HOLIDAY
JANUARY 1968 75¢
REGINA
BACRA Roulette
Colibri
TABU
Hotel Hacker
Blauer Peter
Safari
Erotic Bücher
KABARETT
STRIP UND SEX
KABARETT Sensation auf St. Pa
STRIP TEASE
Entritt Frei
TRAVEL EUROPE 1968:
THE PRINCELY RESORTS
VICTOR BORGE'S DENMARK
EUROPE'S FINEST RESTAURANTS
THE CHELSEA SCENE
WILD AND WICKED HAMBURG

Two submissions for the Holiday *Hamburg cover: (above) original, (opposite) amended, 1968.*

The Holiday *management (Caskie Stinnett, Editor; Frank Zachary, Art Director) could not accept a street-walker, however bored, on their cover, and requested a change, which Searle effected by substituting a naive tourist. A line running down the 'Striptease' poster from the first 'A' in Kabarett shows the left-hand edge of the cut Searle made to lift out the figure of the prostitute, which was subsequently replaced in his original.*

George Feifer's Hamburg article was billed as 'Wicked Cities of the World, Part I', and Searle's drawings as 'A Modern Rake's Progress'.

Above: 'Mislaid Masterpieces: Mona's Sister, Gladys, by Leonardo Da Vinci (1452–1519). Discovered by Searle 1980', *Ronald Searle in Perspective*, London, 1980

Searle's rubric runs: 'Mona (or Monna) Lisa Gherardini del Giocondo's younger and more cheerful sister, Gladys. The portrait was painted about 1510, shortly before Gladys set off for Rome, to seek her fortune – again.'

Above: 'The Casualty', 1976

A picture with a slightly confusing history, explained thus by the artist: 'The original watercolour, given to Léon Schwarzenberg, was called "Cancer", and when the sketch for it was published in the RS album [1978] that was called "Cancer" too. But when I did a lithograph version, the title was changed to "The Casualty" as there was some resistance to "Cancer" being used for the print.' Searle had actually visited this theme before (Punch, 24 April 1957), showing the artist-and-model couple who had carved the heart watching the doctor's examination with anxiety.

Right: Monica at Le Canadel, 1967

Taken on the Searles' wedding-trip, June–July 1967.

Above: Mislaid Masterpieces: *The Raft of the* Medusa, by Henri de Toulouse-Lautrec, 1980

'Lautrec's interpretation,' says Searle, 'should not be confused with that of Théodore Géricault, in the Louvre somewhere ... Lautrec radically changes the emphasis by reducing the casks to bottles and the fifteen known survivors to eleven. Also, less anguishing than the version by Géricault and more in the spirit of his own times, the wrecking of Lautrec's Méduse has taken place on dry land.' Realized in pen, watercolour and crayon.

Right: 'Model with tattooed cheek', Paris, 1961

Dated January 1961, and drawn from life in the studio of Searle's friend Franta Belsky, whose model this was.

Right: 'Scorpio', Zoodiac, London, 1977

Searle rediscovers one of his old jungle enemies, the scorpion. In a kind of exile again in the south of France, he happily obliges himself to lavish the delicacies of accumulated technique on completely imaginative subjects.

Below: 'Full, fruity character', *The Illustrated Winespeak*, London, 1983

Full-blown example of the Arcimboldo Effect: the painter himself perpetrated many faces composed of fruit. A large exhibition entitled 'L'Effetto Arcimboldo' (subtitled 'Transformations of the Face from the Sixteenth to the Twentieth Century') was held in Venice in 1987, without, alas, this exhibit.

Below: 'Fullish body, but beginning to fade', *The Illustrated Winespeak*, London, 1983

This drawing also appears untitled in Something in the Cellar *(1986), and possibly emphasizes one of the reasons why Searle favours champagne.*

Below: 'The nose is fantastic', *The Illustrated Winespeak*, London, 1983

A borderline example of what has become known as the 'Arcimboldo Effect'. Giuseppe Arcimboldo (1527–93) specialized in versions of the human physiognomy made up of other components. This particular nose, however, suggests an unusually benign attack of the alcoholic skin-reaction known as 'grog-blossoms'.

Right: 'Deutschland, Deutschland . . .,' unpublished cover for *Der Spiegel*, 1976

A rich and re-armed Germany lords it over the mangy representatives of Britain, Italy and France. The globe-body has a pleasantly antique feel, as of a Gillray cartoon. Searle today is 100 per cent in favour of German reunification, he says: 'From what knowledge . . . our many trips have brought, I have absolutely no fear of the Germans. Only of idiots like Kohl, of course.'

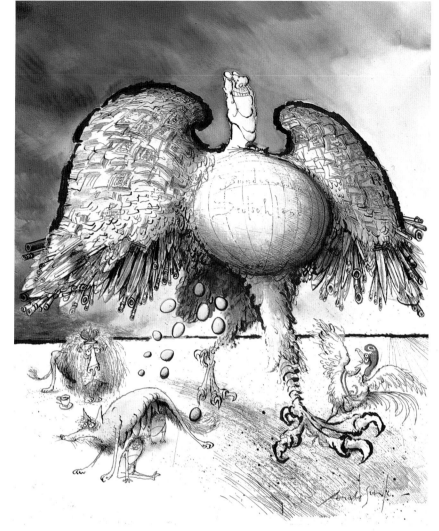

Right: 'The Fool', *Ronald Searle in Perspective*, London, 1980

Part of a series of gnomic tarmac tableaux entitled 'Strictly for the Birds'. Opposing the spirit of antic frivolity personified by the Venetian-Quixotic figure is the life-denying form of the jet fighter, whose proboscis, legs and tail remind one irresistibly of an old tropical foe, the malarial mosquito.

from *Punch*, featuring two solar-topeed matrons strolling through some Middle Eastern *souk*, where the ambience is sketched-in almost in 'straight' reportage style. Here again the possibility of an amalgamation of comic and 'real' styles is suggested, this time in a cartoon (though it has to be admitted that at the time of the drawing's original publication, Searle's Moroccan trip was almost a year ahead, so the 'real' background was not drawn from on-the-spot notes).

It was taken as a sign of great affluence and commercial confidence when Searle started his own publishing house. Perpetua Books was actually never a source of great profit, nor even intended in the first instance as a way of asserting control over the reproduction of his work, though it came to fulfil that function later. At first, it arose merely as a comradely response to an address given by the playwright Christopher Fry to the Critics' Circle at the Arts Theatre, London, in April 1952. Fry, a friend of the Searles (Ronald would continue to illustrate editions of his plays), had been coming under heavy fire from the critics on account of his supposedly facile 'intoxication with words'. He felt he had been misrepresented, and Perpetua was created to publish the persuasive text in which he said so, along with a balancing 'symposium' in which leading critics of the day would describe their 'approach to Dramatic Criticism'. ('My main approach to dramatic criticism,' wrote Eric Keown, 'is the Southern Railway.') Given the title *An Experience of Critics* and decked out with Searle caricatures and his new Perpetua colophon – in which some precognition of Bardot was at work – it was received as 'a highly entertaining experiment' by *Punch* and others, and still provides a storehouse of bluffing defences for the cornered critic.

Even that part of the public which never read a book, bought a magazine or opened a newspaper now had access to Searle's work. It had begun to be displayed on some of the biggest poster sites in London as part of a new campaign on behalf of Lemon Hart Rum. Under the too-neat-to-change slogan 'Have a GOOD RUM for your money', Mr Lemon Hart, a tall, emaciated figure with granny-glasses and a huge chin, was portrayed as

Above: Colophon design for Perpetua Books, 1952

The publishing company was named after Eric Gill's 'Perpetua' typeface, which Searle and Kaye Webb adopted simply because they liked it.

Left: Lemon Hart poster *in situ*, London, spring 1952

The third poster in the Lemon Hart series occupies a magnificently prominent site at the Monument, in the City of London. (It was the first of the genre to appear in this position.) The poster itself measured 37 feet by 34 feet.

Opposite: Poster for Lemon Hart Rum, n.d.

Part of Searle's eleven-year contribution to this advertising campaign; his last Lemon Hart drawings appeared in 1962. The Holmes-and-Watson relationship of Mr Lemon Hart and his friend from Lamb's Navy Rum is distinguished by British stolidity on the latter's side, and a farouche and accident-prone tendency on the part of Mr Lemon Hart. (Photograph by Odhams Press Ltd.)

rendering all his predicaments bearable with a flask of the eponymous product. The figure himself had something in common with Searle's still-continuing portrayal of Patrick Campbell in *Lilliput* (Campbell was that shape), and perhaps also owed a little to Eric Keown, whose foldaway limbs were ever an object of wonder. It is a matter of psychological interest that the incidence of benevolent, plump characters in Searle's work has been low, a fact it is tempting to connect with that time in his life when any well-fed figure automatically identified itself as an enemy. Not even Father Christmas, in Searle's versions, can quite rely on enjoying his usual embonpoint. When the *News Chronicle's* Editor, Robin Cruikshank, got together a volume called *The Humour of Dickens,* using a gallery of illustrators from Ardizzone to Giles, Searle was a natural choice to depict the querulous, spherical beadle, Mr Bumble. That he contributed a spindly Pecksniff to the same volume implies no contradiction; thin men could certainly be villains. Mr Lemon Hart belonged to no moral category. He was an opportunist and, given his little bottle, self-sufficient. He remained so for a dozen more years, during which his original drainpipe-and-winkle-picker look actually became fashionable.

All that it eventually took to kill off Mr Lemon Hart was a refusal on Searle's part to renew the contract that perpetuated him. The schoolgirls of St Trinian's were characteristically tougher to bump off. Their creator was partly responsible for the prolongation of his own misery, by giving way to a suggestion from D. B. Wyndham Lewis, alias 'Timothy Shy' of the *Chronicle,* who had been his collaborator for three post-war years on, of all things, the *Journal of the Hallé Concerts Society* (yet another small entry on the 'deadlines' chart). Lewis proposed writing a narrative, a St Trinian's romance; and since this removed from Searle the burden of inventing yet more anarchistic ideas, he agreed. *The Terror of St Trinian's* became one of the 'publishing events' of 1952; no fewer than 45,000 copies were printed in the month of publication, and the fantasy spilled over into traffic-stopping life in a notorious stunt. A team of suitably costumed 'young ladies', not all of them young or ladies, led by the mettlesome *diseuse* Miss Hermione Gingold, stove in one of the show-windows of Foyle's, the London bookshop, with hockey-sticks, in full view of a battery of press photographers and the newsreel camera of the Pathé Pictorial. Miss Gingold's fit of delinquent rage was inspired, the publicity handout claimed, by the realization that 'her deadly rival on the hockey pitch and in the Stinks Lab., Angela Menace, is revealed as the heroine' of the new book. 'As a reprisal she kidnapped Miss Desiree Umbrage, Head of the School, who, bound and gagged, was balanced precariously on top of a taxi stolen for the raid.' The driver of the 'stolen' vehicle was the future Liberal Member of Parliament for the Isle of Ely, Sir Clement Freud. To Foyle's, the cost of the affair was said (by Miss Gingold) to be £120, a calculated loss which some newspaper commentators found rather shocking, especially when it was revealed that real crime had been consequent upon the fake: about twenty-five books were filched through the hole in the glass. 'Somebody worked very fast,' commented an assistant, probably from the thriller department.

Searle's publisher Max Parrish was understandably eager for a quick St Trinian's follow-up, but this time The Founder put his foot down. He could not oblige. But he did undertake to give Parrish 'a better best-seller' for the following Christmas. Geoffrey Willans, a friend who worked as a journalist for the BBC's European Service, had proposed expanding to book-length the exploits of a character he had featured in sporadic contributions to *Punch* during the Forties: the fanatical schoolboy-chauvinist pig, Nigel Molesworth. Parrish, glumly unconvinced, assigned a total advance of £300, insisting on 'profuse' illustrations from Searle. While Coronation fever raged all round, he set about producing them, buoyed up by Willans' text, whose linguistic misprisions and obbligato of dissent ('chiz chiz moan drone ect.') he found quite unexpectedly hilarious. *Down With Skool* made good Searle's promise to Parrish with another wild success, selling 53,848 copies in the first six months.

Above: 'My veins stand out like whipcords', *Whizz For Atomms*, with Geoffrey Willans, London, 1956

Nigel Molesworth prepares to strike fear into the heart of a weed. Searle's own memories of an unathletic childhood helped him capture the precise delineation of the musculature here.

Left: 'Aktually it is not me it is a weed called Shelley', *Back In The Jug Agane*, with Geoffrey Willans, London, 1959

From a volume published more than a year after the death of Molesworth's originator, Geoffrey Willans. Molesworth, like many funny creations who have made critics feel vaguely ashamed of their laughter, attracted charges of 'whimsy', e.g.: 'The true curse of St Custard's, in effect, is not nigel [sic] but something called whimsy, which has long been the curse of British humor; but readers on both sides of the Atlantic who are willing to dig through a little of that sticky substance will easily get their molesworth' (Time magazine, 10 October 1955).

Below: 'R. Searle reviews his troops', *Souls in Torment*, London, 1953

For once, the girls of St Trinian's line up respectfully to honour a presence more deadly than their own. The elegantly supercilious expression of R. Searle is attributable to the fact that he knows, while they do not, that they are about to be killed off. The designation 'R. Searle', with initial, may owe something to the Lifemanship foundation of S. Potter.

Yet it was almost lost in the profusion of 1953, a year in which Searle produced three books as a contracted artist and three more in which he shared collaborative authorship. The *Looking At London* pieces, published by the *News Chronicle*, were mixed in with a subsequent series from the Webb-Searle team, 'People Worth Meeting'. Some of these were people they did not have to go very far to meet, such as Denys Lasdun who had designed their house; Hilton Tranchell, editor of Changi's 'bolshie' magazine *The Survivor* and now practising as a physiotherapist in a London hospital; and Rowland Emett, *Punch* artist and creator of whimsical, wobbling trains and trams — a draughtsman sometimes confused with Ronald himself in those years by readers too young to distinguish between jolly eccentricity and purposeful satire.

Much the most important book of the year from Searle's point of view was his own

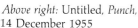

Above right: Untitled, *Punch*, 14 December 1955

Perhaps the climax of Searle's Undertaker Period. Similar, but not identical, to a pair of undertakers called Gabbitas and Thring who went around kidnapping young men and carrying them off to be turned into schoolmasters, in How To Be Topp. *Thring, however, had a bulbous nose. (Gabbitas and Thring is the name of a real agency devoted to the placing of teachers in high-class posts.)*

Right: Searle in undertaker's garb, c.1954–5

Searle writes: 'It was in fact Gielgud's costume in The Importance of Being Earnest, *when he played Algy dressed to announce the death of Bunbury. I borrowed it from [the costumier] Monty Berman for the Chelsea Arts Ball, 1954/5, and John Vickers took a record of it, before I returned it to stock.*

Souls in Torment, a Perpetua publication explicitly intended as a funeral rite for St Trinian's. No more permanent end than an atomic explosion could be imagined, so it was by this means that the school was wiped out, while a future Poet Laureate, Searle's friend C. Day Lewis, provided a suitably doomy dirge. Knowing in advance that this truncation of the girls' career would be perceived as a villainous act, Searle cast himself as the visiting 'Founder', wearing an undertaker's outfit and an expression of fastidious indifference. His eagerness to put an end to the series has helped nourish the theory that their boarding-school universe corresponded by direct analogy to life under the Japanese. This notion has been produced with an air of triumph by subsequent commentators, but it was certainly current at the time and indeed appears in Kaye Webb's own résumé of the St Trinian's years. Certain scenes, certain props – see, for example, the girls dragging the heavy roller under the whip of the schoolmistress – do marry with parts of Searle's experience. A cartoon of merry classmates gathered round a cooking-pot in which an entire cow is stewing must remind us of the POWs' habit of introducing cats and dogs to the same fate. But any interpretation that casts the staff straightforwardly as representatives of the Japanese will not stand up, because the whip-wielding mistress actually strays beyond the normal borders of the St Trinian's logic. The general principle is that the girls and their teachers are very much alike in villainy, and 'in it together'. In rejecting a latter-day proposal for a musical comedy version of St Trinian's (there have been many such over the years, and they still come in), Searle corrected the misapprehensions of the would-be adapter in the following terms: 'The Staff, behind an extremely old-fashioned façade, conceal equivalent excesses and plenty of lesbianism. They insist on good manners at all times, and in all circumstances' [that does not rule out

Below left: 'Bloody sportsdays ..., Lilliput, *May 1952*

Officially the last of the St Trinian's cycle (but see Plates). Note the subtly deformed whipping-hand of the schoolmistress, a satanic portent.

Below right: '"Light duties" for sick men', Changi Gaol, Singapore, July 1944

Prisoners pulling trees as part of the Japanese land-clearing campaign in the Changi area. Guards frequently added to the weight of the trailer by standing on it to oversee the men. This is one of the few instances in which the Changi experience can be seen to have a directly circumstantial bearing on Searle's black humour.

the Japanese] 'but are extremely tolerant [that does]. Even to the point of employing an abortionist-nurse to look after the school crèche, and care for the girls' babies while their mothers are busy in the school lab, refining heroin base.' The girls' rooms, he goes on to say, 'have been described as "smelling like a ladies' powder-room in Port Said"'. What is implicit here is not any sort of rehash of the war experience, except in the sense that it presents a young man's view of women at a time when he was forcibly deprived of women's company: of women as another country, a far-off country of which Searle and his fellows either knew nothing or had forgotten much. From not knowing what females are capable of, it is only a short step to portraying them as capable of anything. But at the same time, the girls are not threatening, but funny; they are not alienated from human sympathy. A St Trinian's girl, Searle explained to his brow-beaten applicant, 'would be sadistic, cunning, dissolute, crooked, sordid, lacking morals of any sort and capable of any excess. She would also be well-spoken, even well-mannered and polite. Sardonic, witty and very amusing. She would be good company. In short: typically human and, despite everything, endearing.' It is in this unusually detached view of what is 'typically human' that the lessons of wartime show.

Right: 'Fair play, St Trinian's, use a clean needle', *Lilliput,* 1950

An example of humour whose blackness has deepened with time. In 1950, the worst one could generally fear from a dirty needle was a badly swollen, infected arm. The size of the syringe suggests that the tableau took its inspiration from the horse-doping scandals of the time. It is possible that the girl on the right is pregnant.

Like the figure he drew for the *News Chronicle* on Coronation Day, remarking 'Seems to be some sort of procession', Searle could not work up much interest in the grander British 'institutions'; but for *Punch* he still made an exception. The *Punch* Table in those days was a closed shop, reserved for members only, on the grounds that technically the Wednesday Lunch was a policy meeting called to decide the content of that week's full-page political cartoon – *Punch*'s weekly 'statement'. Only once in the history of the magazine had a guest been admitted to the normal proceedings of the Table (as opposed to formal dinners for the likes of Garibaldi), and that was Mark Twain in 1907, on an occasion made famous by Twain's declining to carve his initials in the table-top, as was the members' custom, on the grounds that two-thirds of Thackeray ('W.M.T.') was good enough for him. Now, on 7 April 1953, Ronald Searle had become the second guest thus admitted, at the invitation of the new Editor, Malcolm Muggeridge, a self-confessed 'addict' of Searle's work who wished to bind him closer to the magazine. There was also a more immediate ulterior motive in Muggeridge's mind, since the regular producer of the 'Big Cartoon', Leslie Illingworth, had departed to the Continent on holiday, and the Editor was keen that Searle should have a go at replacing him.

Over lunch at 10 Bouverie Street it became apparent to Searle that the rigmarole of round-table discussion and even sketching (on cream laid paper passed round the members) was something of a put-up job; a political line had been taken and treatments considered in advance, in discussion between Muggeridge and his Art Editor, Russell Brockbank. But Searle went along with it, accepted the honour of the 'Big Cartoon', and produced it within the requisite forty-eight hours. It was a commission he would fulfil a number of times more as a holiday deputy, but he never enjoyed the experience of expressing a corporate opinion, or drawing in the stiffened, didactic tradition of *Punch*'s 'policy' cartoon. More interesting to him were the complexities of human relations round the Table, where on his first appearance (which also marked the début of the new Literary Editor, Anthony Powell) he saw Muggeridge uncomfortably flanked by two former Editors, 'Evoe' (E. V. Knox) and 'Fougasse' (Kenneth Bird). An air of bufferishness prevailed which Muggeridge was able only partially to dispel during his brief tenure of the editorial chair.

A pleasant consequence of his high professional standing was that Searle could now award himself the occasional break from his pattern of work. Already widely travelled in places where few tourists would be terribly eager to go, he had so far never had the chance to immerse himself, alone, in the splendours of Renaissance art. In 1953 he put this right. His first trip, in midsummer, was devoted to resting and looking, and taking up contacts provided by Anna Romersa, a long-time minder of the young Searle twins. In Milan, the itinerary began propitiously with time spent in the company of Giacomo Manzù, the sculptor and lithographer, then at work on his famous series of 'Cardinals'. Rome, Naples, Capri and Pompeii followed; Sienna, in time for the Palio; and then the great binge of Florence, taken far too quickly, of course, but as an investment of information for the return visit. Searle enjoyed his solitary wandering, though it left him open to rather haunting experiences like the one that occurred in the Grand Hotel in Milan. He made an immediate note of it:

> The little waiter who brings me my breakfast – a sad, grey, little man with sunken cheeks and pink rims to his eyes – just brought me in some coffee 'for a nightcap'. He hesitated a moment and, slightly embarrassed, said: "Scuse me donta mind, but why do you use your left hand to write? I saw for the furst time this morning that you usa left hand and I look to see whata wrong with the other, but it looka alright to me.

Above: 'Bumble arrayed', *The Humour of Dickens*, London, c. 1952

Dickens' infamous parish beadle, who heard Oliver Twist's appeal for more gruel. 'Another beadle,' Dickens wrote, 'had come into power; and on him the cocked hat, gold-laced coat, and staff, had all three descended.'

I never see it before, except once with a soldier who had the other one offa here' – sawing at his shoulder. I told him I was born left-handed and it was fairly commonplace in England. 'Well,' he said, 'I *never* see it before.' (He must be 50.) Surely left-handedness can't be so rare in Italy – or peculiar to England. Anyway, I seem to recall that Leonardo was left-handed. The waiter went out quite convinced that it was rare and strange – still puzzled that it should happen.

Right: 'The Child-Hater', *Punch*, 9 June 1954

A one-picture short story, distantly related perhaps to 'The Pied Piper of Hamelin'.

It was the waiter who now seemed rare and strange: was this some complicated defence on his part against the superstitions that still attached to the left-hander, or *mancino*, in Italy? Happily, Leonardo's 'Last Supper' was close by for reassurance.

There was time only for a token resumption of the continuum of work, and the publication of *Souls in Torment*, before the second Italian trip came round. This time the whole of October and November were allotted to the journey, which took Searle from Milan right down, through a month's discouragingly awful weather, to Taormina in Sicily, where his 'enormous sketch-block' finally came into its own. At one point Ronald's activities became so intimately intertwined with those of the local fisherman that he used 'the fresh black ink of a newly-caught cuttlefish to sketch the head of one of the men who caught it'. To return to such basics of existence, and to the improvisatory methods of his imprisonment, must have reminded him of the dangers of an over-civilization of his talent. He was entering again into the spirit of exile. His many paintings of Sicily, mostly sold at the Leicester Galleries in 1954 in an exhibition with the no-nonsense title of 'London, Taormina — and the last of the schoolgirls', were watercolours and gouaches; it would take ten years, Searle said, to master oils, and no time would be left for anything else. The look of these paintings was quite 'hot': complex and jungly lines made legible with bold colour. Sometimes one misses the human figure; a preparation seems to have been made for a foreground action that does not occur. Perhaps the artist felt this too; it is certainly a problem he could have wrestled with. As his friends have said of him, it was 'another way he could have gone'. But instead, in December, he went home to his contracts and agreements and responsibilities.

Newton Road was not turning out to be a complete success. Filled with gorgeously multifarious *objets* (the childhood museum re-presented with the artist's eye) and the light admitted by vast horizontal windows, and even a wall of glass bricks in the hall, the house was ideal as a photographic backdrop for visiting cameramen. The Searles had many friends in journalism and underwent the 'ideal couple' treatment more often than most. Their New Year Party came to be quite a celebrated event in the social calendar of London's artists, writers and performers during the Fifties. There are those who, with hindsight, remember these gatherings as 'entirely Kaye's thing', with Ronald a rather withdrawn and even embarrassed presence. Others recall him as a perfectly willing accomplice. The truth is that he was probably just tired. Invitations and decorations were all his responsibility, and he could not bear to fall short of personalizing all the items so that everyone had something to take away (signed and illustrated dusters were one particularly successful motif). But it was in the normal working day that the inadequacies or inappropriatenesses of the house really showed themselves. Sound travelled apparently unobstructed — a switch turned on in the cellar could be heard at the top of the house, Kaye Webb recalled — and the twins' playroom was directly below Ronald's studio. Ronald would be trying to work, it seemed to Paul Hogarth, 'while the twins were fighting with T-squares'. Ronald's own preference was for a radio turned on very low, and meticulous tidiness, an aim in which none of the rest of the household was able to match him.

The house itself was famous — architectural-school pilgrims came in busloads to see it — and so was Ronald; the visiting graphics world seemed to expect him to act as its host. Nobody, not even the artist friends to whom he mentioned the problem, realized how seriously he wished to insist on his privacy. If his family failed to grasp it too, it was very likely because he did not 'explode' enough to let them know. His anger was contained, rationalized, diverted, so that his presence was interpreted by some as universally obliging.

Above: Fisherman, Taormina, November 1953

Searle's journey of self-regeneration took him down the length of Italy during the autumn of 1953, ending on the coast of Sicily. Most of the paintings from this exhibition were sold at the Leicester Galleries, along with the last of the St Trinian's cartoons.

Right: Katie Searle, Ronald Searle, Johnnie Searle, at home, London, early 1950s

In recent years, Katie has been running the Props Department of the Royal Opera House, Covent Garden; Johnnie is a freelance photographer. (Photograph by Tom Blau.)

As one of Ronald's secretaries recalled, it was difficult to know what to do for the best, because 'everything one did was right'. As a father, he was a specialist in treats, sometimes quite punitively disguised, as when he announced to the twins that they were due that afternoon at the dentist's. When the taxi disgorged the miserable children at their destination, they found it was a cinema. He realized that he had complicated feelings about them, and in a beautifully executed 1954 cartoon, occupying a whole page in *Punch*, he rescued some fun from the darker emotions. The balloon-seller whose wares carry children silently upward and away really requires no caption, but as if to acknowledge openly some such potentiality in himself, Searle called it 'The Child Hater'.

He now enjoyed an individually negotiated working arrangement with Muggeridge's *Punch*. For his new series 'The Rake's Progress', scheduled to start early in 1954, he requested from Muggeridge

> a separate rate ... because of the extra research and work involved in this – but more particularly I would like you to consider either taking first serial rights on any cartoons I do for the paper or alternatively letting me retain the book-rights on my work, on condition, of course, that none of it is used for advertising purposes ... It is most likely that our own little 'firm' Perpetua would do the publishing and our margin is too small to allow us to budget for a copyright percentage.

Muggeridge gladly agreed to retain only the first-publication rights 'in all your work except the occasional political cartoon', which Searle would not have wished to republish anyway; and hoped that 'if you will accept this gentleman's agreement, there will be no need for you to fiddle about with the wording on the back of the cheque' (copyrights were normally assigned as a matter of course to *Punch*). Muggeridge also accepted the suggestion of a fee of £75 per episode, which made Searle the best-paid of the *Punch* artists: but the 'Rakes' series was worth it. Cycles of ambition, social advancement and decline had been presented before: William Hogarth's territory had been memorably revisited in the Thirties by Rebecca West and David Low. But the economy of Searle's version, and the accuracy with which he pinned down the milieux in which his upstarts operated, gave the idea new edge. He must have known he was on a winner when the second in the series, 'The Painter', brought from Sir Alfred Munnings, Past President of the Royal Academy, a letter almost incoherent with delight. 'My God, sir, you're a smasher,' raved the Academician. 'Quite the best page — and so *much better* in style than all this Americanized silliness — I've seen for years. Marvellous.' Urging Searle to 'Do another of the sculptor's progress', Munnings headed the letter 'Dear *Artist*', with the noun underlined three times. Searle had hit the spot — and continued to do so, for there was no shortage of volunteers to fuel the series with ideas. Muggeridge passed them on ('Here is a suggestion for a lawyer from John Mortimer') with his own delighted comments ('The last two Rakes were superb'; 'The Rakes get better and better'). When Searle collected them the following year into a Perpetua book that went into a second printing before publication, the Editor may have looked back a little wistfully at his surrender of the book rights.

Even humdrum attendance in the stalls of the West End was now made bearable for

1. Discovers The Wasteland. First verse play published in The Cherwell. Drafts autobiography

2. Captivated by German Youth Movement. settles in Berlin. Shakes hands with W.H.Auden and Christopher Isherwood. Deported

3. Joins International Brigade. Barcelona. Sunstroke. Converted to Yoga. Reading of own poems at Kingsway Hall

4. Dines with Cyril Connelly. Special issue of Horizon devoted to tone poems. Shakes hands with Stephen Spender

5. Dirge, accompanied by Tongan nose flutes, broadcast on Third Programme British Council lecture tour, Friendly Islands. Nods to C. Day Lewis

6. Accepts Chair of Poetry at a Los Angeles girls College. Visits Aldous Huxley. Succumbs to mescalin.

Left: 'The Rake's Progress: The Poet', *Punch*, 24 March 1954

Searle's chief contact in the poetic fraternity was C. Day Lewis, who provided a Preface and a Dirge for the death of St Trinian's in Souls in Torment. *Day Lewis himself had the requisite Oxford and revolutionary-leftist credentials, but is not otherwise to be identified with the figure portrayed here, who conforms to the type George Orwell had characterized as 'the nancy poets'. By the standards of* Punch *in the early Fifties, the prominent bottoms of the German boys made quite a daring reference to homosexuality.*

Right: 'Consequences of putting
Mr Graham Sutherland's latest
portrait on public exhibition',
Punch, 8 December 1954

*Thus titled on its first appearance, but
untitled in* Merry England, *etc. The
House of Commons presented
Winston Churchill with a Sutherland
portrait of himself as an eightieth-
birthday present. The artist had done
nothing to disguise the effects of age
on the Prime Minister, especially in
the area of the sunken jaw and the
loose, corded skin beneath the chin.
Those accustomed to flattery in public
portraiture saw the work as a
caricature. Churchill's wife
Clementine was among those who
took offence, and she later destroyed
the painting privately. The subject
himself, in his speech of thanks, had
described the picture as 'an
outstanding example of modern art'
(laughter).*

Searle and Keown by the travelling they regularly undertook, not just to the Edinburgh
Festival, which was an annual fixture, but to the theatres of Paris and Dublin as well. The
Paris visits settled down pleasantly into a twice-yearly rhythm, Keown justifying the
expense with extra feature articles of the kind he and Searle had already been supplying
from the English provinces. In June 1954 they saw *Hamlet* at Elsinore, as part of a small
group of London critics following the Old Vic Company. The *News Chronicle*'s critic Alan
Dent was there, and Searle drew him in *Hamlet* costume for the paper – not so much a
favour as an obligation, since Searle himself had returned to the *Chronicle* with an 'Exclusive
Saturday Sketchbook' entitled, with perhaps an ominous hint of the tyranny of the
deadline, 'Searle Every Saturday'. This replaced Vicky's topical 'Weekend Fantasia' (Vicky
had just left the paper in a reciprocal huff) with a much larger and more fantastical feature,
very hard on the inventive faculties. Searle went for groups of visual jokes on seasonal
themes: tulips, the seaside, Wimbledon, and (celebrating the end of meat-rationing)
butchery. Stuck for anything more novel one week in high summer, Searle allowed himself

to regress as far as 'The BOYS of St Trinian's', though there was perhaps an excuse for this in the imminent and widely pre-puffed première of *The Belles of St Trinian's*, first and best of an erratic film series. It opened on the last day of September that year at the Gaumont, Haymarket, and its reception must have caused The Founder very mixed feelings. 'Girls will be Searles,' burbled as serious a critic as Paul Dehn. 'And what fun it all is!' 'Run along,' he advised, 'and laugh thy Searlish laughter.'

News Chronicle readers said goodbye to Searlish laughter in the autumn, when the Saturday feature came to an end. It had thrown up some highly collectable images, but the panic for ideas was no fun to face week by week. Searle preferred a series he could prepare for, such as the 'Major Thompson' articles of Pierre Daninos which he illustrated for *Le Figaro* a few months later. His reputation in France had received a curious sort of boost in December 1954, by virtue of the embarrassing non-arrival of five drawings of his intended for an exhibition mounted by *Le Canard enchaîné*. Searle's secretary had arranged for their delivery through the impeccably reliable James Bourlet & Sons Ltd ('By Appointment Art Packers To His Late Majesty King George VI'), but French customs officers working to rule at Orly Airport impounded the works and did not release them in time for the show's opening. The *Canard* personnel retaliated with admirable spirit and pertinence by exhibiting in their place some works by the art world's most celebrated customs official, Le Douanier Rousseau, which they draped eloquently in black crape. Never was Searle more appropriately represented by an exhibit not his own.

It was hard to turn down new opportunities, even when they took him away from the strict pursuit of line. Drawing cartoons for *Time and Tide* he found himself invited to set and judge the magazine's weekly competition, a job that recurred from time to time. On a physically larger scale of responsibility, he took on the task of designing the décor for the Chelsea Arts Ball, on the theme of 'The Seven Seas'. The *Times* came to photograph him at work on 'a series of suspended mermaids'. At much the same time he was photographed preparing the cover for the next Spring Number of *Punch*. By the time the cover appeared – confirming that Searle, like André François, saw Mr Punch as no less mad-eyed and leering than his nineteenth-century prototype – Searle had undergone the delightful but exhausting experience of seeing his designs for a film put through the production process. His director, Wendy Toye, had been interviewed by Kaye Webb some years before and a friendship had developed; she was to remain impartially devoted to both Ronald and Kaye, whose social gatherings she recalled as one of the few places in those days where performers met those alien creatures, the critics, on apparently free and easy terms. A previous attempt at collaboration between Wendy and Ronald had fallen through in 1952: it was to have been a portmanteau film called *The Paper Chase*, a little narrative fugue inspired by the stories on a sheet of newspaper blowing down the street. The replacement notion offered much more in the way of fun for Ronald, however, and in the late summer of Coronation Year he put in the groundwork on costumes and décor.

Late the following year, the film was made: a 'short feature' of twenty-two minutes, in almost hyperactive colour, called *On the Twelfth Day*. Its premise – what if the gift-giving orgy we sing about in 'The Twelve Days of Christmas' literally happened? – ensured a rapid build-up of personnel and wildlife in the studio, where the entire production was colour-coordinated by Searle in such a way as to put a gorgeous sheen of unreal decorative patterning on everything, including the animals. A decade or so later, the whole process would have been recognizable as 'psychedelic'. Turtle-doves had to be humanely dyed and eight cows, imported to accommodate the maids a-milking, repainted daily by the

Above: Ronald Searle and the 'Belles of St Trinian's', *Punch*, 13 October 1954

Caricature by R. S. Sherriffs (1906–60) to accompany the Punch *film review by Richard Mallett, who found the film amusing, but not as an extension of Searle's own humour: 'every outrageous detail is emphasised, explained and clearly labelled "Joke" ... the whole conception seems to be misguided. It's like expecting one of the Searle jokes to seem just as funny with a drawing by Du Maurier.'*

designer in their eccentric uniforms of stripes and spots. Amid all the pandemonium of swans and geese and drummers and leaping lords, one cow, in a striking reassertion of red-raw nature over stylization, managed to give birth.

The film that emerged from these panics was a delight, but for a whole year British audiences were denied the chance to see it. Its awkward length and 'continental' feel – all that colour and no words – meant that the Rank and ABC circuits spurned it. 'May be too English for Venice and a trifle too precious for Wigan,' a reviewer at the Venice Film Festival had correctly predicted. America proved more receptive: NBC paid £15,000 for a showing on New Year's Day, *Life* published a five-page colour spread, Bosley Crowther of the *New York Times* called the film 'a glittering and witty little gem', and Hollywood nominated it for a 'best short film' award. It was not until Christmas week of 1956 that London's Carlton Cinema got around to presenting it to a British audience. Jympson Harman of the *Evening News* called the delay a scandal.

The Toye-Searle partnership had long before passed on to a new project, the musical revue *Wild Thyme*, which opened in Bath in June 1955, earning seven curtain calls and the admiration of a local reviewer for 'some of the most beautiful scenery I have ever seen, by Ronald Searle'. By mid-July the show had arrived at the Duke of York's Theatre in London, greeted by W. A. Darlington in the *Daily Telegraph* as 'a sweet little story with next to no point … but it has life and charm and humour'. The sets again were praised, but the reviewer hinted that the show was too innocent to live in the modern world. It was the age of failed summits and 'security conferences' and the ever more impassioned debate over nuclear weapons. Here Searle could not share the moral outrage of his erstwhile colleagues on the Left. Upon him, in 1945, the 'shadow of the Bomb' had fallen as a blessing, not a curse. And he said so, on BBC Television, in the last *Panorama* of the 1955 summer series, marking the tenth anniversary of the Hiroshima detonation. The programme opened with a dramatized reconstruction of the day the bomb fell, plus film of Hiroshima then and now; and then came Searle, explaining to Max Robertson, through the medium of the POW drawings, the treatment the prisoners had received, and the likely end if it had continued. 'The contrast between the dramatic horror of the opening and the quiet horror of the interview with Ronald Searle was astonishingly effective,' commented *The Listener*. 'It was a contrast between universal catastrophe and individual suffering, between the scream of horror and the understatement ... the fearful opening made us receptive to Ronald Searle's quiet, bitter voice and the terrible story he told.' A letter of thanks from the *Panorama* Editor, Michael Barsley, assured Searle that his contribution had made as great an impression as anything in the programme. Indeed, it seems that Searle may even have rather pre-empted the foreseen climax of the presentation, a debate between the pacifist philosopher Bertrand Russell and General Sir Frank Messervy.

As occasions like this demonstrated, Britain was aware of Searle's talent for reportage, but persistently disdained to call upon it. Again it was the Americans who stepped in. Since 1952, when he began contributing illustrations to their *Holiday* magazine – who cast him at this stage very much as an exponent of olde-English quaintness – he had been represented by an American agent, John Locke, a descendant of the seventeenth-century English philosopher of the same name. The health of the American magazine market should perhaps have sustained a sufficient crop of home-grown artists, yet there were pockets of unexpected opportunity (for example at *Life* magazine) which had maintained a strong wartime tradition of graphic reportage done by distinguished painters but had found itself short of top-class specialists when the artists returned to their peacetime easels. So *Life* tried Searle out on his own patch, covering Winston Churchill's last Prime Ministerial speech in the House of Commons. The journalist Honor Balfour had received

Left: 'Twelve lords a-leaping ...', design for the film *On The Twelfth Day*, 1954–5

Wendy Toye's film was what one might call wardrobe-intensive; everything in it was meticulously yet exuberantly designed. As a graphic artist, Searle expected his audience to make deductions from what they saw, hence the specification: 'One could have long pants or a nightshirt – (overslept).'

Right: Ronald Searle and Wendy Toye on tour, June 1955

The colleagues are signing the scenery of the musical Wild Thyme, *probably at its opening in Bath. Wendy Toye has been much honoured of late, especially abroad, as a pioneer among women film and stage directors. (Photograph by* Bath & Wilts Chronicle & Herald.)

the tip-off that Churchill's resignation was imminent, and it was she who arranged for Ronald to sketch the inside of the empty House, and to sit in the Press Gallery making more sketches while a staffer from *Life* noted the seating arrangements. Ronald took all the information home, worked till morning, and the drawing arrived in New York on the evening of the same day. Even the *Life* editors,' accustomed to stops being pulled out on their behalf, must have been astonished by so wholehearted a treatment of a packed House, with its teetering Gothic shelves of seating treated no less scrupulously than the horde of Members.

Searle was rewarded in October with another urgent job, the Geneva Four-Power Conference: a new kind of foreign assignment for him, and a welcome enlargement of his view of the continent of Europe, where he was increasingly at home. That summer, unusually, he had actually managed a 'proper' holiday, at Le Lavandou in the south of France, with Kaye and their friend Wendy Toye. They could not resist popping along the coast to Marseilles, to see what kind of living quarters had been proposed for the human species by Le Corbusier. Impressive to look at, Ronald thought, but after Changi, not inviting to live in: too much concrete. He was now brandishing a new Leica camera, under whose eye the family fell one by one – even in Cambridge, where sister Olive was snapped with her new baby, Stella, and William Searle immortalized as he approached the end of his working life. Enfeebled at last by emphysema, he had undertaken only 'light duties' for some time, and in the spring of 1956 he retired with the accolade of the Imperial Service Medal for his thirty years' work in the Post Office.

Without understanding its origins, the one-time 'Buller' had come to appreciate his son's talent at least in the measure of the amusement it brought, and also the honour, which was already considerable. On 1 February 1956, Ronald took his place as a member of Mr Punch's Table, carving his initials with a chisel midway along the edge of the large oblong (though by tradition Round) surface. This ceremony was the consequence of a rather more prosaic commercial negotiation whereby Searle, in consultation with Muggeridge, Art Editor Russell Brockbank and Peter Agnew (speaking for the management), had reached what Ronald called 'an agreement for me to become more closely associated with *Punch*'. It was in Mr Punch's interest to rein this contributor in. If paid realistically for his exclusive services, on the other hand, Ronald would find his freelance life pleasantly simplified. He proposed an income of £100 per week from *Punch*, in return for which he would 'abandon all artistic work for other magazines and newspapers in this country and accept no further advertising commissions here', with the exceptions of Lemon Hart Rum

Left: Chelsea Arts Ball, London December 1954

Searle's 'suspended mermaids' in situ at the Seven Seas Ball. Music by Ted Heath's band and others. The centrepiece was the best part of fifty feet high.

('for which a character was created on the provision that it shall continue') and the 'Young Elizabethan children's magazine, in which we have a family interest'. The Young Elizabethan was Kaye's new project. A very spruce revamp of the former Collins' Young Elizabethan, it benefited greatly from Ronald's illustrations and headings, his thoughts on layout, his attendance as a famous prize-giver at 'Young Liz' functions, and his part in supplying regular narratives from the world of St Custard's, where Geoffrey Willans was now propelling Molesworth into the space age. From 1955 to 1958, the magazine thrived as a sort of printed prototype of the children's television programme Blue Peter (which began in 1958), aiming at the post-war baby-boomers of nine, ten and eleven years of age. It would have been unsporting of Punch to interfere with this.

Having examined Ronald's figures closely, in particular the cited '2340 guineas a year paid by the News Chronicle for one cartoon a week', the 'slightly increased offers' made by the Evening Standard and Kemsley Newspapers for a similar series, and his poster-fee of '250 to 500 guineas, depending on the series and the use', the Punch committee decided it must accommodate him. Researching in recent archives, Brockbank had concluded that 'our successful [covers] have been done by François, Ardizzone, Mansbridge, Thelwell, Searle and R.B. [himself]. As to colour pages, he has proved his brilliance in our recent Almanack and I can easily use him more if he is ours.' Brockbank suggested £4500 per annum, which was passed on by Agnew to Searle as an offer of £90 per week, with exceptions granted for Lemon Hart and the Young Elizabethan. Any contributions exceeding the total of weekly payments would be taken at a rate of £30 per theatre drawing; £45 per half-page, £60 per full-page in black and white; £75 for a two-colour cover; and £100 for a four-colour cover or colour page. By Punch's prevailing standards, these rates, even allowing for the component of exclusivity, were enormously high. A full decade later, the going rate for a Punch cover was publicly quoted at only £50. But if the arrangement worked, it would be worth it. What was not foreseen was the size of the loophole represented by the phrase 'in this country'. Searle did not set out deliberately to exploit it, but the attractive work offered him in America would eventually make rather a hollow boast of Punch's 'exclusive' right to his work − not that any public boast was actually made. In Peter Agnew's view, the contract should not be publicized: 'People should learn to look for your work in Punch as time goes on.' This was probably a tactical error. At all events, Searle was on the staff. He took his place at the Table on the bitterly cold first day of February. Russell Brockbank was in the editorial chair, Muggeridge having been delayed on a ferry-boat from France. It happened that A. A. Milne, a Table member, had died the night before. 'They replaced him quickly,' somebody said. Another member remarked, rather in the fashionably disconcerting style of Stephen Potter, that Searle was the first bearded member to join since 1901, the last one having been 'sacked for homosexuality'. Basil Boothroyd voiced gratitude and relief that he was no longer the youngest member. Ronald Searle was only thirty-five. In the traditional way of Punch, he might have been expected to go on appearing at the Table for another forty years. As things turned out, it was hardly more than five years later that he left the Table Room for the last time.

Two big new Punch series followed closely on the clinching of the new deal. Alex Atkinson came up with the notion of inhabiting the style of Henry Mayhew, one of the Victorian founders of Punch, and producing a modern equivalent of his London Labour and the London Poor. There being less outright shocking squalor in mid-Fifties London − less interesting squalor, perhaps − Atkinson concentrated instead on a class more characteristic

Left: 'A Moving Picture Girl', *The Big City, or the New Mayhew*, with Alex Atkinson, London, 1958

First published in Punch *(2 May 1956), as all the 'Mayhew' characters were, with the single exception of 'A Lady of the Streets'. As for the 'Moving Picture Girl', Alex Atkinson's text recorded that: 'Her story was not easy to follow, for she had adenoidal tendencies, and used a provincial accent with which I was unfamiliar . . . Her ambition was to become a "star" . . .'*

of the age: those pathetically defiant strugglers of inner-surburban bedsitter-land, where ambition finally learns to die. With few but striking exceptions, such as a most wondrously innocuous vicar, Searle's character-studies have in common a projecting lower lip that tells of stubbornness giving way slowly to misery. The 'New Mayhew' pieces, later collected by Perpetua under the title *The Big City*, operate right on the line between humour and melancholy; textually and graphically, they tread it with a delicacy that now seems to belong as securely to the long-ago as Mayhew himself. To be made to laugh at the 'type', and yet feel sorry for the reality it stands for, is more than one expects from such a book.

Searle's other series was a solo effort, more grandiose, and a tester for the parameters of his new pay agreement; for the 'Heroes of Our Time' were colour caricatures printed as a centrefold across two whole pages. Among the 'Heroes', there were several (notably T. S. Eliot, in his office at Faber's) who consented to give Ronald a brief sitting, though they must have known that the heading under which they were destined to appear was heavy with irony. The selection actually divided itself between Sacred Monsters and Sacred Cows. Adopting the faded palette of the age of 'Spy' and 'Ape', and toning down something of his natural spikiness in their honour too, Searle produced portraits which were the talk of London for weeks, with variations on the same story being told about each. Perhaps the best-attested is the one about Lord Goddard, the Lord Chief Justice. H. F. (Humphrey) Ellis, the *Punch* writer, found himself seated between Norman Birkett, the eminent counsel, and Goddard at a dinner in the Inner Temple. It was Goddard himself who brought up the subject of his appearance among the Heroes. 'Well I mean to say, I know it was meant to be a rag and all that, but I didn't think much of it. Should have been better than that. It wasn't like me. It wasn't good, y'know ...' By way of gentle dissent, Ellis enquired the Lord Chief Justice's opinion of the other caricatures in the series. 'Ah *well* now, *they* were in a different class altogether ...' Gilbert Harding, the testy television pundit, retaliated on the spot; he gave Searle a sitting, but called him 'Judas' when the drawing was complete. Of the Princess Margaret portrait, *Punch*'s Christmas special, it was said that the Queen Mother had remarked 'Margaret doesn't look like that at men.' The line has the wishful tinge of a *Punch* man's invention, but it was passed on to the artist as authentic.

It was in the preparatory stages of the 'Heroes' series, around July 1956, that the conditions were established whereby one of the oddest episodes in all of Searle's career would literally take over his life. It started when Brigadier Bernard Fergusson marched into the Newton Road house and requested the favour of a very private talk. That Fergusson should turn up was not so strange; he was an old colleague, at *Punch* and in the little magazines, where he had contributed anecdotal adventure stories and the *Strand* magazine's 'Useless Information' column. Ronald regarded him as one of the last of an old school of 'Army poets' – very old, to judge by the glint of his monocle. Once this slightly batty figure had established that the coast was clear at the Searle residence, however, a different manner took over. Waving an identity card in front of Ronald and gabbling an impressively condensed version of the Official Secrets Act, he informed the astonished artist that failure to respect the confidentiality of their meeting would entail penalties dating from a crueller, pre-monocular age. The fact was, Fergusson stated, that there were going to be 'manoeuvres' in the Mediterranean area and, when the time was ripe, Searle was required to come along as a member of the Psychological Warfare Department. For the moment, it would suffice if he accompanied Fergusson to White's, where others engaged in the same notional venture were forgathering. Off Searle went to the celebrated club, where he met 'all sorts of bizarre people', some of them conceivably as bewildered as himself. Restored, still uncomprehending, to his home and studio, he found that nothing had changed except that his phone was now tapped. It was dead whenever he lifted it, but after a loud 'ping', and sometimes an equally audible voice groaning 'Searle's on the line again', it started to work. Otherwise, all remained mysteriously calm.

A busy summer took its predicted course. Ronald and Eric Keown made their annual excursion to the Edinburgh Festival, meeting up as usual with their favourite colleague, the genial Cornishman J. C. Trewin, at the Open Arms Hotel, Dirleton, East Lothian. Trewin was known in this small group as 'The Human Filing Cabinet', because of his perennially bulging pockets. Two years before, Searle and Keown, with the co-operation of the victim, had undertaken a surprise search of Trewin's garb, and discovered no fewer

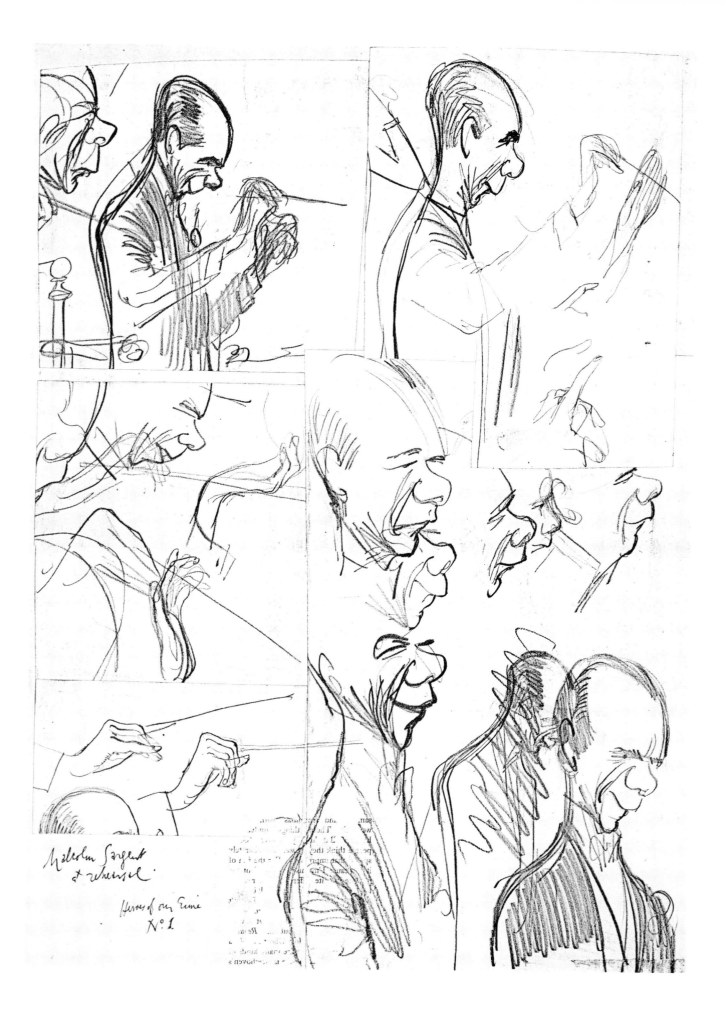

Malcolm Sargent
+ rehearsal.

Heroes of our time
Nº 1

than 117 items in one suit of clothes, ranging from an intact bottle of Disprin, and a virtually empty bottle of same, to – quoting the inventory – 'one half of a metal lizard (tail end missing)', an *Observer* press-cutting dating from 1940 and a sketch-plan of St Davids in Wales. That such a prodigy of plethoric dishevelment should have got on so well with the meticulously organized Searle is a tribute to the open-heartedness, and adaptability, of each.

Back at *Punch*, there were 'Heroes' to be dispatched, and a whole fortnight's trip to Paris with Eric, this time including coverage of the Motor Show and a private visit to the outlying village of Grisy-les-Plâtres, the home of André François. In Searle's absence, the third Molesworth book, *Whizz For Atomms*, was published and on his return he was inducted into the Garrick Club. The newsstands were displaying an invigorating *Punch* cover, Searle's pastiche of Picasso in honour of the master's seventy-fifth birthday. Inside, Searle had rendered several Victorian household favourites (remembered from youth) in one or other of the Picasso styles: the 'Monarch of the Glen' suffered the fate of Guernica. But this anniversary fun appeared against a background of worrying world events, particularly in Hungary, where a state of emergency had been proclaimed while Soviet troops intervened to suppress democratic reforms. It was as the Red Army stood poised for full-scale invasion that Ronald at last received news of the imminence of Brigadier Fergusson's 'manoeuvres'. Searle was to report, the message said, to the War Office at 6 p.m. and bring 'more than an overnight bag'. Reading skilfully between the lines, Ronald packed a week's worth of clothes, topped off the collection with a leather jacket that looked as if it didn't care what happened to it, and presented himself as requested. He had warned his wife that one of these days he was going to have to dash away without explanation, so she was not dumbfounded, but merely dismayed, as he disappeared.

The War Office turned out to be full of taciturn men with bowler hats and umbrellas, and pistols in their back pockets – evidently, Ronald deduced, members of the legendary plain-clothes army of 'Flaming Terrapins'. Everyone shuffled around without speaking, until at last somebody took charge and instructions were issued. Searle was told he was being flown out not to Budapest but, for some reason, to Cyprus. What this had to do with Psychological Warfare he still had not the faintest idea.

A rickety plane took off, full of still wordless bowler-hatted super-troops and Ronald Searle. By Malta the plane had lost the use of an engine and had to put down. Another plane dashed back to London to pick up replacement parts. The group finally landed in Cyprus twelve hours late, to be informed that it was about time too, since the first wave of planes had just taken off to bomb Cairo. The so-called 'Suez adventure' had begun. Now that it was evening, it would be necessary for Searle to travel immediately overland to GHQ at Episkopi, so that he would be on the spot at daybreak. To that end, an armoured vehicle and full escort had been arranged to take him through the Troodos Mountains under cover of darkness. It was at this point that Searle rebelled in defence of his civilian status. Unlike everybody else on the excursion, he was not in the army and not obliged to obey an order, especially when it involved offering himself as a target, however well defended, to Colonel Grivas and his Greek Cypriot rebels, in darkness and on their own territory. There was an uproar at this, but Searle had already made clear to Fergusson his determination not to be drawn back officially into the army, for fear of not being able to get out again – a reasonable apprehension in view of the press-gang tactics that had been used on him so far. So Searle stayed put for the night, in a hotel, on the personal say-so of Fergusson – which was appropriate, since the Brigadier, all along, had

Below: Anti-Nasser pamphlet, for Suez campaign, Cyprus, November 1956

Drawn by Searle in Cyprus for the Department of Psychological Warfare, for use in pamphlets which were subsequently not dropped on Cairo. Colonel Gamal Abdel Nasser (1918–70) had been elected President of Egypt in June 1956 and had seized the Suez Canal the following month, provoking at first merely economic retaliation, and then an Anglo-French armed response.

NASSER
November 1956

been in the position of vouching for the artist personally, against the doubts of MI6. It emerged that the Intelligence men had entertained serious misgivings about Searle since a morning at the turn of the Fifties when he had been observed investing in a copy of the *Daily Worker* on Campden Hill. Even Fergusson was a bit puzzled as to 'what you were up to with all those Lefties', but his faith in the fundamental soundness of his friend had never been shaken.

And the upshot of that was that, as November began, Searle found himself installed in a tent at Episkopi. The Department of Psychological Warfare, as was only appropriate, turned out to be considerably more fearsome in imagination than in reality. For the purposes of the Suez operation, it consisted of Major 'Mike' Wingate Grey; Bill Williams of the Foreign Office; Commander Peter Vine RNR, a former Suez Canal pilot; and Searle, plus Fergusson and a liaison officer. Searle was brought in on general 'Ops', such as the high-handed takeover of the local radio station, which embarrassed him greatly; but his chief responsibility was for the design of leaflets intended to drive a wedge of doubt between the Egyptian citizenry and their leader, Colonel Nasser. Searle drew up some half-dozen. A couple showed Nasser in personal fear of his life; another depicted a triumphant RAF streaming overhead. A couple more, into which the artist had managed to infiltrate a little of the old 'bolshiness' of the private soldier, showed fat generals defended by naive youngsters, or taking their ease in an armchair with a Coca-Cola and a cigar while exhorting others, down a telephone, to fight for every village and strip of land. Oddly enough, the Psychological Warfare detachment was enjoying very much this sort of easeful existence itself, for while the Suez fighting raged, full-dress dinners were in progress at Episkopi, with merry yo-hoing for more wine and sceptical remarks about the quality of the beefsteak.

Below: Portrait of W. Somerset Maugham, *Punch*, 1954

With Maugham's own annotation: 'According to my daughter not a caricature, but a striking likeness.' The drawing was made from photographs, some two years before Searle met the writer at the Dorchester.

Searle's propaganda cartoons were run off in hundreds of thousands on a temperamental printing-press, and prepared for dropping over Cairo. Which fact is more absurd – that they were asked for in the first place, or that they were never dropped? The artist was past caring. A message came from the RAF to say that they were 'too busy' – dropping other things, presumably – to bother with paper. According to Fergusson's account, most of Searle's productions had been vetoed anyway by the Foreign Office presence, on the grounds that they were 'too witty and near the bone' (perhaps the British High Command's own bone was meant). All bar a few copies that survive as collectors' items were dumped into an incinerator; but Searle had not stayed to witness this act. Once it was clear that he had adequately discharged the duty imposed upon him, he gave notice to Fergusson that his time was up. A helicopter was arranged to take him to Nicosia and, having paid a mess bill for £3 6s. 4d. (wine, mostly), he flew off to be ferried onward to London with all speed.

It had been one of those parodistically 'secret' British episodes, undertaken by decent chaps in a rotten cause. As Fergusson's memoirs conceded, Searle 'politically was not in sympathy with the operation', so it had been good of him to go ahead with it. Searle had actually bitten a larger bullet than that, for if there was anyone in the political spectrum he abhorred it was Prime Minister Anthony Eden, who had ordered the expedition, and to whom Searle had taken a violent dislike during a previous sketching encounter. At least Fergusson admitted to having used 'almost blunderbuss tactics' in 'persuading' his friend to take part. What shocked Searle most, looking back on the affair, was that he had been put on alert so many months earlier, a fact that pointed to a long-term collusion between Eden and the military, behind the Cabinet's back. But nothing more came of Searle's role in Suez, beyond a thank-you letter from the Allied Commander, General Sir Charles F. Keightley, GCB, KBE, DSO, expressing gratitude 'for coming out at such short notice and being ready to do so much to help us'. A couple of years later, during one of the periodic re-examinations of the Suez campaign, a couple of Searle leaflets were exhumed and reproduced in the public prints. A *Spectator* reader wrote in to express amazement that a man whose 'inspired grotesques enlivened the *Tribune* of a decade ago' had seemingly succumbed to the same 'Suez-cidal tendencies' as had overcome everyone else. But since Searle was prevented by the Official Secrets Act from defending or explaining his position, the *Spectator*'s editor, Brian Inglis, decided not to publish the letter. The last word in the whole business inevitably belongs to Fergusson, whose own letter of thanks to 'Dear Ronnie' contained the perhaps equivocal expression 'it was great fun having you'. The Brigadier took the opportunity – some might say the liberty – of asking Ronnie ('if it would amuse you') to 'knock off' a Christmas card for his unit. The Intelligence business requires all kinds of nerve.

Back in 'Merry England' (the name of his latest collection, whose publication day he had missed), and facing the embarrassment of explaining his absence with varying degrees of evasiveness, Searle was shanghaied again, this time by Malcolm Muggeridge. A lunch had been arranged with Somerset Maugham and his amanuensis Alan Searle, a rare fellow-clansman. Ronald, who had something of a talent for getting on with difficult elders of the arts (he had lately embarked on a decade-long correspondence with Edward Gordon Craig, the aged guru of theatre design), agreed to go along, and the four men dined

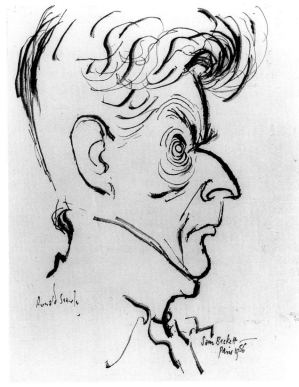

together in Maugham's Corner Suite at the Dorchester. In spite of his atrocious stammer, Maugham was on excellent form, announcing with pride that he had delivered 163 babies and was still qualified to practise as a midwife. Searle found himself entertained even by those of Maugham's opinions with which he was reluctant to agree, such as that the recently deceased Max Beerbohm had been lazy and self-indulgent, building a tremendous reputation on a 'trivial' quantity of writing. Yet Maugham did not denounce the minimalist tendency wholesale, for he had just seen Beckett's *Waiting for Godot* and liked it very much, especially the last quarter-hour which he said 'brimmed' with pathos. This was pleasant for Ronald to hear, as he had recently made the acquaintance of Beckett as well, during a visit to Paris for *Punch*. Eric Keown had asked rather apologetically if Ronald would mind lunching with an old pupil of his uncle's from Trinity College, Dublin days: a playwright, Keown intimated glumly, of the 'dustbin school'. The meeting at Chez Marius went well – Beckett choosing a table near the *toilettes* to accommodate his excitable bladder – and the three diners resolved to meet again. To the end of his life, Beckett kept up a friendship with Searle: he wrote – sparingly – a letter every Christmas.

Only a week had passed since the Cyprus interlude when nature found one of her famous ways of telling a man to slow down. A representative from Valentine's Cards had come down from Dundee in hopes of concluding a deal with Ronald, only to learn that the artist was in appalling agony and could not see him. Stricken by peritonitis from a burst appendix, Ronald was rushed into University College Hospital at tea-time and into the operating theatre by 8 p.m. His surgeon, 'Mac' Maclellan, later informed him, with that jolly sadism to which only the eminent sawbones is entitled, that 'the appendix contained nothing more poetic than PUS. Rich, virulent, super-toxic, pre-antibiotic PUS. And about half an acre surrounding the peritonitis. Another six hours' delay and you would have heard that harp.' (Harps of three different types happened to have featured in *Merry England, etc.*) Ronald's release from hospital was an event now deemed worthy of mention in the 'Invalids' column of *The Times*, along with the latest bulletins on 'Mr Solomon, the pianist', and Mr Robens, Labour M.P. for Blyth. Carrying instructions to 'keep away from nutcrackers', Searle left for Brighton to complete a careful convalescence. The most memorable part of the experience – a living cartoon – had been a hospital visit from Eric Keown, who arrived bearing a bunch of violets but didn't want to admit it. They were concealed inside his umbrella.

Left: 'Messieurs les Anglais, tirez les premiers!' ('Gentlemen of England, shoot first!'), Le Canard Enchaîné, 10 April 1957

The Canard *cartoonists welcome their counterparts, in a 'Franco-English' edition of the paper. The three guests, reading from left, are Ian Peterson, Vicky and Searle. The six caricaturists receiving them are Henri Monier, César, Lap, Grove, Pol Ferjac and Grum. Canard artists tended to remain faithful to the paper. Lap (Jacques Laplaine, 1921–87) stayed forty-one years. William Napoleon Grove (René Nolgrove, 1901–75) started in 1924 and remained until his death. This cartoon was drawn by Pol Ferjac (Paul Levain, 1900–79), who joined in 1939.*

Opposite top: New York skyline, May 1957, *Which Way Did He Go?*, London, 1961

The view from Room 2310, Beekman Tower Hotel ('On Exclusive Beekman Hill'), 3 Mitchell Place, at 49th Street. 'We awoke on Wednesday morning with the whole of New York spread out under our window at the top of this place, sideways on to the UNO building.'

Opposite bottom: New York cop, May–June 1957, *Which Way Did He Go?*, London, 1961

An example of perfect specificity achieved with very loose line.

By Christmas, Searle and Keown were back in the stalls together (the seasonal attraction was Flanders and Swann's *At the Drop of a Hat*), and within a month they were back on the Paris trail. In spite of mid-winter sadnesses – both John Minton and Gwen Raverat committed suicide – Searle had reason to feel buoyant. Sales of his *Merry England, etc.* collection had been excellent (16,000 copies gone in the first ten days) and the financial position of Perpetua Ltd had been consolidated by the publication of the Frenchman Raymond Peynet's 'Lovers' cartoons, which grew into a series. Peynet's taste in cartoon ideas was very much more gushy than Searle's; nor were they at one over the question of André François, whom a whole band of French cartoonists had rather scandalously boycotted on grounds of plagiarism (though it looked very much more like xenophobia against a Romanian immigrant). By maintaining impartiality in this matter, Searle was able to arrange a kind of poetic justice on his friend's behalf: the profits from Peynet's 'Lovers' helped, eventually, to finance a Perpetua collection of François' work. Searle's own reputation in France continued to grow. In *Le Canard enchaîné* he was caricatured, by Pol Ferjac, as the piratical leader of a visiting British delegation, including Vicky, who contributed to a 'Franco-English supplement'. At the time of its publication, though, Ronald was very much on English territory: at the Old Bailey, sketching for the trial of Dr John Bodkin Adams, the alleged euthenasiast, aptly enough for *Life*.

Searle had reached the age of thirty-seven without ever visiting America, where a considerable amount of his work had appeared both in magazines and books (the St Trinian's and Perpetua collections had been picked up by Knopf). Now at last he had a chance to go. The Standard Oil Company of New Jersey had an idea for an animated film to celebrate their seventy-fifth anniversary in business, and invited Ronald over to work on it. It would be a three-month trip – alarming for *Punch*, though they would be mollified with a promise of a Searle 'Sketchbook' from the New World. Searle and his wife sailed over in mid-May, 1957: 'a leezurly trip,' wrote Ronald, 'docking in a cloudburst about

Right: Dr John Bodkin Adams in the dock at the Old Bailey, April 1957, *Life*, 13 May 1957

Dr Adams was accused of the murder, by drugs, of eighty-one-year-old Mrs Edith Morrell, of Eastbourne, a patient from whom he inherited a chest of Georgian silver. After what was at the time the longest Old Bailey murder trial, he was acquitted. It was probably his middle name, with its suggestion of the needle, that helped to make him memorable.

ten p.m.' They stayed at the Beekman Tower Hotel ('On exclusive Beekman Hill, overlooking the United Nations and the East River'), where from the twenty-third floor Ronald sent his reactions to Russell Brockbank at *Punch*:

Overwhelmed I am. What a fantastic place; there's no need for me to tell you anything about it except that I've been knocked sideways...We awoke on Wednesday morning with the whole of N.Y. spread out under our window at the top of this place – sideways on to the U.N.O. building. Very useful in case I need to seek sanctuary.

I ran straight into a series of ... 12 meetings over two days including getting carried up and down the McCann-Ericson building in an express lift that lost its mind every time it passed the fiftieth storey. I just couldn't get out of it.

After sessions with lawyers and all the delightful things that go into making out a contract it became quite clear that I am to stay here until July 24. They insist on ten weeks ...The plan is that I have to work with the film people here for about a month and then, about the second week in June, go to Hollywood to get the actual production moving. I'm doing full-time office hours (much to my disgust) so there isn't much time to tackle anything else except at weekends. I've been trying to get around in the odd hours before dark to look about and get some of the feeling of the place and during this week I shall airmail you enough for the first Searle New York Sketchbook ...

I went down to Wall St–Broadway this afternoon and took some pictures for that possible Royal Visit cover.

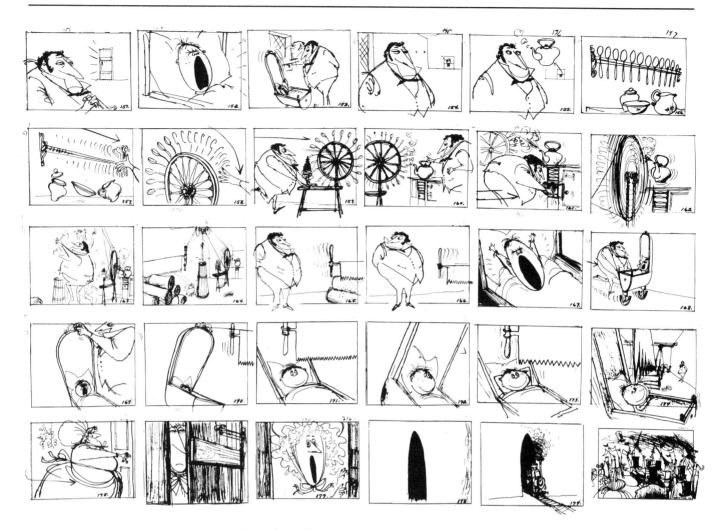

Above: Part of the storyboard for *Energetically Yours*, Hollywood, summer 1957

James Watt discovers the steam engine. Searle's main problem was to persuade the animators working under the direction of Bill Melendez to loosen up their line in imitation of his own. The film was subsequently premièred at the Museum of Modern Art in New York. Aired in the course of the NBC Standard Oil TV spectacular, 13 October 1957, it fell foul of the critics on grounds Searle could do nothing to influence, viz: 'Ronald Searle's lengthy film cartoon on energy started off amusingly but then lapsed into an institutional commercial' (Jack Gould, New York Times, Sunday 20 October 1957).

Brockbank himself was putting together a collection of his own for Perpetua. 'When you have finished the jacket,' Searle instructed , 'let Jean (Ellsmoor, my secretary) know, and she will collect it and pack it and air express it to me ... I can then add the lettering and express it to the printers ...' Kaye, meanwhile, was expressing a monthly thrill-a-minute résumé of their activities to the eager readers of the *Young Elizabethan*. The weeks in Hollywood ('our aeroplane, a Jet Stream Constellation, flew over Oklahoma City') were much the most productive of gossip. The Searles

> bumped into John Wayne in the corridor ... shared a hotel lift with Norma Shearer ... ate our dinner sitting at a table between Jane Wyman and James Stewart ...This afternoon we had a swimming race with James and Portland Mason (and lost) ... [the Masons were old friends] ... and tomorrow we are going over to the MGM studio to see Danny Kaye making a new film called *Merry Andrew*. We've also got a date with a wonderful place called Disney Land.

They were actually shown over the Disney domain by Walt himself; Ronald didn't like him much, but got on splendidly with his veteran animators, especially the extrovert Ward Kimball, who remained a friend. Ronald himself was working with an independent animation specialist, Bill Melendez (later famous for the 'Peanuts' films), and most of his effort went into persuading California-trained animators to step out of their tradition a little and adopt a looser, Searle-ish line. The resulting film, a history of energy called

Energetically Yours, eventually won eleven assorted awards. Some of the wisdom Ronald acquired in negotiating a compromise Anglo-American 'feel' in the animation was later passed on by him, privately, to the Disney team who achieved their own version of the same effect in *One Hundred and One Dalmatians*.

Searle's American visa ran out on 2 August which meant that he had just time to see his children and his studio again before leaving for the Edinburgh Festival. Home from that, he watched over publication of the reissued *Paris Sketchbook*, stockpiled some stuff for *Punch*, and left for New York a second time. He had been booked to enunciate what were reported to be 'the most expensive ten words in the history of American television'. A TV spectacular was being mounted to celebrate Standard Oil's anniversary and Ronald was to appear on it, introducing *Energetically Yours* with the words 'But artists, like children, should be seen and not heard.' For this service, he was to be paid at a rate of $1000 per minute on top of expenses for himself and Kaye. Even American columnists seemed quite surprised by the extravagance of it all – and there was more for them in the story on the night. The NBC show trudged its elephantine way through an all-star bill, including Tyrone Power, Jimmy Durante and Duke Ellington (who gave Ronald his latest album, *Such Sweet Thunder*), until at last Ronald came on to deliver his ten words

of wisdom. But no sooner had he accomplished this and stepped off the set than he was arrested. Immigration officers, acting on a seemingly malicious tip-off, had come to detain him on suspicion of accepting employment without a valid work-permit. Since he had left all his papers, even his passport, at the hotel, he was unable immediately to convince the officials of his innocence. For a few dire moments, he was both stateless and trouserless, as his rented dinner-suit was repossessed at the same time. Some hours passed before the requisite papers were produced and Searle was released from the custody of a department that was not known for its daintiness in human relations. In a gesture of national restitution, the fraternity of cartoonists rallied round and treated Ronald to a more than usually sumptuous dinner at the Lambs' Club, where he was proposed for membership of the National Cartoonists' Society of America, and given a Harry Devlin drawing signed by all present (including Bill Tytla and I. Klein, veteran animators; Otto Soglow, creator of 'The Little King'; and Carl Rose of the *New Yorker*). Good humour restored, Searle flew back to England, where he immediately repacked and left for Paris with Eric Keown.

Michael ffolkes, the cartoonist, remembered Searle producing 'like a machine' in the early post-war years. Nothing had changed, except that now the producer had become a captain of industry. Perhaps the parallel with industrial supply was indeed too close for comfort; Searle was in danger of becoming a non-stop supplier of work, rather than a spontaneous generator of it. Being busy, for a freelance (which Ronald remained, temperamentally, in spite of his attachment to *Punch*), too easily becomes an end in itself. He was everywhere, unmissable. New York, Paris and *Merry England* drawings went on show at the Leicester Galleries in London. A second cinematic scrimmage, *Blue Murder at St Trinian's*, opened for the 1957 Christmas season. In New York's *Saturday Review*, Searle was debating 'The Emasculation of American Humor', a subject he had already rehearsed a year before in a *Collier's* magazine newssheet (he seemed to enjoy taking on the Americans, and talked straighter to them than to anybody). American *Vogue* was carrying a Searle portrait by the photographer Irving Penn. For *Punch*, at Muggeridge's insistence, Ronald had performed radical surgery on the old Richard Doyle cover-design. For a time, his simplified version was re-run at quarterly intervals in different colours, to remind readers – rather in the manner of the *New Yorker*'s annual Eustace Tilley cover – that the

Below: Untitled, *Punch*, 21 May 1958

Marianne, the embodiment of the French Republic, on the point of effecting her own extinction. The drawing was subsequently used as a cover illustration for the French current-affairs magazine L'Express. *'Marianne' was the password of a secret society set up in France during the 1850s with the aim of restoring republican government after the* coup d'état *of 1851. Drawn at the height of the Algerian crisis.*

old tradition was being borne in mind. *Punch* had lately beaten off an approach from Walter Hayes, Editor of the *Sunday Dispatch*, who was eager to enliven a dying paper with a weekly Searle. Tartly evoking its exclusivity clause, the magazine drove him off. Conscious of his rather intermittent availability the previous year, Searle put in his regular weeks at Bouverie Street in 1958, producing his share of covers, and one 'Big Cartoon' that actually seemed to bypass the committee procedure and make a strong personal statement. It came at the time of the Algerian crisis. Marianne, embodiment of the Republic, was seen on the guillotine, pulling the rope that would sever her own neck. This seemed to sum up the French national suicide so succinctly that *L'Express*, Jean-Jacques Servan-Schreiber's new radical weekly, put it on the cover. The great French cartoonist 'Tim' (Louis Mitelberg), just starting at *L'Express* himself, remembered being especially impressed by the drama of the angle of the drawing, and by the fact that it felt exactly like an insider's comment on the situation, and not a foreigner's.

James Thurber visited the *Punch* Table that year, a test-case of Searle's tolerance of good-bad draughtsmen. He was typically exact in his appreciation of the 'sloppy refinement' of Thurber's style, which 'could neither be improved nor, come to that, made worse'. It was 'a form of neolithic shorthand', and a 'deceptive camouflage for the neat little rapier that slid between your ribs exactly where you expected to be tickled'. In fact, he rather preferred Thurber's drawing to Thurber, who, entertained at Newton Road, bent the ears of his hosts relentlessly and required Kaye Webb not only to accompany him to the lavatory but even to help him aim successfully into the bowl. Thurber took his place in a whole summer of disruptive experiences. Some of them Ronald volunteered for, like the BBC TV series *Who's Next?*, in which one celebrity interviewed another, the victim moving on to become the interviewer in the next programme, and so on, in a chain. It was the actress Siân Phillips who chose to interview Ronald, and he chose Cleo Laine: an interesting sequence, of which no scripted evidence survives.

Between the two studio dates, shockingly, Geoffrey Willans died of a heart attack in hospital, aged only forty-seven. He had just left the BBC to give all his time to writing. In a *Times* appreciation, Ronald called him 'the sort of writer who made collaboration sheer enjoyment'. Molesworth, he said, 'concealed behind his mis-spelt observations of life all the wiles of a diplomat in foreign affairs. Willans was delighted to learn that schoolmasters, far from feeling publicly disrobed, were in fact giving away his books as end-of-term prizes.' Two more, *The Compleet Molesworth* and *The Dog's Ear Book*, were in preparation at that moment, and were published in October in another daunting burst of new Searleiana. *The Big City*, the neo-Mayhew book, came out the same month, as did the first instalments of a particularly ingenious *Punch* series Alex Atkinson had recently devised. The premise of 'By Rocking Chair Across America' was that 'Too many books about the United States have been written by men who have spent only a few weeks in the country. This one is different: it is by a man who has never been there in his life.' By this witty means, Atkinson enabled himself to shovel together all manner of prejudices, clichés, misremembered fragments of travelogue and outright inventions about America, which

in some alchemical way managed to add up to a shrewd, if knockabout, critique of the *real* United States. The kind of illustration this project required was right up Searle's street. What was needed was not so much exaggerations of observable reality, but absurdly jostling concentrations of it in one place: a funny dream, perhaps, but one bordering on a nightmare. Where exaggeration was required, it took an organic form; Searle would take a style or taste and show it in the grip of some fantastic growth-hormone. Anybody could have had the idea of making a Texan automobile a riot of carbuncular rococo excrescences, but only Searle, among all his contemporaries, could have made the thing look as if it had arrived at that state by some sort of ghastly evolutionary process.

With this series already established as a hit, and three new books in the shops for Christmas, Searle took himself off to France with Eric Keown for their regular trawl of the Paris theatre. Charles de Gaulle was about to be elected President, and the thought of a soldier in charge had put the country in an interestingly apprehensive mood which Keown was researching for a feature article. Their schedule was full and they occasionally fell behind; for one rendezvous, at the Café Régence, they were particularly late. The contact Keown had been meeting there, a man from French radio, had been expecting to be delayed himself and had asked a young lady-friend to sit in for him till the Englishmen arrived. But when he got there, they still had not appeared, so he went off again to check on their movements, leaving the young lady sitting under a portrait of Napoleon and looking out, rather unwillingly this time, for an unmistakable pair of Anglo-Saxons, one 'ten feet tall' and the other with a beard. As soon as he had left again, this very duo came panting in. Eventually all four sat down together, Keown conversing with the radio man while Ronald made stilted conversation with the vividly pretty, dark-haired lady who was to become his second wife. Monica Stirling, née Koenig, was an artist, ballet and theatre designer, born at Purley in Surrey, of pleasantly complicated German, Polish, French and English stock. Some years before, she had fled to Paris from a failed marriage, and had no thoughts of sacrificing her independent existence. So even though her conversation with the one with the beard soon warmed into a more enjoyable chat, she did not think of him as anything more than a rather unusual new friend. He was much more seriously disturbed by the meeting; within days, in fact, he knew that his life had to change, and in roughly what way. But he also knew that he could not do it all at once – not even if she should suddenly feel as convinced as he did, which he knew she did not. It would all take time.

Ronald returned to England. Having admitted to himself the possibility of another life, and even glimpsed it momentarily with Monica, he began to see his own existence as another series of imprisonments: in a family structure he had not sought, a lively social life he did not desire, and an involvement with publicity he frequently resented, while playing along with it in his dutiful way. In all these areas, the temperamental gap between himself and Kaye had widened; they were two egotistical personalities who, he now saw, could not go on working happily in tandem. His immediate list of engagements happened to include several which made him wonder what kind of 'personality' his home country wanted him to be. First, there was filming for BBC Television's *Monitor* series – a portmanteau programme on cartoonists featuring André François and Osbert Lancaster besides himself. A glum review in *The Listener* called the two Englishmen 'merely frivolous' and praised François, a judgement with which some part of Searle agreed. Then, in January 1959, came a remarkable double, possibly never achieved by even the most avid of publicity-seekers, before or since: appearances in the course of a single day on both the *Desert Island Discs* radio programme and television's *This Is Your Life*. The latter was hardly to be avoided, since the subject of the pop-profile was Canon Noel Duckworth, the army padre universally loved by the prisoners of the Japanese. To his notional desert island, Ronald took the collected works of Gillray, and looked forward to re-activating his Changi-bred expertise in cooking tropical snails. At least, he said, he would not be competing with 7000 others for the available food.

By participating in these exercises, Searle knew, he was colluding in the domestication of himself and his work. He was being drawn into cosy corners of British life into which he should perhaps have been pointing the mocking finger. As Hans Pflug had just pointed out in the Swiss-based magazine *Graphis*, Searle 'has never been regarded as subversive or seditious' by the British. Pflug's analysis of this situation was an odd one. It was the 'healthy self-awareness' of the Briton, he ventured, that prevented him 'from ascribing to Searle's cruel diagnosis the same degree of dangerousness as was attributed to the caricatures of George Grosz in Germany after the First World War'. This appeared to be suggesting that Britain absorbed Searle's attacks with equanimity because it knew what was coming; through 'self-awareness' it had anticipated him. Had this been true, it would have been a poor look-out not just for Searle but for any social satirist in any medium. A far more likely explanation lay in the Briton's blithe insistence on construing all attacks as disguised forms of flattery. Into true complacency, anything can be absorbed (which is the reason why so many politicians' utterances begin with the words 'Of course'). And in the Macmillan era, complacency was the very watchword of government propaganda.

It was a good time to discover a new audience. Germany, as it happened, had just been made aware of Searle by the writer and producer Heinz Huber, and a television show of his called *Hurra für St Trinian*. An unexpected opportunity to develop these contacts arose in mid-summer 1959 when a general print-stoppage closed down all Searle's normal outlets. *Punch* missed seven issues. Searle spent a week in Paris drawing for a *Jours de Franc* magazine feature and then travelled on at Huber's invitation to Berlin, the starting-point of a three-week tour that took him all over West Germany and resulted, a year later, in Süddeutscher-Rundfunk's documentary *Ein Engländer sieht Deutschland*. Searle, stood, unknowingly, at the beginning of a two-year period in which he would seldom stay at home for more than a few weeks at a time, and often returned only for days between long trips. The pattern established itself at once. After the Continent, straight to Edinburgh; three weeks later, off to America again.

It was the nature of the work offered that took Searle back to the United States. His regular illustrative contributions to *Holiday* magazine had been building all through the Fifties, until he had graduated to full-page topographical drawings of English and continental 'sights', and opulent fantasies of hedonism and gourmandise to accompany the high-life articles of Lucius Beebe. The real breakthrough came in July 1959, just at the

Left: 'The Old Bailey', *Holiday,* August 1960

Searle gave an unusually exhaustive account of the making of this drawing in a contribution to Robin Jacques' book Illustrators at Work *(1964). It was commissioned, he said, as 'a light-hearted illustration to a factual article on the Old Bailey ... From the time of receiving the manuscript to the time of posting the finished drawing back to America, there were only three days available for the work ... fortunately, all the background reference I needed was available from a previous commission. [See p. 122 (bottom).] The preliminary pencil work was carried out in detail, working with a B pencil on fashion board with a cartridge surface. Once the idea was fully worked out, which took about three hours, the washes were laid on to emphasise the gloom of the scene, but kept well away from faces or essential fine lines that might be weakened by tone. When the washes were dry, the pen work was added and worked as rapidly and as freely as possible over the pencil to capture a feeling of spontaneity in the line. Working with an ordinary fountain pen to cut out stopping and dipping, and using the back of the nib for the rougher outlines of the dominant figures, the drawing progressed downwards from the judge ... When the whole of the line had been laid over, the washes were strengthened, final touches added, and the odd unnecessary line scratched out with a razor blade. After the pencil work had been cleaned off, broken lines were checked for reproduction. The whole work took about six hours.'*

time of the British printers' strike, when *Holiday* ran 'By Rocking Chair Across America' as a huge summer feature. The book version of this material was destined to perplex some reviewers (a *New York Herald-Tribune* critic thought Atkinson really *believed* Kentucky colonels drank whisky with mint sauce in it); and there were some grumbles from the bald eagles among the *Holiday* readership ('the objective seems obvious – ridicule of everything American': J. Wilfred Corr, Pasadena, California). But overall reaction was so positive ('Best ever. Illustrations great': Mrs Burt Raynes, San Diego, California) that Alex Atkinson was taken on the staff of *Holiday*, while Searle was invited over to enter upon a golden age of American reportage. Las Vegas was his first target. Stopping off first in New York for his first American exhibition (at the Kraushaar Gallery), he travelled to Nevada with Midge and John Locke, his increasingly active American agent, to discover an urban

Right: 'The Complaints Officer', *Russia For Beginners* with Alex Atkinson, London, 26 September 1960

The follow-up to By Rocking-Chair Across America (*aka* U.S.A. For Beginners) *could call upon even more extravagant fancies, since Searle really was unconstrained by personal knowledge of the Soviet Union. France, Spain and Sweden were among the other nations visited by Searle and Atkinson in their rocking-chair, for* Holiday *magazine features.*

landscape that appeared to start where his more overloaded hallucinations had left off. Such blatancy did not tell the whole story about America, but it gave the graphic satirist a terrific start.

U.S.A. for Beginners, alias *Rocking Chair*, was published on both sides of the Atlantic in what for Searle collectors proved a most expensive autumn. Perpetua Books offered *The Biting Eye of André François*, with Ronald's essay in praise of a man who was 'eschewing the sensitive line in favour of the harsh scratch'. François had been known, he said, to tour the post-offices of Paris, robbing them of pen-nibs that were guaranteed to be unusable. Searle now had art-historical plans for Perpetua; he had begun to round up visual material to accompany monographs on two of his idols, Cézanne and Toulouse-Lautrec. Yet another Perpetua book on the market that season was *The St Trinian's Story*, 'the whole ghastly dossier' compiled by Kaye Webb. She was undoubtedly right that a ready public existed for a summary of the besotted decade in which, as the contents themselves showed, so many otherwise stable citizens had dressed up in gymslips and straw hats and gone on pretend rampages through the High Streets of Britain. But The Founder, equally, could not be blamed for taking as little part in the venture as possible. The book could almost have stood as a symbol of the couple's contrary instincts. The St Trinian's monster was now uncontrollable, and the best Searle could do was to stay out of its way. A year later, he was invited to stand for Rector of Edinburgh University, but declined on the grounds that he had 'done the city sufficient scholastic injury'.

Above: Men's Dormitory, Camp Karls-Kaserne, Vienna, 4 November 1959

Searle knew the feelings of desolation and abandonment occasioned by prison life, and found something very similar in the refugee camps of middle Europe. The neatly ranged beds suggest a mental revisiting of the scene at the India Lines camp in Changi (p. 56 [right]), but the transient, 'transparent' figures add a new and touching dimension.

In the last weeks of 1959, Ronald Searle and Kaye Webb worked on their last collaborative effort, another job from the 'unrefusable' category. World Refugee Year was in progress, promoting an appeal on behalf of the '100,000 refugees left in Europe alone'. The office of the United Nations High Commissioner for Refugees invited the two observers to visit camps in Austria, Italy and Greece, and bring back a report. The three-week working journey was as arduous as any Searle had undertaken since the war, and was reminiscent of that time in other ways. Nobody in the European camps was starving in the sense that he had known, but to move among people who felt that they had been left behind by history was an unpleasantly familiar feeling. The drawings he made were fanatical in their excavation of a calm beauty from all the desolation. It is quite clear, looking at them, that this is the same hand that produces the cartoons, but something in the contrast between lines, very rectilinear here and there, very loose when loose at all, speaks instantly of gravity, not amusement. Searle had a habit at the time of drawing 'transparent' figures, through whose forms the background is allowed to show. In these drawings (published as *Refugees 1960*, by Penguin), the effect is movingly appropriate to the transient status of the people depicted. One feels that while they, as individuals, may be moved on, the conditions in which they are held will remain to enclose others. Meanwhile, they exist as ghosts of themselves. *Punch*, to its credit, devoted seventeen pages of its end-of-year issue to the refugee report. Kaye dominated the discussion over its layout; *Punch* colleagues, noting how little Ronald contributed, wondered what was up. But in fact he was as disaffected with *Punch* as with his domestic life. With the new editor, Bernard Hollowood, relations were nothing like as easy as they had been with Muggeridge – possibly because Hollowood, having inherited a 'special relationship' with Searle, now saw that *Punch* was no longer getting the best of it. It must have seemed to him that, by working so much abroad, Searle was taking unfair advantage of the flabbiness of his contract. His discontinuous appearances in the theatre column told their own tale.

Right: 'Sweet Emma' at the Old Absinthe House, 240 Bourbon Street, New Orleans, February 1960

'Sweet Emma' Barrett (b.1898) was known as 'The Bell Gal', because of the jingles she wore on garters round her calves. She had been playing jazz piano in New Orleans since 1923. A red beret-like hat was a fixture in her wardrobe. Towards the end of her career, in the early Eighties, she suffered a stroke which incapacitated one arm, but continued to play quite convincingly, one-handed, at Preservation Hall. Facially, she is flattered just a little by Searle's portrait.

That situation did not improve in 1960. Although Searle was able to accompany Eric Keown on his spring visit to Paris (a city Ronald was now unlikely to pass up an opportunity to visit), he had by that time spent most of February in America again, expanding a 'Christmas Carol' colour-feature for *Life*, and driving down to New Orleans for a *Holiday* feature. John Locke took the wheel, covering up to 600 miles a day. It was Locke who arranged the whole American programme on Searle's behalf. If he paid his own passage over the Atlantic, Searle was not exclusively beholden to any one employer and could work for several in the course of one trip. The most attractive work came from *Holiday*, which by its nature, as a travel-based magazine, favoured far-flung locations. Its Graphics Editor, Frank Zachary, was held in great esteem by Ronald, and its production values were extremely high; issue for issue, *Holiday* must have been one of the *heaviest* magazines ever produced. A year's run is quite a challenge to carry.

Later in the year, America called again (after two intervening Paris trips), this time predominantly with the voice of *Life* magazine, who clearly felt that *Holiday* was getting too much of the pie. The proffered topic, they knew, was irresistible: the Presidential Election campaign, Kennedy versus Nixon, starting with a week on the road with Kennedy. He was difficult to pin down, caricaturally; his features were 'too balanced', Searle complained, so that 'all you have to work with is his hair. It took me the better part of a week before I could get the hang of his face.' It never did come completely right: pouchy faces – Kennedy's, Churchill's – found some inbuilt resistance in Searle's psyche. Nixon, by contrast, baggy rather than convex, was an ideal subject. His nose, Searle remarked, 'is an absolute treasure'. His suits were usually too small for him. 'He made them seem even smaller by buttoning all three buttons.' The itineraries swung all the way from Billings, Montana, to Albuquerque, New Mexico, by way of Austin, Texas, which was billed at its border, Searle swore, as 'The Spam Capital of the Universe'. (By a rather disgraceful irony, it is now the home of a substantial body of his work.) Then it was back to New York for follow-up work on the feature. *Life* was generous with expenses, but did insist on attendance at the office for final touches. Those finished, Searle put all the glee of liberation into a superbly mischievous portrait of Khrushchev for *Holiday* and allowed himself to relax a little. Thurber, that Broadway season, had agreed to save his own faltering show *A Thurber Carnival* by appearing in it, so Searle celebrated by seeing

Below: John F. Kennedy, *Life*, 31 October 1960

'All you have to work with is his hair,' Searle lamented. A single week with Kennedy took him from New York to Minneapolis, Duluth, St Louis, Springfield, Chicago, Indianapolis, Terre Haute, Evansville, Louisville, Cincinnati and Washington. The original Life *caption, 'And thanks for the hat . . .', signalled Kennedy's embarrassment at receiving this seemingly irrelevant headgear.*

Left: John F. Kennedy campaigning, October 1960

From Searle's photograph it is clear that he could get as close as he liked to the future President. In view of what happened to Kennedy in November 1963, it is quite alarming to see him overshadowed by a brick building of much the same vintage as the Texas School Book Depository. Which of the many cities visited this was, the photographer does not recall.

the show with the Lockes. He hung around for Election Day, dined with the *Time* and *Life* publisher Henry Luce, and left at last for England – land of *Punch*, the still-continuing Lemon Hart posters, and yet another St Trinian's film, *The Pure Hell of St Trinian's*, all too aptly named now that scriptwriters had buried the original idea. It opened just in time for Christmas, the last Ronald Searle spent in England.

In 1961, he was voted Cartoonist of the Year by the National Cartoonists' Society in New York, but he was naturally not at home when the news arrived. It was only the end of April, but already he was completing his third foreign trip of the year: two to Paris, followed by another *Life*-sponsored excursion, this time for the trial of the Gestapo chief Adolf Eichmann. Searle made the journey by way of Beirut, where two newly-married friends, 'B' and Theo Larsson, were engaged in a slightly *Casablanca*-flavoured import-

Right: Nikita Khrushchev, *Holiday,* February 1961

Khrushchev (1894–1971), appointed First Secretary of the Soviet Union's Central Committee in 1953, was credited with a peasant cunning rather than the suaver arts of statesmanship. At the time of this splendid drawing, he was in a phase of disconcerting the West by proposing various disarmament and test-ban negotiations. Drawing a Time *magazine cover to commemorate the (failed) four-power summit meeting of May 1960, Searle had called the Russian leader 'that incredible public-relations man Khrushchev'.*

export business in stoves. A fellow-guest at the dinner-table was introduced as Kim Philby. He turned out to be extremely drunk but very entertaining, confirming Ronald in the belief – formed by a fairly impressive acquaintance with intelligence agents of one sort or another – that whatever other talents a spy may have, he must give rather better value, socially, than the average fictional spy appears to do. The Larssons drove Ronald down to Jerusalem, dropping him at the Mandelbaum Gate, and he spent the rest of April in the courtroom in the company of the insignificant-looking Nazi functionary in the glass booth. Searle did not much enjoy the Old Testament flavour of the proceedings, but passed some off-duty moments with one of his fellow-reporters, James (later Jan) Morris.

Back home in London for ten days, he managed to fit in a couple of *Punch* theatre drawings (including one of the *Beyond The Fringe* quartet which became a book-cover in 1989) before packing his bags again. Large bags were required, because Frank Zachary of *Holiday*, answering the challenge of *Life*, had laid out two months' worth of travelling assignments in America. Ted Patrick, the Editor of *Holiday*, had just administered an angry rebuke to the proprietors of 'London Fog' overcoats, whose advertisements were using the 'Morbid Anatomy' format (a sketch plan with funny captions) which Ronald had pioneered in *Holiday* several years earlier. In a letter to *Advertising Age*, who had praised the ad-campaign unaware that it was larcenous, Patrick commented: 'The artist for London Fog might at least have had the grace not to copy Ronald's style (for one thing, he'll

Above: Adolf Eichmann at his trial in Jerusalem, April 1961, *Life*, 17 July 1961

Arrested in May 1960, the Gestapo chief Eichmann was put on trial for crimes against the Jewish people, found guilty, and, after appeal, hanged on 31 May 1962. Searle deepened his knowledge of what the court proceedings brought to light by visiting surrounding towns and kibbutzim to meet survivors of the Holocaust. In court, Searle said, Eichmann had the demeanour of a 'horrible little functionary'; it was 'difficult to associate him completely' with the horrors he had perpetrated.

never come near being the artist Ronald is) and the calligraphy of the headline. Or if his powers of invention were so meagre as to demand this, he should at least have given a credit line to Ronald Searle, or *Holiday*, or both.'

With this tough-talking endorsement in his pocket, Ronald set off for Provincetown, Massachusetts, Atlantic City and the State Department, Washington, all of which would feature in forthcoming *Holiday*s. There was time to thank Ted Patrick for his support over a lunch at the 21 Club, along with Frank Zachary, the sportswriter and humorist Roger Angell, and the comic poet Ogden Nash; and on 18 July Searle flew home, carrying the newly-published Eichmann edition of *Life*. As he arrived in London, the 120th Birthday issue of *Punch* was being distributed. Somewhere along the way, Searle had managed to concoct a couple of pottily appropriate full-page cartoons, involving cut-ups of the work of Tenniel and George du Maurier. Eric Keown welcomed him back to six weeks in the stalls. He took a last look at Edinburgh.

On Saturday 9 September Ronald packed his suitcases again. This time nobody had asked him to. The family was away for the weekend. He wrote his wife one of those letters that begin 'By the time you read this ...', and left Newton Road for the airport. On Sunday 10 September 1961, he arrived in Paris. His drawing had saved him once, and this was the way he would save it in return. He never lived in England again.

Right: 'Layman's Guide to the Journalist's Anatomy', *Souls in Torment*, London, 1953

One of Searle's 'Morbid Anatomies', or annotated sketch-plans, with punning intemization of features. This was the format purloined by 'London Fog' overcoats in their advertisements. No apology was obtained, but by threatening a lawsuit, Searle's agent, John Locke, managed to persuade the company to desist.

SIX
Which Way Did He Go?
(1961–75)

Everybody went into a kind of shock. Perhaps it never quite wore off. Kaye Webb was stunned. Never having imagined that the marriage had become meaningless to Ronald, she preferred to believe that he had been lured away, and blamed herself for not realizing how attractive he was to women, how much he had been 'chased'. In Paris, however, the persuading had all been on Ronald's side. His children, aged fourteen now, did not find it hard to accept at first that Daddy had 'gone off to France for a while', since he had been abroad so much in any case in recent years. Ronald's feeling had been that they, at least, were young enough to adapt, whereas he had only one possibility before him. This was perhaps to overestimate their chances of understanding his needs. Even Ronald's friends had trouble defining his state of mind. David Arkell, looking back on these events in a 1986 article, wrote: 'For a start he needed to eliminate family responsibilities, and social demands.' But in revising the piece for inclusion in a book he repented of the toughness of this formulation, substituting: 'For a start he needed to reduce social demands on his time and energy.' Perhaps the first version faced the facts more squarely. Viewed in one way, Ronald's departure was the one ruthlessly self-interested act of his life, and it caused a lot of pain.

Above: Monica and Ronald Searle, Paris, 1967

Photographed in the year of their wedding and looking perhaps at the future, and the past, respectively. (Photograph by André Chadefaux, Paris.)

Had he been starting a new life simply on his own account, there might not be much more to be said. But of course, he was escaping not only *from* but *to* – to Monica, into whose little flat at 2 Rue Antoine-Dubois he moved himself and his few portable belongings. From his 'drawing self' he was stripping away all the circumstantial encrustations of the years. His talent he regarded, rightly, as something entirely different from his career, much of which he had just given deliberately away. Monica would have to give away hers as well. Fortunately she had the kind of abilities – artistic, linguistic, culinary, decorative – which can flourish without 'professional' recognition. She also had a tigerish temperament when put-on by the outside world. Each would be needing every bit of support the other could provide.

Ronald really had started again, appropriately enough in a student quarter of Paris, the *sixième arrondissement*, right opposite the university Medical School. All income from England was cut off at first. An outstanding bill from the Inland Revenue would have made the prospects even more unpleasing – it was for £2300 – if Ronald had not decided in advance to part with one of his most beautiful possessions, catalogued by Sotheby's, with whom he had lodged it, as 'a magnificent Benin cast bronze head of a deceased oba [chief]'. This marvellous artefact, from an ancient African kingdom now incorporated into

Right: Costume design for *Acte sans paroles,* 1971

The design was made for Deryk Mendel to wear in a projected film of Beckett's mime, but the venture was abandoned.

Nigeria, had been found by Ronald lurking in the corner of a moribund antique shop in 1946. He had paid off the considerable price of £95 in instalments, with his army pension. At auction, the head raised £2800, just enough, once Sotheby's cut was taken, to satisfy the taxman. The Benin head later changed hands at least twice more, passing through an American collection back to Africa, at a reported price of half a million pounds. It would have been heartbreaking to think of such a possibility in 1961. Ronald and Monica were lucky to find a friend in Mme Marcelle-Marie Methlin, of the Restaurant des Beaux-Arts in the Rue Mazarine, who gave them credit for a while, a gesture repaid by Ronald in drawings which still hang thirty years later in the seemingly unchanged dining-room. The name of the establishment appears in unmistakable Searle capitals above the door.

Ronald had come to Paris with the conviction that the city would not let an artist starve, but there was not much point in hanging about to see if it was true. His first commission took him to Berlin for a week, to see the infamous spectacle of the newly-built Wall, and report on it for *Nouveau Candide*. To his surprise, *Punch* took some Berlin drawings too; he had thought that 'the subject might be a bit sombre for the paper'. Writing from Berlin to Bill Hewison, the new *Punch* Art Editor (and very much a Searle follower in his early stylings), Ronald broke the news that 'it looks as if I am going to be up and down the Continent for some time to come on various projects, so you'd better forget me for the theatre drawing until I know what's doing'. What really was doing,

Left: The Benin Head, London, c.1960

The valuable bronze head (left) resides on its plinth at 32 Newton Road. 'Actually, I never did make much money,' Searle recalls, 'and was always having to sell things off to fill the gaps.' The fifteenth-century head, however, was much the most prized of the possessions sacrificed: 'the thought of it still makes me weep'. Searle's tapestry can be seen on the wall behind him. A bottle of Lemon Hart rum stands on the sideboard. (Photograph by George Konig, undated, c.1960.)

hardly anybody in England knew. By a horrible irony, October's *Woman and Home* carried a huge article on Ronald, and by an old friend, Betty Frank: half a dozen pages' worth presenting Ronald and Kaye as the happy smiling couple (once again) in their ideal home. His Perpetua collection, out in November, was called *Which Way Did He Go?* Among the answers were New York, New Orleans, Germany and of course Paris.

A series had been devised by which he could keep *Punch* supplied while 'on the move'. The 'Imaginary Portraits', as he called them, or 'Searle's Eye View', as *Punch* preferred to bill them, presented famous figures as their reputations suggested they ought to look, rather than as they were. They ran on until the following September, scoring several bull's-eyes but never quite convincing their creator. *Punch* was dropping out of the picture, and *Holiday* coming to the fore, not least because in America Ronald and Monica could live on expenses as they went. First-class travel and accommodation were always laid on, because Ronald needed room to work, but the life of luxury ended abruptly when they returned to Paris; an allowance of £50 per month was the best Ronald could extract from legal negotiations with England.

He left with Monica late in February 1962 to take a look at Florida and Alaska on *Holiday*'s behalf. Not long after their arrival in America, news came through that Alex Atkinson had died of a heart attack in Philadelphia. Ronald attended the funeral there, on his forty-second birthday. 'It has left a great gap, I am afraid,' he wrote to Bill Hewison at *Punch,* and the remark was true of his own working life as well as of humour in general. The 'Rocking Chair' feature, lately transferred to *Holiday*, had spread as far afield as Russia, Sweden and Spain. The day before he died, Atkinson had sent Searle the third instalment of a quite different series, about sex. Atkinson died at forty-six, even younger than Geoffrey Willans.

Among the palms and balms of Florida, Ronald fell upon the wrinkled senior citizens with an extra venom, though without immense exaggeration. As a later reviewer remarked, 'the old buttressed against reality by great wealth make him angry enough to give us them straight'. Alaska posed unusual problems, such as sketching at −25°C and trying to keep to a schedule in the season of blizzards. Trying to keep up as best they could, Ronald and Monica took advantage of a short break in the appalling weather by hiring a tiny Beechcraft plane to take them to the village of Fort Yukon, on the Arctic Circle. *En route,* they remembered that a painter friend from next door in Paris − Valerios Caloutsis, of 4 Rue Antoine-Dubois − had an exhibition opening at the Redfern Gallery in London the following day, and that a good-luck cable would be in order. From the Fort Yukon airfield, accordingly, a tractor dragged them through mud and snow to the N.C. (Northern Commercial) Trading Store, a one-man emporium full of Indian youths clustered round an enormous central stove. Having ascertained that it was possible to send a message, they wrote it out, filled in the 'Name of Sender' box and handed it over to the manager. His first reaction was amazement − 'not THE Ronald Searle?' − followed by a curious serenity. 'Good,' he said, 'I've been waiting for you. I knew you would come.' Emptying the store of its Indians and locking the door, he introduced himself as P. J. Doyle, and took Ronald and Monica through to his living-quarters where, he said, 'I have all your books ready for you to sign.' He had about twenty of them, plus a sketchbook which, said P. J. Doyle, he had also kept in readiness so that Ronald could do a quick sketch of his dog. The animal sloped in − it was an Irish wolfhound, three feet tall − and stood around while Ronald drew and P. J. Doyle opened a bottle of champagne which, naturally, he had kept by for this moment. 'But how on earth did you know we were coming?' asked his visitors. 'I dunno,' said P. J. Doyle, 'I just knew that one day you would come here.' They flew back to Fairbanks with a birchwood ladle, an Indian caribou-skin bag, and a very strange feeling about the Yukon Territory, which nobody before that day, not even themselves, had known they were going to visit.

Six months into his self-exile, Searle's timetable looked almost as densely packed as before. Three more magazine tours were undertaken that year, to Dublin, Berlin and, for *Fortune* magazine, the Volkswagen works at Wolfsburg. *Fortune* tended to see Searle as a pipework specialist. When they sent him to cover the installations of the Slochteren and Schildmeer natural gas field in Holland, followed by two more chemical plants in the summer of 1963, he gave them up. Searle had begun an association with the animator Ivor Wood, celebrated later for 'Postman Pat' and such, but then working at *La Comète* studios in Paris, producing advertising shorts for television quickies which still turn up in the odd hole in European broadcasting schedules. In the summer, Wendy Toye and her team came to Paris to discuss designs for a new film, *The King's Breakfast,* shot at Shepperton that autumn.

There was as yet no reason for his English audience to feel deprived of Searle. Michael Joseph published two handsome but flawed editions of Dickens − *Oliver Twist* and *Great Expectations* − in which a text doctored by a great-granddaughter of the author ('for people who find him long-winded') was made unwarrantably desirable by Searle's superb drawings. He had always been right for Dickens, because his sense of the portent of appearance matched the novelist's. Having seen a Perpetua *Christmas Carol,* published just after Searle's exit from England, 'we didn't really consider anybody else', said the Michael Joseph office. Searle, for his part, found Dickens exhausting to do. 'Ideally Dickens should have no illustrator,' he once wrote. 'By tradition he always has.' In a *John O'London's* interview about the Joseph project he must have terrified the more casual extemporizers among his graphic colleagues by revealing that 'the first two weeks were spent indexing the descriptions of characters and breaking down the book into detail'. To the readers of a more specialized journal, he confided that

> Technically the drawings are deliberately fussy and nervous in line — a direct reflection of the exploratory sketches which were made during the second reading of the book and were, so to speak, hot from the 19th-century oven. The limitations were: that the drawings could only be in line and were to be reproduced in a small book on poor-quality paper. Which they were.

Despite the dissatisfactions of a lifelong enemy of complacency, however, these remain cherishable volumes, as long as one can forget Miss Doris Dickens' avowed rule of thumb as editor: 'When I meet a phrase like "luminous conception", I change it to "bright idea".'

Clearly no holidaymaker in France, Ronald had to come to terms with residential requirements and apply for a *carte de séjour temporaire*. More *temporaire* than he could have wished, it ran for just six months, but removed the problem in time for him to receive the first deputation from his family in August 1962. Johnnie and Katie came over for the first part of the month, staying at the Madison Hotel, while the 23rd was a mad day given over to a lightning tour of Paris for Ronald's sister Olive. She arrived at 6.13 a.m., left at 10.03 p.m., and spent very little of the intervening time not looking at a famous Parisian vista. Ronald returned the compliment with a quick visit to Cambridge, resuming the *train-train parisien* just in time to receive Eric Keown doing his *Punch* theatre stint, just like old times. Pierre Dux as Mephistopheles in *Faust*; Louis de Funes in *La Grosse Valse* — they made the round of four such shows, and as many restaurants, in a nostalgic binge which was good to look back upon when, a few weeks into the new year, Eric Keown died. The bad news reached Ronald when he opened *The Times* on his return from Marseilles, where he had been sent on a rush job covering *pétanque* for *Sports Illustrated* of America. 'The last time I saw him,' Ronald wrote to Bill Hewison, 'he was very happily settled behind a glass of wine at the end of a well-rounded meal — which leaves me with an enjoyable picture of him. So I am probably luckier than most. But it is a great loss after all these years.' Keown had been a great tutor in enjoyment, especially of all things French (he was barely dissuaded, it was said, from stipulating in his will that his ashes should be scattered over the vineyards of Château Lafite). Their last shared feature, 'A Face Lift for Paris' (André Malraux, in charge of culture, was having the capital scrubbed) appeared a month later in *Punch*. After that, Ronald's links with the magazine quickly perished. A couple more covers and it was all over. By the time the Business Manager, A. V. Caudery, was sent across to try to persuade him back, Searle had priced himself out of *Punch*'s league. One hundred pounds per cover was no longer attractive when American magazines would pay many times as much.

Still perfecting the art of living on expenses, Ronald and Monica took on a three-month American tour, in the course of which they managed to visit Palm Springs twice, for *Holiday* and *Sports Illustrated* (it was baseball's spring training season). One month into their trip, their Paris neighbour Valerios Caloutsis got through to them on the telephone with the news that a much larger and more suitable apartment had become available in his own house, No. 4 Rue Antoine-Dubois. On 23 April 1963, after dining with Ronald's 'fellow-terrorist' Charles Addams in New York, they arranged through John Locke's office to send off the necessary deposit; ten days later, Caloutsis called to confirm that the apartment was theirs. However, so full was the work schedule that they could not move

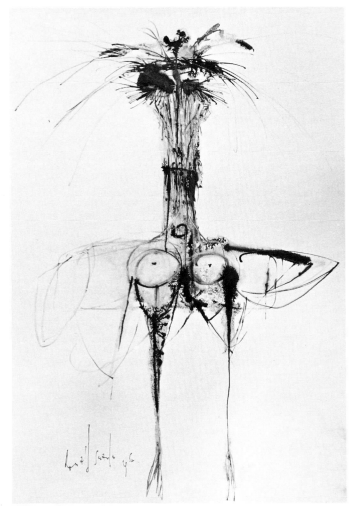

Above left: From 'Anatomies and Decapitations', 1962–6

This example is dated 1962. Some of Searle's American audience viewed the series as a parade of Rorschach ink-blot tests, more suitable for psychological than artistic analysis, and it is true that difficulties with women ('birds' is the term suggested by this picture) are suggested by the occasional violence of the treatment.

Above right: 'On the Bayswater Road', London, 1950

A more figurative ancestor of the previous picture but at some points (eyes, breasts) quite closely related. With her pony-tail and tight pants, this young professional lady is very much in the vanguard of fashion. The Bayswater Road lies half-way between Searle's former addresses at Bedford Gardens and Newton Road, and just south of Moscow Road.

in for another five months. The German *Kristall* magazine had joined the queue of employers and Ronald was 'up and down the Continent' very much as he had predicted. He was living determinedly in the present, while the past dropped away. A letter came to say that old Dr Rabel, the Searles' pre-war lodger, had just died in Cambridge, shortly before Oxford University Press published her pet project, an annotated selection of the works of Kant. She had asked Ronald Gray of the University's German department to send Searle a copy. 'She used to speak of you fairly often,' Gray wrote. 'She enjoyed your books, especially the travel ones, but was firm in denouncing your St Trinian's trend. I mention this not for the criticism but to recall her to you. She was very glad to have the bundle of ballpoint pens you sent her some time ago, but so covered her papers and books with greasy kettle and paraffin stoves that the pens seldom worked in the end.' Rabel had not changed.

She would have been delighted to see how little irresponsible levity was detectable in Ronald's latest 'trend' – though she would have had to travel far afield to witness it, for his 'Anatomies and Decapitations', premièred at the Bianchini Gallery, New York, in October 1963, were never exhibited in England or collected in book form. Over the previous couple of years, he had produced seventy-three of these large, disturbing explorations in ink, wash and watercolour, in which he was aiming to 'unmask' the human personality in a new way. Some of his friends found the technique he adopted shocking, and still shake their heads over it. It is as if they feared the loss of control implicit in the runny textures, the sheet anatomical marshiness and capillaried bloat of these figures, which though evidently human – and even in odd cases mistakenly proud of it – look most alive when revelling in a sub-human grotesqueness. They are both dissolute and dissolving. Such frankly stated horror of the body – the watery female body predominated in the collection – defeated many observers at the time. *Graphis* properly hailed the 'Anatomies' as *'un aspect nouveau de son art'*, but the accompanying essay by Ben Shahn, though eloquent, came in the nature of an endorsement of all Searle's gifts, rather than an excited reaction to this new form of comment. Perhaps even Searle himself was perplexed by what he had done. 'I know I am only on the fringe,' he wrote, when the exhibition was later transferred to Bremen, 'but for me it is the most exciting personal development in all the years I have spent exploring the medium of graphic art ... It is the curse of the satirist that satire is basically a parasitical art – only thriving where there is weakness. The frailty of human character is my mushroom bed.' It seems a pity that these first fruits of his liberation from 'popular' fame did not meet a better fate. Most of the 'Anatomies' are stored away in Vermont, in the care of John Locke, who is among those who feel that they are monuments to a dark period in Searle's morale rather than to a breakthrough in his analysis of human nature. Yet to see one of these pictures close up is to witness a fascinating struggle between liquefaction, a letting-go, and Searle's characteristic assertion of the chaos-limiting line. Perhaps their time will come again.

Those were certainly days of anguish. A resolution of the family difficulties seemed more remote than ever. Most of Ronald's possessions had now been forwarded from London, but attitudes had otherwise hardened on both sides, and Kaye would not grant the desired divorce. Wranglings would ensue which one very distinguished lawyer was moved to describe as 'Balzacian' in their ferocious complexity. Ronald stayed on the move, ranging from Vermont ski-resorts to Reno, Nevada; all over Germany again; and finally to Booker aerodrome in England for work on the film *Those Magnificent Men in their Flying Machines, or How I Flew from London to Paris in 25 Hours and 11 Minutes*. When premièred a year later, the movie turned out to match its title in long-windedness, but the combination of a jaunty theme-tune and Searle's title-sequence got it off to the best possible start. Collectors of Searleiana were delighted by the issue of a souvenir programme mocked-up as an issue of the 'Aeronautical Gazette Illustrated', and including a full 'Art Portfolio' of Ronald's aeroplane drawings. If the film had retained a bit more of the string-bag tenuousness of the artwork, at the expense of some British 'robustness', it might have been a classic.

Frank Zachary was now in charge of *Holiday,* and agitating for more Searle; in the first two months of 1965 alone, Ronald and Monica flew to destinations as far apart as Casablanca and Hawaii in Frank's employ – though not exclusively, for Ronald still filled up spare days with whatever work John Locke could get. Returning from Hawaii to New York via Los Angeles, he met up with Miss Laddie Marshack of the *TV Guide,* the huge-circulation listings-booklet to which the new television generation was addicted. Since television already dealt in images, which quickly became all too familiar, there was little a magazine could add, visually, to the information a viewer already possessed about his favourite programmes, unless a fearless caricaturist took them on. Searle was perfect for this; his covers, for the first time, made readers reluctant to throw away their *TV Guide* at the end of the week.

At the Kunsthalle in Bremen, the first-ever Searle retrospective had opened, but the artist at that moment was guying the clientèle at Grossinger's hotel in the Catskills for

Right: S. J. Perelman and Monica Searle at Erwinna, Pennsylvania, 14–15 February 1968

From the Searles' overnight trip to Sid and Laura Perelman's Pennsylvania farmhouse. 'Retired today to peaceful Erwinna, Pennsylvania,' Sid once wrote, 'Perelman raises turkeys which he occasionally displays on Broadway, stirs little from his alembics and retorts . . .'

Holiday. New York was now their working base for so much of every year that Ronald and Monica had taken to sharing an apartment with the Lockes. Hotels had begun to pall (aside from which they were quite sticky, in some parts of America, over the matter of accommodating couples who were not strictly married). So they maintained a whole kit of household effects, which saved them the expense of eating out so much; and since rent was deducted at source by John Locke on his agency accounts, they did not feel the loss. Their range of acquaintance in New York City was already impressive – indeed, in a sense it was virtually limitless, since one of their firm friends was Irving Hoffman, the press agent, a sort of journalistic pilot-fish to the shark-like doyen of gossip, Walter Winchell. Hoffman (whose activities contributed much to the character Sidney Falco, played by Tony Curtis in *The Sweet Smell of Success*) was the kind of operator who made a tour of all the restaurants and clubs in the morning, dropping in a few dollars on hat-check girls and waitresses in exchange for information on tête-à-têtes, to be retrieved in the afternoon.

Some people thought of Hoffman as a threat; but then it was quite the vogue to see Searle in the same terms. His new book, the panoramically all-American *From Frozen North to Filthy Lucre*, carried the kind of endorsements ('Beware of Searle': Friedrich Dürrenmatt. 'He is a great and dangerous and frightening man': Al Capp) which must have recommended Searle to Hoffman as a fellow-spirit. Hoffman certainly loved Ronald's work, in spite of eyesight so appalling that he was forced to enjoy it from a range of about an inch. In fact, Hoffman was dogged in his pursuit of all that was best in art. He once camped outside Picasso's gates with such unbudgeable persistence that eventually the master was obliged to admit him and listen to his requests. All Hoffman wanted was something – anything – created by the hand of Picasso. The artist obliged by handing over a sheet of paper on which, he said, was everything he had ever written. It was an alphabet. But at least it was a Picasso alphabet. In some ways, Hoffman struck Ronald as all that was worst about a certain bulldozing kind of American, yet he couldn't help liking him, and even helping him on occasion: when 'arrested' by the immigration officers on the Standard Oil show, Ronald ensured that Irving got the story first. Hoffman could afford to reciprocate generously, for he was employed not only to get things into gossip columns but also to keep other things out, most particularly any scandal involving the film mogul Darryl F. Zanuck, who visited Paris quite often. Ronald and Monica would entertain Irving and Irving would respond with some extravagant treat at Zanuck's expense – on one occasion an entire bucket of caviar for three, consumed in the courtyard of the enormously distinguished Hotel George V.

Searle's *Frozen North* book carried a whimsical recommendation from Groucho Marx, who disclaimed any knowledge of art ('I know ... that Toulouse-Lautrec walked around on his knees') but insisted that 'it does not need the curator of the Museum of Modern Art to tell the world that Mr Searle is a genius'. He repeated the diagnosis, or charge, at a press conference at London airport ('I think he's wonderful'), adding that Random House had paid him $250 for saying so (it was actually Viking Press). The moral of the tale, said Groucho, was that 'you really don't have to know anything about a subject in order to make money'. Of that great generation of Jewish-American comedic talents, the one Ronald knew best, by far, was S. J. Perelman, whom Malcolm Muggeridge had brought round to see him at Newton Road in the early Fifties. Sid Perelman had his irascible side and was given to uttering extended monologues which often turned out to be trial runs for future articles; but he had a genuine affection for Ronald, triggered at an early meeting when the Englishman asked his way to 'the cloakroom', a term which delighted Sid by transporting him instantly to his favourite literary territory, amid the rapiers and intrigues of Baroness Orczy.

Perelman became increasingly Europeanized in the Sixties and showed up often in Paris with his wife Laura. It is tempting to imagine what might have happened if they had all got round a Left Bank dinner-table with another friend of Ronald's, Samuel Beckett. The acquaintance with Beckett had been reawakened through Monica's friend Deryk Mendel, a fellow-inmate of 2 Rue Antoine-Dubois, who had done much to get her established there. Mendel was a dancer, choreographer, mime-artist and stage director, and Monica had designed a couple of shows for him. Among his best-known presentations were those written for him by Beckett, including the mime *Acte sans paroles*. They found their readiest audience in Germany, where Mendel was also engaged in production at the Berlin Opera. Every so often, Ronald and Monica would fly off to Germany – 'almost like groupies', Mendel recalled – to attend one or other of these premières, in Berlin or Ulm, and raise a glass with Beckett and Mendel.

There was no chance to converse on these occasions, but over one of their rare dinners in Paris, Beckett would sometimes talk quite gravely about writing. One of the central problems he faced, he said one evening, was that of wringing the precise meaning out of a word. As Searle noted at the time, 'he said that he didn't go along with Joyce's settling for invented words when the existing ones were inadequate. He (Sam) fought for precision with what existed.' Searle might have advanced a parallel argument in favour of figurative art. Speaking of 'the disastrous mechanics of trying to capture on paper the exact image that was in your head, the loss during the journey from the brain, down the arm, to the written word', Beckett put forward the example of Giacometti, 'who felt that his life had been a disaster because he had never been able to realise the "feel" of the image in his head'. To Searle, these words so exactly described his own situation that he adopted the example of Giacometti thereafter in explaining himself to interviewers. His affinity with Beckett's characters, in their stubborn mad resolve to go on going on, he had proved more than twenty years before, in his captivity. The Beckett plays could almost have been written in commemoration of the mental realities of that state.

Ronald and Monica started their New Year travels earlier than usual in 1966. In New York by 4 January they moved on to California and the *TV Guide*, and a memorable encounter with a nocturnal storm of tumbleweed on the way back from a weekend in Tijuana, Mexico. One of Ronald's topics for caricature was the *Man from UNCLE* series, reintroducing him to the actor David McCallum, whom he had last known as a Shakespearian striver in the ranks of Stratford-upon-Avon. Both men, in their way, were being borne along in the gaudy parade of the Sixties, a decade which increasingly usurped the role of the satirist by caricaturing itself. Searle, at least, had been spared the spectacle of 'Swinging London', where his old colleague Vicky had just committed suicide and, hardly less dismally, *The Great St Trinian's Train Robbery*, fourth in the film series, was about to open. Small glimpses of Searle's current work had been given in the *Sun* newspaper – a broadsheet then, and still respectable – but the casual British reader was losing sight of him.

The converse was not the case, for Ronald made ten separate journeys to Cambridge and back in 1966; but the reason for these was sadly personal. His father had fallen seriously ill with something obviously more urgent than his familiar emphysema, and it was not long before cancer was diagnosed. William Searle, like his son, was a stoical patient. Old Cambridge friends like Gee Horsley of the Art School were impressed by the extent to which Ronald was prepared to drop everything – each weekend for a while – and return to Cambridge to help, making himself responsible for conferring with surgeons and ferrying the patient back and forth between Addenbrooke's Hospital and Collier Road. For the first time in years, Ronald was in London on the publication day of one of his books: *Haven't We Met Before, Somewhere?*, a comprehensive view of Germany and Germanism, with text by Heinz Huber. 'Another chapter in the British-German love-hate relationship,' the *Times Literary Supplement* called it, 'a rich commentary on prosperity, half-taken democracy, Munich burpiness and leaden sensuality.' While this review was being penned, Ronald and Monica were taking an essential holiday in Le Canadel and its neighbouring countryside. The previous year, they had been rather taken with a hilltop village they had found at the foot of the Provence Alps. Now they returned, with a view to finding some small hideaway, out of reach of editors and enquirers and people with books to be signed. Nothing came of this research at first, but it was not wasted effort.

November and December were frantic months. Ronald made four trips to Cambridge, meeting his children there, and also Olive and her family. Grandfather Searle's latest operation had left him desperately ill, but the crisis passed. In between times, Ronald had mounted his first French exhibition, at the Galerie La Pochade. One of the elders of Surrealism, Philippe Soupault, wrote a little programme-note for it, reaching a familiar conclusion: '*Prenez garde à Ronald Searle, cet homme est dangereux!*' It seemed characteristic of European and even American observers to relish the expectation of the unexpected from Searle, while Britain preferred to have more of the same. He had overhead a *bonne femme*, Soupault said, 'fat as a pumpkin', standing in front of a Searle drawing and asking plaintively '*Où va-t-il chercher tout ça?*' ('Where does he get all this stuff?'). Soupault could not but agree, he said, and ask the same question. The show helped inaugurate a series of Searle lithographs, published at first by La Pochade, and later by the artist himself in association with his printer, Michel Cassé. First to be issued was 'The Square Egg', which happened also to be the first drawing of Ronald's to be published by the *New Yorker*. The way it happened was typical of the ups and downs of the year. For some months, Ronald had been contributing cartoons – perhaps better defined as scenes from a re-ordered

Above: Doctored postcard, 1970–1 (Le Sacré Coeur, Paris), unpublished

Searle's talent for embellishing postcards is regularly exercised. Elephants appear in the meadows near his home village, and the Eiffel Tower is revealed as a drilling-rig for an underwater champagne deposit. This example comes from his own archive.

universe – to the *Figaro Littéraire*, which after a period of quiet acceptance had suddenly terminated the series on the grounds that it was 'not literary enough'. In no great hopes of success, Ronald parcelled off his unpublished stock to the *New Yorker*, whence all work he had previously sent had been returned. This time, however, they took a whole dozen in one go, publishing them at regular intervals through 1967. Searle had met the *New Yorker*'s Art Editor, Jim Geraghty, on his latest American journey, so perhaps it was the personal contact that made the difference. Curiously, Searle did not, as he put it, 'knowingly perpetrate a gag cartoon' for more than twenty years thereafter; but what the *New Yorker* could not extract from him in cartoons, it made up for in covers. The register in which Searle naturally worked – funny situations, but too full of troubling ambiguities to be called jokes – suited the *New Yorker* cover perfectly, and in an increasingly eccentric gallery of chosen artists he has remained the most reliably distinguished since his cover début in 1969.

Walter Winchell's syndicated American column in mid-December of 1966 carried one of his typically zippy and heartless gossip-lines: 'British cartoonist Ronald Searle of *Punch* and his mate Kaye are asunder. She's a director of a bookhouse . . .' Premature in a legal sense, the item was more or less true. The lawyers had finally reached an agreement, and Kaye Webb's petition had appeared in a list of undefended suits to be heard in the High Court. With characteristic determination, she had established herself as the head of the Children's Publishing Division of Penguin Books responsible for the Puffin series. Ronald knew nothing of the progress of the divorce proceedings. After paying yet another call to Cambridge, for his parents' golden wedding anniversary, he left on his customary January–February tour of the States; and it was there that he saw the *Times* announcement – as stony-faced a piece of prose as Winchell's had been slangy:

> Mr Ronald William Fordham Searle, the cartoonist, offered no defence in the Divorce Court yesterday when a decree *nisi* was granted his wife, Kathleen, a director of Penguin Books, of Newton Road, Bayswater, W., because of his desertion. They were married in March, 1948, at Kensington, and have two children. The court's discretion was exercised in respect of adultery admitted by Mrs Searle.
>
> Judge Mais approved a proposed arrangement between the parties whereby Mr Searle, upon decree absolute, would transfer his share of their jointly owned home, said to be worth about £20,000, to his wife in lieu of maintenance. Mr Searle was ordered to pay the costs.

Three more months were required finally to solemnize the decree. During that period, Ronald visited Cambridge three more times, first for his father's seventy-first birthday, and later, in mid-April, to share his last days. William Searle died on his daughter's birthday, 18 April, in the evening. He was cremated and the ashes were scattered under a flowering almond tree. Ronald stayed another week, looking after the formalities and comforting his mother. Then he returned to Paris, leaving Olive and her family to take the widow on a sentimental pilgrimage to Glengarriff in Ireland, where she had first met her soldier husband.

Notification of the Divorce Absolute reached Ronald in May. The following day, he requested the British Embassy to accommodate his marriage to Monica. A certain amount of human error would attend the festivities. Ronald and Monica arranged to have messages incised on the inner surface of the rings they exchanged. Making the most of a fifty-fifty chance of a bungle, the engravers put the messages in the wrong rings. Happily this was corrected in time for the ceremony, which took place in the British Embassy in Paris at 11.45 a.m. on 16 June 1967. Announcements were posted, and a very small table of friends, including David Arkell who happened to be in town, gathered that evening for a celebration dinner at the restaurant Gachoucha. It was not long before the news filtered over to the New York office of *Time* magazine, who found a place for it in the 'Milestones' column. 'Ronald Searle, 47, scalpel-sharp cartoonist' was reported as having taken a wife 'Monica Stirling, fiftyish, British novelist (*The Boy in Blue*)'. 'Sir,' cabled the groom in response, 'However much I may enjoy her books, I have never met Miss Monica Stirling, British novelist, in my life and I am certainly not married to her.' Monica Stirling, fiftyish, was equally insistent that she had 'never met Mr Searle'. *Time* sent apologies and best wishes to all the wronged parties – the present Miss Stirling, the former Mrs Stirling, and Ronald – the extraordinary thing about whom was that they all lived not just in Paris but actually in the same *arrondissement*.

Had Ronald been a newly-married man in the conventional sense, it would have been indelicate of Frank Zachary to send him off to Hamburg to cover the notorieties of the Reeperbahn. But he wasn't, and Zachary knew that there were not many artists he could trust to do an acceptable job on striptease, prostitution and sado-masochistic display. What he had failed to take into account, however, was Ronald's new un-British frankness in these matters. The drawings *Holiday* received from the pleasure-domes of St Pauli proved to be more adventurous than they had bargained for. They sent them all back, with a request that bare bosoms be somehow adorned and token fringes elongated into skirts. A full-page colour picture of a tart, positively roaring with boredom in a doorway,

148

was rejected as cover-art, and a male tourist in similar circumstances called for as a replacement. This was uncongenial work for an artist used to telling the truth as he saw it, and Searle for once took the short-cut and added stick-on emendations which spared the Americans' blushes. When the drawings were restored to him, he peeled them off again and republished the pictures in his own collections as both he and nature had intended. 'They told me they would be acceptable if I put tassels on them,' he told a visiting British interviewer. 'But they accepted perfectly a fantasy drawing of a man being held down and whipped by four prostitutes in a shop window, a bridle in his mouth.' The licentious were at least more consistent than the censors.

In spite of all, it had been a sound editorial instinct to send Ronald to Hamburg: a vision of human appetites openly tormented by professional manipulators of sensuality was bound to appeal to the Hogarth in him; and the Grosz, with an eye for 'leaden sensuality'; and of course the Lautrec, always accepting and at ease among the low-life. From Ronald's own 'working-class-proper' days, perhaps, came a faint but abiding astonishment at this apparently woman-dominated panorama of 'sin'. If anything in the real world corresponded to the special mayhem of the long-defunct St Trinian's fantasy – a mayhem without consequences, outside the 'moral' world – it was the mass showbiz orgiastics of the Reeperbahn, with its pocket-picking broads and all-girl wrestling.

In magnificent contrast stylistically, though some of the implied content was not so

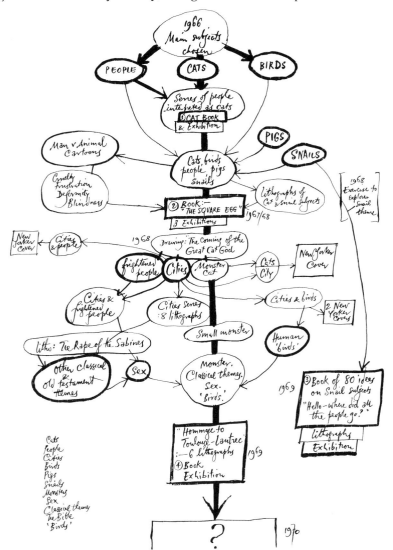

Left: Sketch-plan of Searle's thematic development, 1966–70, *Cartoonist Profiles*, November 1969

Searle demonstrates his father's ability to make an attractive tree out of unlikely materials. He supplied the following gloss to Cartoonist Profiles: *'The apple tree . . . was compiled out of curiosity in an attempt to answer the editor's question: "What routine do you go through to dredge up ideas." [It] covers the area of ideas only, as opposed to other work made alongside: book illustration, cinema animation and so on . . . I work with no fixed market in mind. Some ideas may best be expressed in lithography, others as large water-colours, others in pen. When they have been sufficiently developed I start worrying about placing them . . . The only factor I watch is: that whatever I do is thought of as an international idea – that it will have equal appeal in any of half-a-dozen countries. Or be equally rejected.'*

different, came the cat drawings which Searle had been assembling for a Christmas book to be published almost simultaneously in England and France. For some time he had been looking quite deliberately for a graphic lingua franca in which to express universally comprehensible comments on personality – human personality – and the cats were the solution. Nothing a human face could communicate was beyond the range of a Searle cat's expression, and his/her body-language, or fur-language, was perhaps more outspoken in its scope, from deep, round serenity to spiky, jagged neurosis. That there was a ready market for funny felines among people who actually liked cats did the drawings no commercial harm at all; cat-lovers almost unfailingly invest their darlings with imagined human qualities anyway, so there was no impediment there. Some of them would have been shocked, no doubt, to learn that Searle in his time had eaten cats. He has always been frank about the whole question. 'I don't like animals particularly, any more than I like children. Certain animals, certain children, yes, but I see no need to be *global* about it.' Searle has never left any loose sentimentalities lying around the world. Equally, he has never played the professional ghoul, except in fancy dress – and once, in real life, by accident. Just after their marriage, he and Monica were invited over by the rather dreadfully overpowering *couturière* Ginette Spanier, directrice of Balmain, and her doctor husband Paul-Emile Seidmann, the lure being the presence of Noël Coward. Going up to the Seidmanns' apartment, Ronald somehow cut his hand on some stained-glass decoration in the lift, but so neat was the cut that he did not notice the dripping blood. La Spanier hurried them straight through into the presence of the Master, and it was only as he stuck out his hand that Ronald noticed it was drenched in gore. 'My God, I do apologise,' he stammered, 'I seem to be covered in blood.' 'Of course, dear boy,' Coward replied. 'When one meets Ronald Searle one *expects* him to be covered in blood.'

Within a few months, it would be no uncommon experience for Parisians to stagger home injured, as *les événements* of 1968 got under way. At first, the year took its normal course, with the Searles spending six weeks in New York. Their one long excursion took them to Winnipeg for negotiations with the Hudson's Bay Company over a tricentennial celebration book. Social demands in New York, as usual, were of the kind Ronald liked – the intimate meeting with friends rather than the lavish bash. André François was in town again, and there was lunch with Irving Hoffman at Lindy's. The Searles even travelled out to Erwinna, Pennsylvania, to spend a night with the Perelmans in their farmhouse. Ronald had just drawn a memorable cover for the *Saturday Evening Post*, a right-facing profile (more natural for the left-handed artist) of President Lyndon Johnson, with his Indian-elephant ears. Just as it was published, in early February, Ronald heard from Germany that his collaborator there, Heinz Huber, had died, at the age of forty-five. Four partners gone, three of them younger, at the time of their death, than Searle was now. He had evidently been marked for survival. In later years, he did advise potential co-workers, not completely tongue-in-cheek, that they were not doing their chances any good.

It was from his mother that he had inherited the potential for longevity, but she did not have the taste for solitude that Ronald had possessed. He had to make repeated compassionate visits to Cambridge in the spring, while in Paris shooting was in progress on another neo-Edwardian comedy film. *Those Daring Young Men in their Jaunty Jalopies* (mercifully retitled *Monte Carlo or Bust* for British consumption) not only re-ran the whiskery jollities of the 'Magmen' but also borrowed shamelessly from another 1965 film *The Great Race*, which had likewise featured early automobiles and Tony Curtis. The

Montmartre leg of the filming was completed just in time to escape the turmoil of the student uprisings now brewing in the city. Street battles began to break out on 6 May. The Searles, in Rue Antoine-Dubois, lived at the very heart of the trouble, and their lives for a time were made very uncomfortable. Ronald's daughter Katie arrived to stay on 10 May, which happened to be the first night when barricades went up in unmistakable assertion of the students' revolutionary stance. Ronald and Monica did manage to sneak Katie out to the decadent luxury of Maxim's, her choice for a twenty-first birthday treat, but strikes and disorder were spreading every day; when the time came to put her back on the plane to England, all the Paris airports were closed, and there was nothing for it but to accompany her, for safety's sake, all the way to Brussels in a taxi. Back in Paris, Ronald conferred urgently with the cartoonists Siné and Wolinski, who wanted him to participate in the newly-founded and savagely anti-establishment magazine, *L'Enragé*. Searle faced a real difficulty here. He could agree with some of what they said, and undertook to support them privately; but it seemed to him improper that a guest in any country should seek to interfere with what was going on internally. It was painful to maintain neutrality while riot police were beating up girls under his very window in Rue Antoine-Dubois, but Searle knew in any case that any protest would have brought a volley of tear-gas straight into his studio. As it was, the flat was often filled with the stuff as it gusted down the narrow streets from the battlegrounds around the nearby Odéon. Mornings were usually safe outside, but by late afternoon a detectable tension in the neighbourhood sent the locals back behind their shutters.

Never seriously disconcerted by such a minor degree of confinement, Searle sat at his desk and found himself absorbed in exploring the unusual theme of snails, which as far as he knew had never received much friendly attention from artists (Günter Grass had not yet discovered them). Searle's own affection had centred, so far, on *Helix pomatia*, the edible snail, a French delicacy of course, but one which he had got to know in the course of cooking and eating some of the tropical varieties during the war. A snail had appeared in his work occasionally as an object of terror or ill-omen, wearing a mellophone on its

Below left: From *Hello – Where Did All The People Go?*, drawn 1968
One of the products of Searle's semi-imprisonment in his flat during les événements *of 1968. As may be seen in the chart on p. 149, pigs and snails more or less coincided, so it was inevitable that they would mingle, if not necessarily as intimately as this.*

Below right top: Same, 1968
The exclusively 'feminine' shapes of the snail encourage a fantasy association with a (female) eye. The theme of blindness would shortly be broached by Searle (see p. 152 (top right)).

Below right bottom: Same, 1968
Highly ingenious 'explanation' of snail-configuration in terms of female anatomy. In this is the answer to the question 'Where did all the people go?' – they went into the snails.

back, or spelling out 'Beware' to a suburban gardener in its trail. Now, perhaps, the creature was a kind of topical reference to Searle himself, a man forced to shrink back temporarily into his shell. But, as always with Searle, meanings are not programmed into the exploration of shapes and textures, but are expected to emerge from it. Some of his snail images are no more than craftily realized doodles, momentary pursuits of an image-association or pun. In others, where what you might call an 'intercourse' is set up between the horn-like exterior and the soft, shapeless, deliquescent yet erectile interior body, the drawings are provoking in a way that encourages the viewer to question his unconscious. Freud, in a rare pronouncement upon the dream-image of a 'giant snail', identified it as 'a perfect female sexual symbol'. Searle's versions present, perhaps, a more hermaphroditic picture, though with a strong tendency to the feminine: a huge snail with dugs, giving suck to some piglets; snails bosomed and basqued and gartered; and even a woman kneeling in such a posture as to resemble the ambulant mollusc. Most striking of all, perhaps, are those snails where the whorl of the shell is replaced by an unmistakably feminine eye – for here the eye, too is revealed as a female-genital pun. In the whole book, the normal human figure appears only once, giving scale to a mammoth snail in eighteenth-century rococo style. It was this that led Searle's friend, the thirty-year-old graphic artist Roland Topor, to suggest the title *Tiens! Il n'y a personne?* – translated, when Tony Godwin took it on for Weidenfeld in London, as *Hello – Where Did All the People Go?*

That was a question often uttered by tourists in Paris during August, when the natives traditionally vacated their city for the seaside. August came early in 1968. Many people with an excuse to avoid further trouble invoked it and got away. After particularly rough nights of battle in their area during mid-June the Searles took a break in Cambridge; another in July; and finally decamped gratefully to Rome where Ronald had more work to do on the *Monte Carlo* film. *Paparazzi* buzzed about on the fringes of the location set while Ronald made a lightning sketch of the starlet Mireille Darc, and Tony Curtis did the same for Ronald. *Il celebre artista* would shortly be in front of the cameras himself, filmed at the Café Flore for a French TV documentary directed by the writer and playwright Remo Forlani. *Le Petit Monde des Humoristes* was flatteringly chosen by ORTF-2 to be shown on Christmas Eve. There was, indeed, hardly a corner of western Europe where one was entitled to be unaware of Ronald Searle in late 1968. Exhibitions of his work opened in Zurich and Baden-Baden; there were two more in Paris. Britain saw the publication of *Take One Toad*, a choice collection of weird but authentically recorded medieval remedies – a book which reintroduced into Searle's output the genre of the slim, if large-format, collector's item. More important was *The Square Egg*, a collection in which the 'dangerous' Searle of whom the public had been warned first revealed his aggressiveness. Cat and snail interpretations were present in the book, along with pigs, who represented sometimes a dim outsiderishness, a pathetic desire to join the big boys, and elsewhere the sniggering, gloating narcissism of the person who really thinks he has ingratiated himself with someone important. But it was the themes of 'cruelty, frustration, deformity, blindness' – named by Searle in a sketch-plan of his thematic progress – that really dominated the book: the blind man who dreams of an eye, the man borne aloft by whipped butterflies. There was sickness and perversity in such jokes, but it belonged to man and not the jokes. Laughter was made as hurtful as Searle could presently make it, because in laughter there was always hurt. To those viewers who did not insist on the Searle they had first thought of, it seemed fair enough.

Even England was taking an interest in these developments. Within ten days of the pub-

lication of *The Square Egg*, Searle was visited by Philip Speight's film-crew from BBC-2's *Late Night Line-Up*, who were accorded the very rare privilege of admittance to his studio. The still-extant film includes a glimpse of him sketching with his Mont Blanc fountain pen and excerpts from the Ivor Wood animations of the time. It was perhaps the most relaxed of his television interviews, in spite of the overload of autumn exhibitions and flights to Rome and Berlin. It was on the way to Berlin that the Searles happened to find themselves more or less in the middle of Dizzy Gillespie's band, who were heading for a jazz festival. After some pompous business commuter had treated one of the musicians without the respect due to an artist, and received in return a sharp verbal pasting from Monica in her impeccable German, the Searles fell into conversation with Jimmy Owens, young star of the trumpet section, who proved to be a man after Ronald's own heart: a virtuoso improviser with a style of his own, yet so deeply grounded in academic and practical training that he would never be at a loss in any sort of musical company. Owens met the Searles shortly afterwards in Paris, they met his family on their next New York trip, and a friendship born in an unpleasant moment on an aeroplane still endures.

In New York, plans were finalized for an edition of the Baron Munchausen stories, illustrated by Ronald with a lunatic braying dynamism he could not have achieved without the 'Anatomies and Decapitations', where many of the apoplectic and bloodshot effects were pioneered. Roland Topor, in Paris, introduced Searle to his publisher, Jean-Jacques Pauvert, who had taken on a whole stable of cartoonists, including the virulent anarchist Siné. Pauvert agreed to publish not just the snail drawings, but Searle's Hamburg sketchbook as well, which in its raw state communicated a much less filtered view of the

Above left: 'The Masochist', *New Yorker*, 19 August 1967

Included in The Square Egg, *this drawing was entitled 'Le Masochiste' in Searle's Bibliothèque Nationale Exhibition, although 'sado-masochist' might cover the fullest extent of this elegant perversion. It was one of the burst of cartoons accepted by the* New Yorker *after Searle's arrangement with* Le Figaro Littéraire *had been terminated.*

Above right: 'Gourmet', *New Yorker*, 7 January 1967

The horror of the fly settling on one's food remains with Searle here after more than twenty years — as it does today. He cannot bear to 'share a room with one', a phrase which comes alive in a particularly vivid way in this drawing. (Included in The Square Egg.*)*

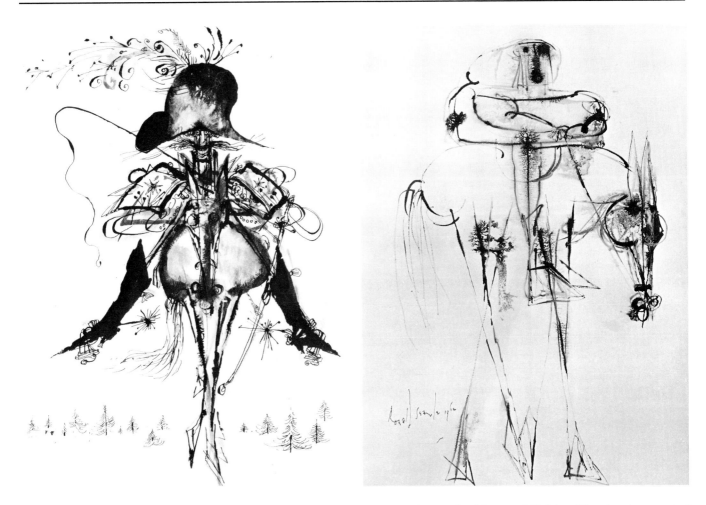

Above left: From *The Adventures of Baron Munchausen*, London, 1969

Baron Munchausen sets off on his journey to Russia. The berserk quality of his narrative is matched throughout by Searle's drawings, some of whose technique arises directly out of the disturbed and disturbing qualities of the 'Anatomies and Decapitations' series of 1962–6.

Above right: From 'Anatomies and Decapitations', 1962

An example of the groundwork which enabled Searle to approach the Munchausen illustrations with the requisite manic glee.

Reeperbahn experience than had the doctored tableaux of *Holiday*. The drawings, noted the *Times Literary Supplement*, 'are beautiful, made with exactly the right mixture of involvement and detached criticism'. The *T.L.S.*, or its reviewer, had been alert enough to pick up the French edition of the work, which did not appear in Britain until a year later under the title *Secret Sketchbook* — no doubt chosen with an eye to interesting its audience in something simultaneously naughty and fashionably 'underground'. The heyday of the underground magazine had now arrived, but that form of subversion held no attraction for Searle. To the BBC's *Line-Up* team he had given an interesting summary of his position in relation to the various publishing possibilities:

One of the main reasons why I enjoy living here is that whilst the interest in 'fine art', if you like, which held such an important place in France, has moved to America, it's becoming a centre [here], and a great centre, of a movement towards a new form of graphic art, graphic satire. In fact, I think it's going to move in an extremely powerful direction, because graphic satire must thrive in opposition, and here there is a certain climate of opposition. It can't come from America, in the sense that the dictates of syndicates, the dictates of the advertisers, are always apparent; a magazine can't stick its neck out too far, if it's going to lose public. The only possible thing one can do is to work for the so-called underground magazines, but again that doesn't achieve anything, because one area in which there is almost a total lack of communication, for me, is in underground publications. Whereas literature has made such vast strides forward, in the sense of saying what it wants to say, there is no artistic or graphic possibility of saying what has been said in, for example, *Last Exit To Brooklyn*, or *The Naked Lunch*, two books that I feel are the most extraordinary puritanical documents, bringing a terrifying indictment – if one could say, graphically, what has been said by those two books, just to pick an example, then I think that the way is open for a vast movement in graphic satire.

That was the encouraging way of putting it. To the American readership of a new publication called *Cartoonist Profiles*, a few months later, Searle was keener to impart the kick-up-the-pants version: ' ... graphic humour is lamely tottering along behind. In the main it is bogged down with conservatism, unoriginality, self-satisfaction, a strong resistance to experimentation and an underlying devotion to minor domestic trivialities'. This was probably not the kind of message of support the magazine had expected when it asked Searle to 'pass on his reactions', but that, of course was part of his point.

It would be quite wrong to give the impression that Searle was, then or now, a haughty loner who administered nothing but disgusted rebukes to his colleagues. He had participated more than most in the camaraderie of the profession, privately in latter years, but at that time in cheerful open session. In 1969 he began attending the annual proceedings of the Société Protectrice de l'Humour, founded three years earlier by Searle's great friend and fellow-artist Jean-Pierre Desclozeaux. Born not far from Avignon, Desclozeaux arranged the Société's junketings there every July, and the Searles continued to attend through some extremely trying times. These were about to begin.

Ronald and Monica had kept up their reconnaissance of their favourite village in Haute-Provence, and a place they liked had become available. A deposit was paid, a loan arranged with a bank down in Nice, and within weeks the beginnings of their hideaway were secured – a shell only, nothing remotely habitable. However, all through the process, Monica was suffering strange body pains which seemed to worsen as the autumn progressed. She had been seeing a homoeopathic doctor for back trouble anyway, and sought advice in that quarter, without raising much effective interest. The matter was shelved while Ronald discussed a new film version of *A Christmas Carol*, a notion which had been bobbing up and falling back for over a decade, and a string of friends trooped through Paris: Ivor Wood, Ronald's favourite animator; his London agent, Hope Leresche; Tony Godwin, the publisher; a number of graphic satirists, including Hans-Georg Rauch, Roland Topor and Jean-Marie Kerleroux; Ronald's old partner in reportage, Paul Hogarth; and, for the last time as a couple, the Perelmans. Ronald never saw Laura Perelman alive again – she died the following spring – although, a decade later, she brought him a message in a manner that might have impressed even P. J. Doyle of Fort Yukon.

By December, with Monica still in pain but closer to hearing the verdict of a competent specialist, Ronald was enjoying renewed notoriety with his *Hommage à Toulouse-Lautrec*, book and exhibition, which took the French by surprise, They themselves had not, on the whole, cared to go too deeply into the story of the tiny crippled aristocrat and his nuzzling intimacy with the girls of Montmartre – certainly not in the form of graphic fantasy, at any rate. To see a version of Lautrec's own detachment applied to himself, to see him dwarfed, more than nature had already dwarfed him, by the vast indifferent thighs of tarts and chorines, would have been shocking at any time, but to have the experience at the invitation of an Englishman was unprecedented. One critic otherwise friendly to Searle's *oeuvre* confessed himself *'profondément choqué'* by the Lautrec material, which he saw as successful, but *'odieux'* in its success. Had it not claimed to be an *hommage*, he said, he would have found it more acceptable – yet there was nothing ironic about the title Searle

Below: 'Samson Demolishing the Temple', *Hommage à Toulouse-Lautrec,* Paris, 1969
The English title of the book, The Second Coming of Toulouse-Lautrec, *emphasized the fact that in its pages the crippled artist was being given a wishful second chance: he was even pictured proudly standing on legs of a normal length. A series of the drawings carried jocular biblical titles. Samson, it will be recalled, became a prisoner of the Philistines – willingly, in this case. Four pages of these drawings were published in* Playboy *(December 1969). José Ferrer, who had played Lautrec in the film* Moulin Rouge, *wrote in to say 'I would love to play [him] again if Searle would direct as he draws.'*

had chosen. He had been rendering homage to Lautrec most of his adult life, and publicly at least since 1960, when he devised and narrated a *Monitor* feature, entirely in praise of the artist, for BBC Television. The tribute, as it happened, was not only genuine but rather well-timed, since it coincided with efforts to persuade the French Ministry of Culture to promote Ronald's case for a new kind of residence permit, guaranteeing a much longer stay without bother of renewals. Sure enough, three days after the opening of the *Hommage* exhibition at La Pochade, the Ministry intimated that in principle it favoured the request of M. Searle, *'qui par la valeur de ses oeuvres mérite d'obtenir une suite favorable à sa demande'*.

This good news was almost instantly obliterated by fears for Monica's health, indeed her life. Her condition had been recognized, on the evidence of physical examination, as both rare and deadly. On the last afternoon of the year, while the rest of the world was bidding farewell to the Sixties, she went in for X-rays. That same evening, cancer was diagnosed and confirmed. It was a particularly venomous form of breast cancer, very quick to spread throughout the system. Immediate treatment was essential, though no hope could be held out for its success. January tickets to New York were naturally cancelled, and on the 5th Monica's radiation treatment began. Five days later, an operation followed. David Arkell, a most faithful friend, rushed over from London 'to be of some use as a telephone answering service, whilst Searle either lived at, or dashed back and forth from, the hospital'. He stayed a vital fortnight. When radiation resumed, it was in

Right: 'I can't help it, I had a dominating mother', c.1972

From 'A Few Complexes (Twelve pen drawings on the theme of Frustrations and Complexes)', included in Ronald Searle *(1978). Drawn in the depths of Monica's illness, and overtly alluding to the medical assault upon the body, this is a drawing in which the anger implicit in the earlier 'Anatomies' seems to be fully mobilized. An influence from the Picasso of* Guernica *survives.*

monstrous doses, to seal off a whole area; no pussyfooting curative dose would ever work.

Into this whirling world of desperation dropped an extraordinary letter from England. Addressed to Messrs Geoffrey Willans and Ronald Searle, it came from Viscount Molesworth. Ronald thought it was a joke, but enquiry showed that the sender, right enough, was the 11th Viscount Molesworth, writing from a flat in Highgate. His complaint involved the book *How To Be Topp*, in which the addressees had used his name, the nobleman pointed out, from first to last. Since he had a good name to live up to, he strongly objected to its being used for trading purposes, especially as his ten-year-old son had recently been called Nigel by his schoolmaster. Molesworth closed with a threat to refer to his London solicitors if the perpetrators did not desist. It says a lot for Ronald Searle's self-possession and command of irony — for his 'frightening' detachment, indeed — that he was able to reply by return of post, in the following terms:

Dear Sir,

Thank you for your letter addressed to Mr Geoffrey Willans and myself, which has been forwarded on to me here.

Your splendid name is shared by many humble thousands, and it would be difficult to say which of these lower ranks, called Nigel, inspired Mr Willans to create the character of 'Nigel Molesworth' for *Punch*, sometime towards the end of the last war.

Alas, we shall never know, as Mr Willans died at an early age some years ago. Happily his books go on after all these years, to the delight of several generations — and a legion of Molesworths.

They also help to support in a small way his widow and children who were left behind in rather reduced circumstances.

'Nigel Molesworth' has entered the ranks of English folklore, and after a quarter of a century of activity I am rather mystified that he has not previously brought himself to your attention. However, I am sure that Mr Willans, were he still alive, would be the first to say that he is happy you have been spared the previous 24 years of anguish due to the invention of his fictitious character.

Yours sincerely,

Ronald Searle.

It was a delicately presented correspondence-stopper — a remarkable one, considering the reserves of feeling that might have been vented at such a moment. Senior specialists had estimated that Monica Searle had three months to live. One doctor declined to administer any particularly radical treatments, as the cause was known to be lost.

Ronald's fiftieth birthday slid by with scarce festivity. He forced himself back to work, making quick dashes to London to confer on what had now become *Scrooge*, a musical starring Albert Finney. In the Searles' French village, another tiny house had become available, heaped up, in the medieval fashion of the place, against the one they already had. Fully intending that life should go on, they signed to buy it — an investment in the hoped-for future. Monica was still in danger; but at last one doctor had emerged from the pack with a radical proposal that seemed to offer her something in exchange for her unwillingness to take conventional advice and give up the ghost. The new man was Léon Schwarzenberg, a name not widely known in English-speaking countries. In France, by contrast, a poll published at the end of 1989 named Schwarzenberg as one of the four most popular men in France. An off-and-on member of the government at the Euro-level of *ministre délégué*, he came to his present eminence from the saddest beginning. In 1944, he was refused permission to take up medical studies in Toulouse on the grounds that he was a Jew. His two younger brothers were informed against and shipped off to the Mauthausen concentration camp where they died. It is not so much a sense of guilt that helps to form the French public's attitude to Professor Schwarzenberg, as a feeling of gratitude that after an experience so bitterly alienating, he chose to stay and serve the country of his birth.

In 1970 he had reached the stage of experimenting with new and powerful drugs, developed in association with the pharmaceutical company Roche. No guarantees could possibly be attached to their use. Their efficacy was unproven, the duration of treatment uncertain, and the side-effects imponderable. Monica agreed to have them – a glowingly irradiated guinea-pig. Léon Schwarzenberg took over personal control of her treatment and chemo-therapy began. Ronald's ten-year residency card was received. Monica's three months were already six.

To Barbara Nicholls, assistant to *New Yorker* Art Editor Jim Geraghty, Ronald wrote in July, agreeing to the sale of a cover-art original. 'It might help to pay some of the medical bills here,' he said. A short respite from the medical onslaught had been arranged:

> The doctors are allowing me to take Monica away for a little while (near Avignon) from Monday – for the first time since Christmas. We shall stay as long as we dare – or rather until she is called back for the next treatment . . .
>
> As our life has been more or less revolving around the battery of specialists and their treatments it has been very difficult since Christmas to settle long enough to really think out ideas. However, the indications are that the battle is being won and that gradually things will become a little more flexible. At least we have the news that they decided last week not to do a second operation. So with that black cloud lifted the future seems a great deal less fluid. So, I hope to be able to get down to some ideas for covers again and what appears will be whisked over to you . . .

The Searles stayed five days at the Hôtel le Prieuré, Villeneuve-les-Avignon, helping Desclozeaux protect humour, and even managed their usual holiday at Le Canadel; but travel was otherwise restricted to Ronald's overnight dashes to Birmingham, where his mother had moved in with Olive after her three years of unhappy solitude in Cambridge. The Collier Road house was cleared out and closed, by Olive. Ronald's presence was not needed. He had spent one day in Cambridge that June, while concluding the *Scrooge* work. He has never been back since.

The news of Monica's condition, travelling round the world, had brought the best out of the cartoon community. Charles Schulz sent his good wishes in 'Peanuts' format; and the old team of animators at the Disney studio, led by Ward Kimball, painted her a 'Monica Mouse', based defiantly on the original Minnie, and not the modern plastic one, which they said they hated. Even Sid Perelman, when he called early in 1971, forsook his usual line of banter for some more confessional reflections, though Monica happened to be in bed, too ill to hear them. Encouraged by a matutinal bottle of champagne, Sid set out on an immense monologue in which he revealed that he was moving to London to avoid his 'bouts of manic depression' and the danger of being 'isolated' in New York. His own wife had died nine months before – of a cancer originating in the breast – and now, he said, his psychiatrist had told him to 'go out there and make all the contacts you can through love'. The man had then repeated the advice in more earthy, layman's terms –

since when Sid had been contacting with the utmost energy. He had lately had the galling experience of being mistaken for Groucho Marx by most of the Atlantic-crossing passengers on the S.S. *France*, an ordeal akin to one Ronald had undergone in New York in 1965 while being photographed by Arnold Newman. After the more formal portraiture was completed, Newman asked Searle to retreat to the pristine backdrop and 'draw one of your trains'. It was instantly apparent that Newman thought he was dealing with Rowland Emett. Searle signed his name rather pointedly on the cloth to put Newman right, and quit the studio, to the sound of the photographer's groans.

Ronald was able to return to New York in January 1971, explaining his position to those who needed to know, and calling in at Radio City to see the *Scrooge* film. Twenty years later, in spite of some unexpectedly characterless Leslie Bricusse songs, it survives quite well, with at least a flavour of Searle seeping from the title sequences into the live action and special effects. Reviews at the time, however, ran mostly along the lines of Sid Perelman's famous outcry against art-movies, 'Small Is My Cinema, Deep My Doze'. Sid at that moment was being visited by the inspirational notion of travelling round the world in eighty days, following the same route as Phileas Fogg. Setting out from the Reform Club on 5 March 1971, with his six-foot Texan secretary Dianne Baker as a travelling companion, he took the overnight train to Paris and appeared the following noon at a lavish lunch, hosted in their apartment at the Crillon by Emmeline and David Bruce, who was conducting the Vietnam peace talks in Paris on behalf of the United States. Also present were the Searles; their good friend (and Sid's) Mary Blume, the journalist; Lady Hesketh, a particular fan of the circumnavigator; and Janet Flanner, 'Genêt' of the *New Yorker*, who paid Monica's powers of recovery an odd but unmistakable compliment by making a pass at her. As she left at the end of this strange event, Flanner seized Ronald's hand and exclaimed 'At last! How I've longed to meet you!', which she had done at least twice before, and not long ago. For Sid, it was a batty beginning to a doomed trip, for the further east he travelled, the more morose he became, until he fired Mrs Baker in Hong Kong. She retaliated by getting her account of the journey smartly into *Harper's Bazaar*. To the no longer globe-trotting Searles, it all came as a rather comforting reminder of the joys of staying at home.

Perhaps because he had stood still long enough to receive them, prizes began to be rained on Ronald. He had experienced bursts of award-winning before, especially around 1959–60 in America, and the *Prix de la Critique Belge* had come his way as recently as 1968. But the award of domestic French prizes marked a different sort of appreciation, an acceptance of Searle's way of thinking, critical as it was, as part of the French social fabric. The annual July visit to Avignon brought two awards, the *Prix d'Humour du Festival d'Avignon* and the *Médaille de la Ville d'Avignon*. 'Incontestablement,' declared a local paper roundly, '*Ronald Searle est le plus grand parmi les grands du monde de l'humour.*' This opinion was gaining ground. Three months later, Searle received the *Grand Prix de l'humour noir 'Grandville'*, named after the early nineteenth-century illustrator who appeared alongside Daumier in *Charivari*. The prize was awarded for Searle's snail collection of a good two years before. Black humour, no doubt, matures slowly. The *Prix Charles Huard de dessin de presse*, added in 1972, came in the form of six volumes of the magazine *Le Rire* from the early years of the present century – a welcome notion except in demands it made on shelf space in the flat. Already Ronald had had to hire a room, opposite the Café Flore in Paris, to house the overflow.

Ronald's own contributions to the book-stack had dwindled to the odd small-scale collector's item. It was neither anguish nor inactivity that accounted for this seeming reticence, but a change in the nature of the output itself. From his travels, Ronald had been accustomed to bringing back pen-and-ink work which lent itself readily to inexpensive publication in book form. Now, a studio-based life encouraged an expansion of technique into areas more suitable for transfer to lithographic reproduction. It was a move towards large colour pictures; the sheer exuberance of dress and commercial design at the time, vulgar though much of it was, demanded a response, and Searle relished the newly-expanded vocabulary of the period ('I love the way colour has opened out,' he told an interviewer). But at first it was only the assiduous continental gallery-goer who took the full measure of Searle's spontaneous creation during this time. On the commercial side, the chief beneficiary of his new working patterns was the American magazine reader. On a three-week trip to New York in January 1972 – the tenth and last of these mid-winter migrations – he lined up an impressive list of editors; at the *New Yorker*, the *New York Times*, the *Saturday Review*, *Sports Illustrated*, and the *TV Guide*. *Holiday* had lately collapsed under its own weight, but Frank Zachary had moved on to *Travel and Leisure* and was open for business.

These reassuring contacts made, Searle returned to Paris and the familiar uncertainties of Monica's treatment. Schwarzenberg and three colleagues conferred once more – Ronald noted it as her thirty-ninth medical – and a new treatment was chosen, commencing with five consecutive days of injections. At times during these years she was dreadfully low, with a blood-count to match, living not day by day but minute by minute. Her neighbour Deryk Mendel remembered her lying in bed watching the second hand of the clock going round, and literally resolving to get through its next circuit of the dial. The future did not look inviting anywhere, except perhaps in Haute-Provence, where a sort of topping-out ceremony had been performed on their premises. However, the place was still far from habitable, so during their tour of inspection they had to stay at the local hotel.

Below: Untitled, *Paris-Match*, January 1973

Searle in the process of entering the Bibliothèque Nationale, with some of his current creations. The artist awards himself the same vertically arranged goggle-eyes as the stupider forms of animal life; ten years later, such eyes would become a fixture in his work (see Chapter 7). The matching eyes of the naked girl and the snail which (uncharacteristically) is first to reach the top of the steps take us back to the drawing reproduced on p. 151. Searle retains the right to use the whip.

Then, in June 1972, news came that Ronald had been invited to present a personal retrospective at the Bibliothèque Nationale. He was the first living, foreign artist to be accorded this privilege, but that fact in itself does not communicate, to non-Frenchmen, quite what a startling, indeed galvanizing honour this invitation represented. The French have a pride in their academic institutions that is in no way matched by an Englishman's feelings about the National Gallery, or even an American's about the Library of Congress. Perhaps Buckingham Palace or the White House would be nearer the mark. Searle had been admitted into one of the citadels of Frenchness – and he would enter, as his friend Remo Forlani put it in *Paris Match*, not by the tradesman's entrance but 'by the great door'. In consultation with Jean Adhémar of the Bibliothèque, Ronald learned that three whole floors would be available to him, plus the intervening marble stairways, and that apart from walls a dozen imposing showcases, in brass, mahogany and plate-glass, would be at his disposal. The wall-space Searle filled with 259 catalogued exhibits, almost all from his European years, though some of the showcases contained sketchbooks, publications and memorabilia from as far back as wartime. But even as they apportioned these items to their spaces, Ronald and Monica began to feel that the whole opulently framed display was liable to look, in its earnest sobriety, rather out of key with the absurdities happening in the pictures themselves. Accordingly they undertook to devote the ground-floor showcases to what the museum labelled (in faultless tiny white script on grey card) *'Documents et objets biographiques sur l'artiste.'* Combining Dada, Surrealism, memories of Ronald's childhood museum and plain English mischief, these exhibits included a filthy stained rag littered with dead bluebottles ('Handkerchief of the artist, utilized between 1965 and 1970'); a squashed spectacles-case ('Working-glasses accidentally sat on by the artist c.1965, after a hard day'); an abominably greasy necktie, annotated with details of three meals whose remains appeared on it, and the names of the restaurants where they were consumed; and a plaster cast of Ronald's remaining lower teeth, taken by his dentist, and po-facedly billed as 'One fifty-third of a bust of Ronald Searle by Professor Raymond Leibowitch, Paris. *Membre de la Faculté ...*' , and so on. At least half the visitors, Ronald was later told, had treated this anarchic junk with the utmost gravity, apparently on the assumption that because such pathetic fragments were all that remained of Searle, he must have died in penury.

It was actually the Bibliothèque Nationale themselves who were short of money. They hadn't any left over for a proper catalogue, and proposed a photocopied sheet instead. To the Searles' cartoonist friend Desclozeaux, this seemed a monstrous suggestion, and he volunteered at once to organize a proper book-format catalogue. His instinct, as founder of the Société Protectrice de l'Humour, was to look for strength in numbers; and so it was that a fine catalogue was published, after just a couple of weeks' hectic work, by a consortium called 'Les Amis de Ronald Searle'. This became a real company, listed in the *Journal Officiel* as a non-profit-making concern, which recouped money from the sale of the catalogues (more than 2000 were sold) and placed it in an account for the future use of young artists who, at the time of their first exhibition, found themselves short of the wherewithal for printing or framing. This excellent and benevolent notion might have remained the keynote of the entire event if the exhibition had run its scheduled course, 26 January to mid-March. But it was extended until the end of the month, and on 16 March the darker side of human nature asserted itself. Two pictures, including the one reproduced on the cover of the catalogue, were somehow detached from their robust moorings on the walls and sneaked out of the building, never to be recovered. On the penultimate day of the show, amazingly, it happened again, and a 1957 *Punch* drawing of New York's Chinatown disappeared for ever. The Bibliothèque Nationale, having failed to insure itself against such eventualities, was obliged to 'buy' the now notional works from Searle, who thus came to be 'represented in the Bibliothèque Nationale', as he later put it, 'by three phantom pictures'.

In the midst of the brouhaha — 30,000 law-abiding customers for the exhibition, any number of press and television interviews, and an official visit by the British Ambassador — Ronald had completed a third transaction in Haute-Provence, attaching another little contiguous cottage to the odd-shaped conglomeration he had already assembled. Yet a fourth element was added in the summer of 1973, leaving the Searles with the makings of a complete house and studio all stuck together upon the underlying rock, a cellar beneath and a couple of sun terraces at the top. Two more years would pass before they could spend their first night under its jumble of roofs; but they were still as enchanted as ever with the village, where they were content to stay as lodgers during the visits while the long process of negotiating with builders got under way,

In spite of his exhibition triumph, the strains of the time had told on Ronald. Photographs show a thin, wary Searle, even a little bird-of-preyish around the head, like his aquiline friend Beckett. The tremendous peaks and troughs of Monica's health were wearying, and it was difficult to cope with such a spread of effort: keeping an eye on all the builders, medical men, and publishers (the Italians had just joined the list with *I Disegni di Ronald Searle*). Galleries were a saga in themselves, for in the year to January 1974 he had been represented in no fewer than eight exhibitions of one sort or another, in France, Austria and Germany. Only in one instance did control pass too far out of Searle's hands, and that was in an animated feature based on Gilbert and Sullivan themes, on which he finished his key-drawings and background drawings midway through 1974. This renewed collaboration with Bill Melendez's Studios looked inviting — seventeen years had passed since *Energetically Yours* — but standards and techniques had coarsened in the animation business; and at feature-length, Melendez's son Steve and his team were unable to maintain the style set by Ronald's characteristic prototypes. Of the issued film, *Dick Deadeye*, the *Observer*'s critic remarked that 'the gloriously nibby quality of Searle comes through only in the backgrounds', a fact that showed up cruelly in the book that was cobbled up from 'cels' of the film. One's eye rejects the vulgar waviness of the lines in which the figures are drawn, and wanders contentedly over the distinguished backgrounds instead.

John Pett, a TV producer who had covered the Nationale exhibition as an item of cultural news, and returned a year later with a grander proposal, now reappeared again with all the paraphernalia of the BBC's *Omnibus* team to film a serious reappraisal of Searle's career. A party drawn from the 'Amis de Searle' was filmed dining at the Restaurant des Beaux-Arts, Ronald was interviewed alone, and Russell Braddon and Malcolm Muggeridge offered their now historical views. It was odd that no draughtsman was invited to estimate what difference Searle made to the whole practice of graphic satire; instead, Muggeridge was allowed to get away with remarks like 'All humour is religious', and to compare Searle with a gargoyle on a cathedral spire. Searle appeared momentarily needled by some of the questions — about his leaving England, the dread St Trinian's and the 'arrogance' of the satirist — but as they were not included in the soundtrack, one cannot tell in what tone they were asked. Pett appears at one point to have commented that Searle did not laugh much, which (though it drew a laugh) must have helped convince him that England was still a place where any distinction drawn between a satirist and a

Above: Ronald Searle in his studio, 4 rue Antoine-Dubois, Paris, 20 January 1973

Photographed by Robert Doisneau (of Doisneau-Rapho) as part of the build-up of publicity to the 1973 exhibition, Remo Forlani visited Searle on the same day to interview him for Paris-Match. *Searle's mother-and-child photograph appears in the far corner of the room; his* Graphis *cover at top left, above a copy of the* TV Guide. *(See Frontispiece for more detail.) The curious horse-shoe shape alongside Searle's head is an upturned rainbow on a cover supplied for* Vista *magazine of New York, September 1972 — the last exhibit, No. 259, in his one-man show. In the foreground lies what was to have been the centre panel of a 'Horselovers' Triptych'. This piece, then titled 'Chambre Rose' was the only one to go into a lithograph edition, under the title 'Pegasus returns'.*

comedian would be regarded as precious, or even 'arrogant'. The programme was best in its reminiscent vein, for it included Braddon's moving description of Searle at death's door in 1943, and from the artist himself the interesting revelation that on his return to England after the war he used to keep one finger held awkwardly back from his pen with sticky tape, so as to force himself to hesitate, and cut out the dangerous fluency with which daily drawing through the war had left him. He described his departure for France in 1961 as a similar handicapping process. In a way, though he did not say so, he was now undergoing another.

A British reviewer, in *The Listener*, summed up by saying that 'Searle is so taut and versatile that anything may be expected of him', but at the same time intimated that he had found the tautness worrying. Searle, he said, had a 'jumpy, nerve-strained manner. He blurted out assertions about his work and life in general as though his arm were being twisted.' This of course was written in ignorance of the kind of strain Searle was suffering. In the early part of 1975, Monica spent three whole months laying abed in the dark, on 'a permanent drug trip', her blood-count down to almost nothing. It would have been abominable even if conditions in the Rue Antoine-Dubois had been ideal, which they were not. They never really had been, for the actress Micheline Presle lived at No. 6 – through the bathroom wall – where she had installed a swimming-pool on the fifth floor of a seventeenth-century house. Her hi-fi equipment and what sounded like a Hammond organ were stacked up against the wall; and since the actress's life began when she returned from the theatre at night, appalling noises would come through in the small hours.

That was just annoyance; harassment was a different matter. Notice had come from the young and ambitious landlord that he wished to install a lift in the building (raising its rent-category in the process), a proposal which the Searles resisted. A nuisance campaign was begun, in which scaffolding was erected outside the house, radios left blaring by windows. At one point the roof was taken off – all this with Monica facing the worst crisis in more than five years of the drug campaign. On 11 April 1975 a formal letter of expulsion arrived. The Searles could have taken the matter further – they did consult the eminent lawyer Maître Suzanne Blum about it – but the assault on their nerves had been too well timed. They were exhausted. Ronald was convinced that Monica would die if they had to endure much more of the same. So they resolved to get out of Paris for good. Down in Haute-Provence, workmen had assured them that their house would be ready in September. They waited until then, and went. Their plane took off at 4 p.m. on 10 September 1975. He had not intended it, but the date happened to be the fourteenth anniversary of Ronald's arrival in France.

SEVEN

Moi Searle
(1975–90)

The difference between the latter fifteen years in Ronald Searle's life and the fifty-five previous ones is that things have been gradually dissuaded from happening to him. He, meanwhile, has been able to establish the rules whereby he happens to them. Exile alone had not wrought the changes hoped for in 1961. True, Paris had proved more interesting than London in its expectations of Searle, and more alert in its appraisal of his work, but in its day-to-day demands on his time it had become, if anything, more insistent than anything he had known. His availability had become his enemy again. Perhaps because he destroyed it so much more casually this time, in a seemingly instinctive flight from persecution, the loss of it never bothered him.

Naturally the house in Haute-Provence was not ready at all by September 1975, so that the Searles were obliged to spend 1200 francs per month renting a place from a friend, M. Sandrini. A load of their most precious possessions followed them down from Paris, though the flat in Rue Antoine-Dubois was not actually closed up for another eighteen months. Valerios Caloutsis and his wife Effie, who lived in the flat above and faced the same harassments, agreed to look after the place, in return for which the Searles hired a member of Maître Suzanne Blum's office to press the demands of both households for compensation. In the end, the greedy young landlord — whom they had known as a child in the house — had his way, though the compensation was paid.

Just to prove that no living-space guarantees one against every sort of invasion, their still-unfinished abode gave notice of its fallibility within three weeks of the Searles' arrival in the south. An advance load of archival material and desirable objects had been parked, for safety, in a locked alcove whose floor was six inches below ground-level — as was proved when they found their boxes sitting in six inches of water. Eighteenth- and nineteenth-century books; antique dresses once worn by Monica's distant forebears in Berlin; many years of patchwork crafted by her — much of the hoard was instantly ruined. Other items rotted later. Fortunately Ronald and Monica had begun to lay down wine in their cellar, so that the drowning process could be extended to include their sorrows.

Ronald tried out the flight arrangements from Nice with a quick business trip to Munich, where for several years past his newest work had been making its public début at the Gurlitt Gallery; they were anxious now to put on their seventh Searle exhibition. Monica was ill and did not go, but the distance she had placed between herself and her medical minders seemed to have made oddly little difference. Her blood-specialist, Michel Dauge, had visited shortly after the move and lined up a local practitioner, trained to the requisite Institut Pasteur standards, to administer treatments if necessary. Schwarzenberg, too, dropped by before the end of the year. All the doctors were willing to fly in at a moment's notice in case of emergency — Monica had always been treated at home rather than at

Above: Self-portrait, 1989
Showing all the occupational hazards of the trade: prehensile appraising lips, weakened eyesight, drawing-board posture, dishevelment — and self-criticism.

Above: Ronald and Monica Searle at home, Haute-Provence, September 1976

The Searles outside their home in Haute-Provence, from which they are 'virtually impossible to budge', photographed by Claudia Desclozeaux.

the *cancérologues'* control centre in the Paris suburb of Villejuif – but their visits thereafter were paid invariably out of friendship rather than necesssity. A part of Monica had begun to think of the whole exercise as 'a great hoot', while realizing how the strain of it had worn her husband down.

The Searles slept in their own home for the first time, experimentally, in December 1975, but only in the following March did they begin to move their personal effects into the house. They became officially resident there, for the purposes of French law, on 1 April 1976. These were natural moments for drawing deep breaths of southern air and looking back at what the last few frightening years had produced in the way of work. Ronald had chosen 100 pictures from the decade 1965–75, which in consultation with his Berlin friends – Prof. Dr Henning Bock, director of the Prussian National Gallery (Gemäldegalerie, Staatliche Museen Preussischer Kulturbesitz) and Prof. Dr Alexander Dückers of its Prints and Drawings Department, the *Kupferstichkabinett* – he arranged to exhibit in early 1976. A certain amount of fanfare was unavoidable, with the press conference and television coverage, but Searle found private consolation in his access to the museum's stored collection of drawings. This time it was the hundred or so Dürers that monopolized his attention; on another visit, Dückers made available the Botticelli illustrations to Dante. It was becoming difficult to call a man a 'cartoonist' who not only had such enthusiasms but was invited to pursue them *à titre d'hommage*. His Berlin exhibition went on to tour five German towns, while in Manhattan Barbara Nicholls, late of the *New Yorker* and now a gallery-owner in her own right, was putting his American work on show. Four years had already passed since he last visited New York, and almost a decade more would go by before he saw the city again. He had worked up, not surprisingly, 'an aversion to long journeys'.

Whereas the citizens of Berlin, Hanover, Stuttgart, Mainz, Recklinghausen and Ober-hausen were now in possession of some facts about Searle's recent development, a wider reading public was not, so negotiations began with the publishers Rowohlt-Verlag over ways of putting this right. It was going to be difficult to keep up with the artist (who had sixty-nine paintings ready for Gurlitt of Munich by December 1976); and an eye would have to be kept on his new excursion into three dimensions. In 1973, Pierre Dehaye, Director of the French Mint (La Monnaie), had asked Searle in the aftermath of his Bibliothèque Nationale exhibition to design a self-portrait medal for eventual issue to subscribers. In Britain, where the concept 'medal' is almost entirely bound up with the monarchy, patronage and the approval of the state, the tradition of the art-medal is very weak; but the continent of Europe has kept alive the Renaissance practice of striking medals as personal expressions of the urge to commemorate and celebrate. Searle's *auto-médaille*, struck in June 1974 as a limited edition and subsequently issued as a general release, displayed his most famous self-portrait sketch of that period, a quite unjustly cruel three-quarter profile with giant, insect-eyes-cum-spectacle-lenses, a pulpy-looking mouth, and the left hand gripping a pencil with more force than confidence. Pierre Dehaye went on to approve a whole series of Searle medals in honour of 'Six Fathers of Caricature', none of whom (Carracci, Ghezzi, Hogarth, Gillray, Rowlandson and George Cruikshank) belonged to the French tradition at all. The same open-mindedness led Dehaye eventually to accept the proposal that La Monnaie should strike a medal in honour of Admiral Lord Nelson. The French Mint had issued many a medal in salute to their national victories, but a state medal depicting the orchestrator of one of France's most notorious defeats was quite unprecedented. That the resulting Nelson appeared with a bulbous nose, a cockeyed hat and a general air of having just been issued a double rum ration, must have mollified the Club Français de la Médaille just a little.

Searle's early medals were drawn rather than modelled: incised, that is, as designs in the flat metal rather than upheavals of it in relief. This permitted him to immortalize a delightful 'cartoon' line, particularly in the case of Carracci, who is seen boggling with dismay at the realization that his own great pudding of a nose had been replicated in the features of his rebellious-looking baby son. But these performances did not enter quite as fully as they might into the spirit of the art-medal as a sculpture in miniature; they could be seen, but did not ask to be felt. Following the flight from Paris, however, Searle did progress to three fully worked dimensions, submitting each medal design in the form of a clay maquette, and these were a literally outstanding success. Sculptural forms held no terrors at all for an artist whose celebrated line had for so long implied it; and as each maquette was the size of a large plate, Searle had every opportunity to include – and to expect to emerge in the sized-down bronze – his characteristically scrupulous yet eccentric detail.

Dehaye was fortunate in having found a medallist whose untroubled command of the idiom was matched by his strong feelings about possible subjects – who ranged, in the field of caricature, from Romeyn de Hooghe, seventeenth-century Dutch pioneer of militant political satire in graphic form, to Otto Dix, the German satirist, who had died as recently as 1969. Searle's scholarship in these matters had been refreshed by his participation in a vast and sumptuous history of the genre, *La Caricature, Art et Manifeste*, in 1974; but among his medal subjects were some who lay outside the scope even of such an apparently inclusive tome – De Hooghe was one, and another was the extraordinary Mexican-Indian José Guadalupe Posada (1852–1913), an engraver, printer and pamphleteer whose political imagery, designed to impress a largely illiterate public, ranged from traditional folk symbols (chiefly skeletons) to completely personal visions. In an essay on Posada in the *Bulletin du Club Français de la Médaille*, Searle revealed that the Mexican had anticipated him in the depiction of a giant snail, a symbol of progress dragged along

Left: Lord Nelson, design for commemorative medal, French Mint, June 1980

Struck in bronze and silver, limited edition of 100 examples. On the reverse is depicted the death of Horatio Nelson (1758–1805), with sobbing Britannia, at Trafalgar.

Above left: José Guadalupe Posada, design for commemorative medal, French Mint, 1978

Struck in honour of the Mexican printer, engraver and propagandist.

Above right: Obverse design for Posada medal, French Mint, 1978

The design is based on the calavera, *a Mexican popular image favoured by Posada, and sold particularly around the time of All Saints' Day, in which performing skeletons mock various aspects of the behaviour of the living.*

by an impatient populace. On the medal, Searle's version of Posada's head, worked up from the two dim extant photographs of the artist, is a magnificent creation, heaving itself out of a background of capering skeletons realized in his own style. Fat, baleful and even slightly bullying, Posada's face offered just the sort of mass of convexities that in the past has shown resistance to Searle's style; but here the improbable jowls loomed out with absolute authority, their polished bronze slopes almost suggesting the sweaty sheen of a fat man in a hot climate. These caricatural medals spoke so directly to the eye that they made contemporaneous medal-portraits, done in 'straight' styles, look rather like the coinage of some doctrinaire republic of Eastern Europe.

Searle drew particular satisfaction from those of his modern European subjects – Dix, Grosz, John Heartfield – which brought him into contact with the families of these artists. The responsibility of achieving a caricatural likeness without giving offence, often while working from photographs provided by the families themselves, was a heavy one. But the rewards were great, in sheer relief alone, when a positive verdict came back. Sometimes a correspondence would bring an unexpected and useful insight into the subject himself, as when Martha Dix emphatically denied that her husband had ever regarded his work, even partly, as caricature. Looking at people, she asserted, Otto Dix saw more or less through them, and what he painted was the impression he received. Frau Dix sounded a very decided character, so it was cheering to hear, from her address in Otto-Dix Weg, Gaienhofen, that the expression of Dix on the medal was 'very typical, and I like the ears'. 'You made me very happy,' Searle replied. To Gertrud Heartfield, widow of the raucously satirical specialist in anti-Nazi photomontage, John Heartfield (Helmut Herzfelde), he sent some words of explanation as to his design:

> For the front of the medal I have tried to give the impression of a man of action, poised not with a rapier but with the equally effective weapon, scissors. Sizing-up the enemy, intense, and in control.
>
> In the background, a three-dimensional version of one of John Heartfield's – to me – most biting montages and typical of his marvellous work ...

For the back of the medal I have again made a three-dimensional version of that Nazi wolf, which seemed to me to sum up the focal point of your husband's struggle to reveal the fascists as they are.

Both compositions seem to me satisfactory although, naturally, to interpret a two-dimensional original in relief poses technical problems, and forces minor adjustments, as clay is not as fluid as photomontage ...

So, I speed these pictures to you in fear and trepidation ...

Sensing the genuine anxiety behind this, Frau Heartfield replied with a compassionate telegram to say that the front of the medallion pleased her very much. A month later she reported that it had taken her a little while to get used to the obverse, which looked very grim – 'but so was fascism'. The whole process posed an unusual challenge to Searle, in that he was avowedly anxious to please a known audience of one. It was not at all like trying to please an editor (to whom it would have been useless, for a start, to explain what one's *intentions* had been). Almost all of his other work produced an impact he never saw on people from whom he never heard; but in these instances, nerve-rackingly, he needed to hear at once. A discouraging word might have destroyed Searle's faith in the work; the 'fear and trepidation' were not rhetorical.

To be involved in honouring George Grosz, whose work had introduced him in 1939 to the possibilities of pictorial rage and scorn in a twentieth-century context, was an even greater responsibility and pleasure. The shape of Grosz's career – politically motivated to a savage degree in Weimar Germany, then wilfully docile and quiescent during an unsatisfactory American period that ended with a final brief return to Germany – remained controversial. It was said that he had repudiated his early work for the wrong reasons, gone over to a flabby middle-class enemy he had once detested, and failed in any case in his accommodation to the bourgeoisie. Searle, who had also seen the worst too soon, and struggled to reconcile disenchantment of many kinds (including the political) with aesthetic delight, was in a better position than most to understand his predecessor's difficulties.

Above left: Otto Dix, design for commemorative medal, French Mint, 1977

Dix (1891–1969) was a powerful social satirist during the Weimar Republic, devoting an academic technique to the depiction of the horrors of a society heedless of its own decadence. His work was suppressed by the Nazis, and its continuing social realism found greater favour after the war in East Germany than in the West.

Above right: George Grosz, design for commemorative medal, French Mint, 1977

Grosz (1893–1959) was perhaps the most deadly of Berlin satirists because of the economy of his technique: a simple outline of a fat profiteer or a crippled war-veteran sufficed to carry the weight of his disgust. Detesting Nazism, but unsure that the far Left offered the best vehicle for resistance to it, he emigrated to the United States, but never rediscovered an appropriate tone for his productions. He died a few weeks after returning to Berlin.

Above left: John Heartfield, design for commemorative medal, French Mint, 1977

Helmut Herzfelde (1891–1968) changed his name during the Great War, as a gesture of protest against the Kaiser's 'Gott strafe England!' ('May God punish England!'). His ultra-modern 'photomontages' expressed some of the most direct anti-Nazi propaganda ever devised, though the method was too vivid and dangerous to find favour in post-war East Germany, where Heartfield later settled.

Above right: Obverse design for Heartfield medal, French Mint, 1977

This design was felt by his widow to be very grim, 'but so was Fascism'.

Their temperaments had a certain amount in common, as one could feel in the essay Searle contributed to the medallists' *Bulletin*:

> By nature he was an outsider and, even as a convinced communist, he could not convincingly swallow a party line that glorified the proletariat as privileged representatives of all that was pure and good.
>
> Basically he was misanthropic, recognising that Man, whatever his class or political flavour, was equally capable of being squalid, sordid and bestial. He also had to admit that Man could be equally good. This conflicting combination in him enabled him to turn a global, if jaundiced, eye on the scene around him. As much as he might pretend to be single-minded, he could not escape the exigencies of his art or his infallible instinct for hitting the nerve of his subject.

Every man who looks into the life of another is liable to find what looks like a chunk of himself, waiting to be described; there was a fair-sized nugget of Searle in this.

Approval in principle for a Grosz medal came from the artist's son, Peter Grosz, of Princeton, New Jersey, and the finished article went into production in 1977, the same year in which Searle provided a *Gedenktafel*, or memorial plaque, for the wall of the house in the Charlottenburg district of Berlin where Grosz died in 1959. Revealingly, Searle could not bear to depict Grosz simply as a staring portrait head; he had to be following the dictates of line, as Searle himself did. The rectangular metal plate was engraved with a drawing of the pipe-smoking Grosz concentrating fiercely on the completion of a group picture of his typical Weimar revellers and *mutilés de guerre*. This was unveiled in a pavement ceremony that included a speech from Alexander Dückers, in which the *Kupferstichkabinett* director reminded the throng of Grosz's contention that draughtsmanship could indeed be a weapon against brutality and stupidity, as long as it was wielded by a clear-minded will and a schooled hand. Searle was standing by to approve these words, which he could have written himself. Peter Grosz, who attended the ceremony, gave him a page from a Grosz sketchbook dated 1912/13 – a sturdy nude, and again, gratifyingly like the ones Ronald had drawn at a similar age.

The same month-long trip – their last absence of such a length from their southern home – took the Searles to Paris, where the novelist Martin Amis spent a day profiling them for a Sunday supplement. They met, evidently, in the Restaurant des Beaux-Arts ('the restaurant walls were adorned with Searles; the proprietress had often fed them in less prosperous times'), and Amis likened the occasion to trying to eat on the Centre Court at Wimbledon: 'Like many couples who have become committed to one another in times of stress and uncertainty, they talk to you simultaneously, finishing each other's sentences, improving on each other's phrases . . .' Searle was a 'springy, alert but delicate-looking man' with angular features and a 'duellist's beard . . . he doesn't look like an artist, exactly – more like the intelligent art-master of an old-fashioned school'. More and more, Searle was being appraised by people who had never known a time when he and his drawings were not there; they always communicated a slight surprise that this institution had a continuing life of its own. Amis was amazed at how freely all the subjects he had trained himself to avoid were voluntarily aired: 'Monica's breast cancer for instance . . .was equally discussed (she held up her arms in triumph).' There was time in the day only for a quick riffle through Searle's work – some of it cats – so the piece emerged as a personal reintroduction to Searle himself, and an explanation of why Britain appeared to have lost him. The explanation did not include the fact that yet another St Trinian's film was under discussion, but then Ronald very likely did not mention it.

Nor would he have insisted that Amis invest in his latest (and almost last) collaborative book, *Paris! Paris!*, with its text by the American novelist Irwin Shaw. For one thing, the book was not really a collaboration at all; it might have been better described as a coincidence, or better still a mere simultaneity. Shaw and Searle had simply been brought together within the same covers; they did not confer at all. If they had, Searle might have raised the odd doubt about the sticky mixture of self-serving anecdote and litanistic cliché that made up Shaw's text. Searle's drawings were split off into sections of their own, setting up pockets of resistance to Shaw's view, and printed (as Searle was able to say ten years later when the drawings were rescued for a volume of their own) very much too small. To avoid all pseudo-partnerships of this kind was the lesson. The only one Searle subsequently entered into was *Too Many Songs by Tom Lehrer with Not Enough Drawings by Ronald Searle*, whose great fault was the aptness of its title.

Returning to the south for Christmas 1977, the Searles were followed down by a television crew from the French TF1 TV channel. It was Monica's turn to be the star. Her Professor, Léon Schwarzenberg, had co-written a prize-winning book, called *Changer la Mort*, about the progress of the fight against cancer; and the TV producer Igor Barrère wished to present some of the living evidence for the optimism expressed in that work. Monica readily agreed, in the knowledge that among the French public the subject of cancer was not yet discussed with the rational detachment on which the nation otherwise prided itself. In fact France was more than averagely taciturn and superstitious about it. The programme, *Monika, Christophe et d'Autres* – Christophe was a boy who had contracted cancer through an eye injury at the age of six – was transmitted the following April, and opened up a useful discussion in the press. Cured, and 'serene', Monica was quoted as describing her state as 'paradise, with hell tacked on *here*' – gesturing to the breast still on fire from the bombardment of radiation. If she had showed courage, she said, it was the courage of the coward: she was 'such a coward that she did not dare despair'. In a

Above: 'La Place des Amis Réunis',
Paris! Paris!, with Irwin Shaw,
London, 1977

*A composite square in which a large
number of Searle's friends are saluted
by name. Among them are the graphic
artists Jean-Pierre Desclozeaux,
Roland Topor, 'Tim' (Louis
Mitelberg), André François, Hans
Georg Rauch; writers like David
Arkell, Mary Blume, Remo Forlani;
medical professors Léon Schwarzenberg and Jean Hewitt; film
actors Pierre Etaix and Deanna
Durbin (Mme Charles David) and
'Mô' (Monica Searle) and her sister
Marion. (Drawing used as endpapers
for* Ah Yes, I Remember It Well . . .,
1987.)

small but pleasantly practical way, the liberating effect of the programme overflowed on to the Searles themselves, for on the morning after its transmission the whole village seemed to be clamouring to congratulate Monica on her contribution, and indeed her recovery. Much of the local suspicion of this slightly mysterious and self-sufficient foreign couple was dissipated in one salutary evening.

If Ronald's own health had a weakness, it was in the bronchial area, where he was troubled by regular infections and wheezes. All through his career, he had been a steady smoker – pen in left hand, cigarette in right. Now, as if to reassert that he, too, had a body, he fell ill for a whole month. The cigarettes were laid aside for the duration of the bout, and never picked up again. He was back at work just in time to deal with the advance rumblings of an avalanche of proofs from Rowohlt, publication of whose retrospective Searle album was scheduled for October, with French and English translations following a month later. This was much the bulkiest Searle collection so far. Its 236 listed items made it comparable in scale with the Bibliothèque Nationale exhibition; and the selection was preceded by sixteen pages of biographical apparatus, including a brief survey of his early work, and his own tersely jocular timetable of events ('1967: Father died. Divorced. Married Monica. Married by *Time* magazine to another lady'). The selected work, most of it printed full-page and in colour, at last revealed the themes with which Searle had been working – in pen and watercolour, inks, or six-colour lithography – over the previous decade. The classic features of a Searle earthscape had certainly changed. In

place of the hectic but friendly architectural binges of his tourist-Gothic reportage days, an abstract plain now predominated. The sense of horizon was perhaps his one major inheritance from the work of Steinberg – though Searle's play with the intimidating expanse of sky liberated by this low cut-off point (in which, perhaps, some memory of the vast East Anglian flatlands played a part) showed a quite unrelated exuberance. In these 'painted desert' pictures, some creature in the foreground is always getting things wrong. A grey man reads a grey newspaper while the rising sun is filling the sky behind him with a riotous blah of colour. A 'sensitive' pig, by contrast, is moved to tears by a similar heavenly spectacle, but does not seem to notice the muck in which it sits. A blind man shuffles trustingly into the future, unaware that his guide-dog is a fanged demon with three tails and that the hot pink glow of the firmament swarms with weird moons.

These scenes struck some observers as preachy, a conclusion perhaps encouraged by the book's opening essay, a ponderous apologia by Henning Bock, rendered almost unreadable by translation into English. Mark Boxer (the cartoonist 'Marc'), writing in the *New Statesman*, quoted Bock as revealing that 'Searle is no longer interested in mocking individuals.' This struck Boxer as

> sad news ... His subjects now tend to be cosmic ... sadly Searle has forsaken being
> funny for being 'meaningful'. The trouble is that Searle draws a stereotyped world
> which he hasn't looked at properly for a long time ... His standard businessman
> belongs to the pre-war world of [John Phillips?] Marquand; Hollywood has updated its

Above left: 'The Camembert Connection', *Paris! Paris!*, with Irwin Shaw, London, 1977

Sights, sounds and above all scents of a typical Parisian cour. A fascinating test-piece for students of advanced trickery in perspective.

Above right: From *Paris! Paris!*, with Irwin Shaw, London, 1977

Paris-registered 2CV in a typical predicament. The appearance of the owner suggests a location close to the Searles' home in the student quarter on the Left Bank. The architectural authenticity of the doorway makes all the difference to the effectiveness of the scene.

prototypes better than he has ... Searle's work over the last ten years makes rather bleak viewing, often rendered trivial by being pretty, his symbol of merit a blancmange rising sun. Although a cartoonist can be exasperated by man, he should still be amused and intrigued by him.

This was quite the most unfriendly review Searle had received in a long time. 'Marc' spoke, of course, as a cartoonist of the social gadfly type, priding himself on his familiarity with the latest fashionable snobberies; but to cast Searle as a failed competitor in the same race was unfair, and even under-informed in view of Searle's continuing critique of the prosperous West German business world – a satirical undertaking quite as aware as anything England was producing. As for colour – and Searle has tended to be plagued by critics who, seeing his colour work, have suddenly discovered that they were devotees of purist pen-and-ink – the supposedly trivializing 'prettiness' it imposed on the work was more often notable for ironic excess: colour overdone to make a point. Those sun-filled skies, far from symbolizing merit, were vulgar rather than beautiful: their obviousness made man's unawareness of them all the more remarkable. In other cases, colour marked the garish overreaction of a universe molested by man; these strange beauties were symptoms of disease. Nature is forced into all manner of perversion in this collection. Amid a world of junk, butterflies are attracted by the floral pigmentation of a hairy hippie's uniform, or flowers painted on the label of a tin can on a garbage dump. If this was preachy, then the sermon was timely – well ahead of its time, in fact, since such messages are only now, in the closing years of the century, credited as realistic warnings. Searle, typically, advanced the idea into the inverted absurdity of a situation where we are 'so alienated from nature by modern urban life that we panic when a tendril or a little paw manages to emerge from the concrete' (thus Ronald Blythe in *The Listener*). But the point about these re-emergences lies in their aggressiveness. A strong premonition pervades the book that Nature will revenge herself in 'unnatural' ways – the giant rose falling on the terrified city, the outlandish bloom that bursts up through the desk of a businessman (who, looks all too well-accustomed to the post-war world). Nature's ability to fight back with new and deadly weapons is now respected as a factor in all our policy-making. Searle was among those who got there first.

The review he had been waiting for came from Richard Holmes in *The Times*:

It still remains, of course, fundamentally, just a collection of contemporary cartoons; but a collection of such technical brilliance, such endless fantasy, and such moral questioning, that the overall effect is much larger and more problematic than I, certainly, ever believed was possible in this essentially minor genre ...

It is notable that Searle's most nearly evil creations – the bloated businessman with face like a sack of drowned kittens, or the psychopathic prisoners (yes ...) of the truly terrifying 'Some Complexes' series – almost invariably have no eyes. Either they are blanked-over with the pebble-spectacles of egoism, or the mascara of lust, or the flesh-folds of greed. Or else they are simply empty orbits, burnt out by power, or gouged out by cruelty – self-inflicted wounds. If you still have eyes to see, the cartoonist seems to say, then you still have hope – and possibly grace.

This was getting much closer to the real complexities of the drawings – especially when Holmes, in analysing the blind-man-and-dog painting, pointed out that it was funny 'most of all because the monster is so much better adapted to his apocalyptic pantomime world, and so much more endearing, than the pitiable man'. Endearing monsters; man his own dupe – Searle had entered a realm of un-English paradox, though there were still those at home who could appreciate it.

Reactions to the book confirmed what sales figures had already been telling Searle: that his most heartfelt work remained too challenging for the 'popular' market, and would not keep him fed and clothed. A statement from the publishers Librairie Arthème Fayard, detailing returns to 31 December 1977, showed that over the previous ten years his book *L'Oeuf Cube et le Cercle Vicieux* – alias *The Square Egg* – in which the 'cosmic' Searle had begun to show himself, had sold a total of 949 copies. It was no wonder that in the meantime there had been cats and *More Cats* (1975), and *Searle's Zoodiac* (1977) with its extended vocabulary of animalisms, realized with almost overpowering elegance. And all the time, a regular tide of parcels swept across the Atlantic to feed the art editors of the *New York Times* and *Travel and Leisure*, *Money* magazine and *Sports Illustrated*, *Vista* (the magazine of the United Nations Association) and the *TV Guide*. John Locke in New York was keeping a whole continent of possibilities open. Yet perhaps Searle himself was more closely in touch with Manhattan than anyone imagined, through his own improbable lines of communication. What else are we to make of an incident that occurred on a pleasantly mild night of 17–18 October 1979, while Ronald lay in bed between sleeping and waking. He has described it thus:

> Suddenly an old friend appeared before me, looking like a gently spotlit figure on a darkened stage. I felt no surprise at all. She was, as always, relaxed and friendly. Her arms were folded across the jacket of her well-travelled tweed costume showing off nicely the choice selection of rings she was wearing. Only one finger moved, to tap ash from an ashless cigarette. (She always tapped more than she smoked.)

Left: 'Atlas', 1979

The gormless animal kingdom admires an almost equally gormless (and much more miserable) Man for shouldering the Great Burden of Doubt. (Made available as a lithograph through the Galerie Cassé.)

The apparition was Laura West Perelman, sister of the writer Nathanael West, and wife of the inimitable Sid. She had died in April 1970.

> But here she was, nearly ten years later, very much alive and looking me straight in the eye. With her usual laconic American drawl, she spoke, coming directly to the point as usual:
>
> 'RAHnald, Sid's dead,' she said. Then she was no longer there.
>
> In the morning, before I had even got to my coffee, the telephone rang. My sister-in-law was calling from London,
>
> 'Sad news, I'm afraid. I've just heard on the radio that Sid Perelman has been found dead in his hotel room in New York . . .'

Sid had died at the Gramercy Park Hotel during the night of the 16–17 October. Searle describes this as 'a very *small* ghost story: but it certainly impressed me at the time'. He still awaits Sid's explanation.

At every level, it seemed, Searle's object had been achieved: rather than requiring his presence everywhere else, the world was coming to him. Flesh-and-blood visitors were received strictly by appointment and invitation only, and knew better than to bring along either children or animals (though the photographer Brassaï, a friend from far back in *Lilliput* days, did turn up with both his wife and a cat, for which unique exception was made). A visitor from a brand-new generation of acquaintance was John Goelet, owner of the Clos De Val vineyards in the Napa Valley, California, and the Taltarni Vineyard of Victoria, Australia. Searle's bilious approach to wine ritual had already shown up strongly in his illustrations to George Rainbird's *The Subtle Alchemist*. He kept in personal touch with developments in the wine world by drinking them. For his admirer Goelet he was the ideal man to give promotional material a character and authority, and fun, no other producer could boast. Signed to a contract in 1978, Searle began two years later to explore a territory he found to be rich in hyperbole, hypocrisy, double-talk and sheer mystification. To expose all this on behalf of a product he approved was a pleasure: and, unlike much of Searle's advertising output, the wine material would prove splendidly collectable for book purposes.

As he moved into the Eighties (spending his sixtieth birthday accompanying Monica to Paris for some dental work), Ronald could afford to entertain the agreeable feeling that he had given the world so much to get on with that it was having difficulty keeping up. In Germany, Rowohlt had just issued a revised conflation of the Hamburg and Toulouse-Lautrec drawings. In England, *Wildcats of St Trinian's* (cunning of them to get cats into it) was about to kill off the genre, perhaps definitively. The French Mint stood ready to issue a medal in commemoration of an English subject they may never have heard of before Searle told them – 'Tim Bobbin' (John Collier, 1708–86), a caricaturist and satirical writer of whose reputation precious few Englishmen are aware either. Searle also had the great pleasure of designing a medal in praise of his old friend André François, issued in the autumn just as the latest Searle cartoon collection, *The King of Beasts*, was appearing in London.

This apparently slight, unpaginated book was in its way quite a style-setter. Searle had long ago given up hoping that the mass public could be weaned away from the delusion that its adored animals were in fact intelligent. His only recourse was to depict a gallery of animals who behaved stupidly even by animal standards, completely failing to live up to the stereotypes laid down by language – 'brave as a lion', 'wolf in sheep's clothing',

Ronald Searle *The Ruhr*
1963

Right: 'Wine Ceremonies of the World: South Africa. Colourful Ceremony of Offering Limited Recognition to the Black Grape', *Something in the Cellar*, London, 1986

Enthusiasts for his earlier Winespeak found an unexpectedly strong political content in this 1986 collection, the majority of whose colour originals are held either in the Cooper-Hewitt Museum, New York City, or the private collection of Mr and Mrs John Goelet.

Opposite: New York Times *poster campaign, 1985–6*

The theme of the campaign was 'reader involvement'. Searle says: 'I delivered my first poster in July 1985 and the campaign went on for about 18 months. About ten were finished and used, out of the twenty ideas I proposed.'

There's no 𝕿𝖎𝖒𝖊𝖘 like the present.

Irresistible
The New York Times

Feb. 17, 1973

THE NEW YORKER

Price 50 cents

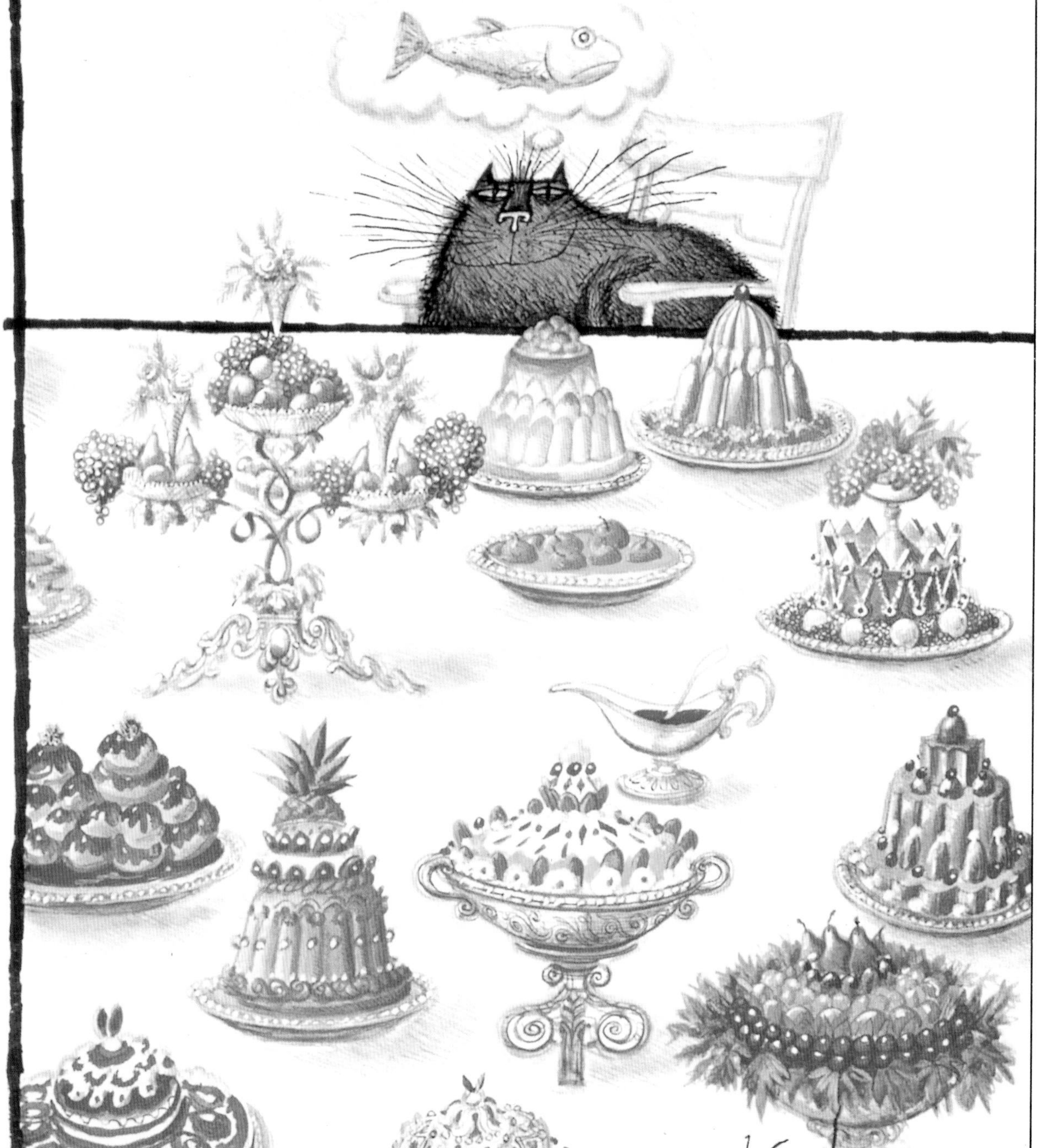

THE NEW YORKER

June 5, 1989   Price $1.75

Opposite: New Yorker cover,
17 February 1973

In an interview with the cartoonist
Mel Calman (Radio Times, 12 June
1975), Searle stated that he 'got the
idea for the fish "thinks" bubble last
of all'. The drawing was published in
Ronald Searle (1978) with the title
'They're all against me.'

Left: New Yorker cover, 5 June 1989

Now that happy relations have been
restored between Searle and the New
Yorker *his appearances on the cover
are quite frequent. He says (13 June
1990): 'I find that I have done more
covers for the New Yorker (31 since
1969) than I did for Punch (23
between 1955 and 1964).'*

Below: Saturday Evening Post cover,
10 February 1968

Another of Searle's subliminally
refreshing right-facing profiles. The
Post *had been in difficulties, and had
cut down from weekly to twice-
monthly at some times of the year in
1962, when P. G. Wodehouse wrote
to Searle: 'I have long been an admirer
of your work, and I remember those
splendid illustrations you did for my
serial in Collier's. What a shame
that paper has gone. It looks as if the
Saturday Evening Post were going
that way, too' (P.G.W. to R.S.,
1 August 1962).*

Left: 'Flat Cats', 1975

Woven into the general cat-theme are
a number of 'encounters' in which
dull, conventional humans are
confronted with confident, usurping
cats, whose repertoire of sociability
seems much broader than their own.

Above left: 'A Bigger Slash: Hommage à D. Hockney', unpublished except as lithograph, 1984

The 'hommage' is genuine enough, as Searle admired Hockney's draughtsmanship, but his view of the poolside ambience is perhaps more jaundiced. The authenticity of the angle of the falling figure's membrum virilis is for aerodynamicists to argue over.

Above right: French Revolution Bicentennial Postcard, 1989

Revolutionary étude, *1789–1989.* Métro *entrance design by Hector Guimard.*

Left: 'Some corner of a foreign field that is for ever England ...', 1981

Said by the artist to be a 'Telescopic photo, taken through the ladies' room of a well-known Port Said hostelry.' This is a terrible revenge by Searle on his creation: this poor girl, probably a 'swot' briskly exported in the white-slave traffic, need be no more than forty years old.

Right: American Express publicity folder ('Travel Related Services'), 1989

It is the opinion of the Chief Executive Officer of the Direct Marketing Group, Travelers' Cheques, as expressed in this folder, that 'as long as the Card-member continues to receive significant and measurable value, both real and perceived, *the relationship will flourish.'* Searle's contribution belongs to the 'perceived' category.

Below left: 'Loquacious parrot convinced that it is teaching man a basic vocabulary', *The King of Beasts and other Creatures,* London, 1980

The drawings 'seem merely capricious', said Tom Wolfe in the New York Times, *'until one begins to fit the beasts to their human counterparts'.*

Below right: 'American bald eagle suddenly realizing that its leanings are basically Marxist', *The King of Beasts,* London, 1980

Human counterparts to this particular type are perhaps rarer now than they were in 1980.

and so on. What almost all his gormless beasts possessed in common, from the 'out-of-touch unicorn unaware that it is a myth' to the 'exhibitionist donkey about to make an ass of itself', was a pair of contiguous eyeballs, often arranged vertically for added imbecility, and denoting an innocent hopefulness bordering on the clinically brainless. Searle had used this effect before, particularly in his depiction of birds, whose brains were proverbially tiny anyway, and to humans when deprived of their powers of ratiocination by greed or lust. But the success of these frogspawn eyeballs in *The King of Beasts* seems to have recommended them to Searle as a permanent weapon in his armoury of scorn, with the result that man and beast have shared this ocular affliction ever since. In the latter-day Searle cartoon, not even the most rarified of intellectuals can expect to find his eyeballs confined within the perimeter of his face – although the occasional pretty girl gets away with it, saved by her eyelashes.

Under the more attractively doom-laden title *The Situation Is Hopeless*, the book was published in the United States the following spring, receiving the accolade of a front-page notice in the *New York Times Book Review*. The piece was written by Tom Wolfe (billed as the author of *The Real Stuff*, which will not have pleased the author of *The Right Stuff*), who reckoned the book to be Searle's fiftieth, counting collaborations. Nevertheless, it was worthwhile reminding readers what Searle had done:

Searle created a new approach to caricature by combining the highly conventionalised, two-dimensional drawing that came out of French modernism with a peculiarly British attention to details of costume, furniture, architecture, ornament, facial expression, gesture and the bric-à-brac of social life. The contradiction between the simplicity of line and the clutter of the content tends to make even the most pointless Searle drawing funny.

That was as plain-speaking a summary of Searle's contribution to the medium as anyone had yet brought off, and it was backed up by evident familiarity with the *oeuvre*:

His modernist line and British eye for social detail achieved their consummation in [the] drawings collected in the book, *Which Way Did He Go?*, in 1961. They rank among the finest drawings of cities since Doré's London drawings of 1872.

The animal jokes in the volume under discussion, Wolfe explained, 'seem merely capricious until one begins to fit the beasts to their human counterparts'. Of the four lions included, two were:

dishevelled and rather neurasthenic monarchs. One is a 'feeble-minded circus lion basking in the belief that it is the King of Beasts.' These three may have a special meaning for Searle's British audience, which finds itself no longer in the Twilight of Empire but in that sort of radioactive black light popular in the yobbo discos of Manchester.

That last detail, of course, was highly characteristic of Wolfe himself, and his own (British-inspired?) attention to the 'bric-à-brac of social life'.

Searle had seldom been reviewed with such intelligent acceptance. The piece probably ensured by itself that he would receive that year's 'Illustrator of the Year' award – a 'Reuben' – from America's National Cartoonists' Society, which was duly accepted for him by Les Lilley, Chairman of the Cartoonists' Club of Great Britain, at the Plaza Hotel in April 1981. These proceedings constituted something of a *rapprochement* between Searle

Opposite: 'Pollution', 1972
Gnomic pen-and-watercolour suggesting the unnatural beauties of a diseased universe.

and the American brethren after a certain awkwardness had arisen between them in 1974. It was an old story, relating to a Reuben Searle had won, but not been present to collect, fully thirteen years earlier. In June 1974, *Cartoonist Profiles* reprinted a version of the tale which, it said, 'apparently has been told around various barrooms in recent years', concerning the Reuben for 1960. According to legend, Rube Goldberg, cartoonist and designer of the Reuben statuette, had attempted personally to deliver the object to the winner at 'Searle's palatial digs in Surrey [*sic*]'. So palatial were they that it was only by giving 'three polite down beats on the massive bronze knocker' that Rube had been able to announce himself – whereupon a liveried butler opened the door, asked him to wait, and returned at last with the message: 'Mr Searle said to thank you for this award. He is sorry, but he is too busy to see you. Good day, sir.' Searle was invited to supply his own version, which he did with a wearied patience, 1974 being not the easiest of years in which to spare energy for such a task. He had characteristically filed away all the dated documentation concerning the award, and was able to show convincingly that neither he, nor his agent John Locke, had realized that there was a Reuben to collect; they had thought there was one Reuben only, kept for the purposes of symbolic presentation. At his most formidable when offended, Ronald concluded his reply with an extension of the imagined scene, as poor Rube Goldberg was turned away from the mansion door:

> No doubt a surly gamekeeper hurried that frail figure through the massive gates (Bronze. What else?) of the grouse-covered drive, making a final brutish gesture with his umbrella to hasten the departing chauffeur-driven car and uttering uncouth oaths into the rapidly thickening fog until he could no longer be seen . . .
>
> What a pity it is not a good story. It lacks wit, humour and inventiveness. One would have hoped for a higher standard from the cartoon profession. Alas, the ability to draw is not necessarily accompanied by intelligence and imagination.
>
> Anyway – does the story matter? Yes, it does, for one reason. On this occasion, the NCS chose to give their award to a non-American artist for the first time and it is disagreeable to be accused unjustly and inaccurately of being churlish about it.

In and out of his work, Searle suffered fools with a patience whose surface glittered with the steely possibility of something more painful. Sometimes he gave up trying to explain himself and simply refused to co-operate, as in the case of the annual nomination he received – throughout a whole decade – as Canada's 'Cartoonist of the Year'. Mr Robert LaPalme, of the International Salon of Cartoons in Montreal, wrote year after year to declare Searle the winner of the poll, and with unchanging resolve Searle turned him down. No lack of enthusiasm for Canada was involved – he had spent more time there than most international satirists do – but only a distaste for the network of obligations involved in accepting the award, including presence in Montreal, supply of a one-man show of originals, donation of one original to the permanent collection, duty as president of the Salon jury and general availability for all ancillary functions and promotions. For tourist-class plane fare and $200 pocket-money it was not the kind of thing a travel-weary Searle was keen to go in for, and he did not. Canada finally gave up on him in 1984. 'I suppose it must have seemed rather arrogant to all those colleagues who generously . . .voted for me, but before such propositions I cringe . . .'

Ronald had lived more than twenty years in France. Aside from a December visit to Berlin or Vienna on gallery affairs, his trips abroad had become rare. All his work was dispatched from his village by post, a process which involved not only the insecurities we all experience with postal services, but actual restrictions on the work itself, in that no postal packet could be accepted in France if it exceeded 90 cm in combined length, width and thickness. To fit some drawings into packet size taxed the ingenuity even of an ex-professional parcel-packer like Ronald Searle. 'I have been known,' he admitted, 'to fold a large picture in half to get it away, and leave it to John Locke to invisibly-mend and remount his end ... In fact, 90 per cent of the time I drew to fit the packet.' (The later introduction of the Chronopost system solved this problem entirely.) Local conditions otherwise had little effect on output at all, save during forty-eight catastrophic hours in August 1982, when huge fires came close to invading the village. Ronald and Monica, doing her best with her weakened arm, stood in a chain of visitors and passed water-buckets, while forty square miles of land were burnt black, right up to the threshold of the village square.

Searle was still coughing amid the ash and vestigial fumes from chemical extinguishers when the *Sunday Times* appeared, in the person of Philip Norman, to carry out another check-up on behalf of the British public. Searle was photographed bracing himself moodily against a carbonized tree. If British readers wished to hear that he was fretting to get back to them, the news was bad. 'He gets up at six,' Monica reported, 'fetches the bread and reads the paper. Then he works for 11 hours. It's all he ever wants to do.' The work went through the same editorial hoops as ever. He often got rejections, Searle told Norman. 'I haven't had a *New Yorker* cover accepted for about two years.' (The reasons for this, which he did not enumerate, had to do with the appointment of a new Art Editor, Lee Lorenz, who took a more active line than his predecessor, Geraghty, in requesting changes to submitted work. A frost descended on the relationship for a few years — now happily thawed again, though Searle and Lorenz still have not met.) When asked about the younger generation of British satirists, Searle had always previously championed Gerald Scarfe and Ralph Steadman. Possibly because his own influence was more evidently at work in Steadman, he now came out in favour of Scarfe:

> People have no right to be revolted by anything he draws. He has to draw it like that because he's *seen* it, he knows it's there ... You *have* to agonise. Scarfe does — I can tell when he comes to see me. I know *he* looks placid, too. That's the trick, you see. Inside, you have to agonize. If you're an artist and you ever once feel pleased with yourself, you're dead.

In the course of the interview, Searle mentioned the 'Changi memory' which commonly afflicted survivors of the experience with odd pockets of forgetfulness. He had lately found he'd forgotten about some of the drawings he made there. 'I looked at them again and felt quite upset, I'd forgotten how awful it was.' The time had come to do something about this legacy of reported experience. In the summer of 1983, forty years after the Siam railway slavery, Tessa Sayle, his agent (since 1976, taking over from Hope Leresche) arrived to cart back some 450 items for the consideration of the Imperial War Museum. A few months later, an agreement was signed whereby the drawings and some relevant objects — brushes, badges, hand-made POW paintbox — were deeded to the museum while remaining available to Searle in his lifetime. If he hoped by this means to get the material out of his life for ever, he was thwarted, for a book was immediately proposed which would keep him immersed in it for many a sleepless month.

Tessa Sayle also took back the clay models for his George Grosz medal, to be deposited at the British Museum. Mark Jones, the young Assistant Director of the Department of

Coins and Medals there, was keen to begin his own collaboration with Searle, and to take under the protection of his department the 'plasters' of any medals already struck in France. In October 1983, Jones went down to Haute-Provence and picked up the clays for Searle's Otto Dix, Edward Lear and James Thurber medals, and also new models for a Dickens medal to be issued to subscribers by the British Medal Art Society. The partnership's beginning was timely, for Pierre Dehaye of La Monnaie was ousted in a politically inspired row the following spring, leaving Searle without his chief supporter at the home of French medals.

Early in 1984, Ronald noted that he had not set foot in London for ten years – and that had been a day-trip, concerning the ill-fated *Dick Deadeye*. Yet he had a bestseller in Britain at that moment. *The Illustrated Winespeak*, subtitled 'Ronald Searle's Wicked World of Winetasting', had sold nearly 30,000 copies in its first two months, doing much to put Britain's Christmas bingeing into cautionary context while savaging the reputations of the professional wine-mystificators, 'that grotesque international band of snobbish inarticulate sponges, who are incapable of thinking beyond their incestuous little circles'. In the book, the images were left to speak for themselves, but in a note produced for circulation elsewhere Searle revealed that the relationship between himself and wines had been a longer and more dramatic one than might have been imagined:

> Throughout a childhood of nights punctuated by exploding bottles of over-excited elderberry, turnip, parsnip, potato, dandelion and other lethal brews concocted by my mother (a simple country girl from remotest Wiltshire), many were the family suppers that would end with me under the table pressing my spinning head on the chilly lino, to prevent it flapping its wings and circling East Anglia. No one actually fathomed why I should get flushed and have dizzy spells after a substantial meal and a mere handful of health-giving home-made natural tonic shots, containing nothing more than baker's yeast and unsullied garden produce. Probably left-handed cussedness. Either way, the lining of my stomach was on its way to non-existence before puberty struck. Add a little wood alcohol, which I unknowingly drank in Singapore, and you will understand why, for health reasons, my doctor took me off my regular, delicious cognac that I had been taking for health reasons.
>
> I don't drink whilst I am working. But when work stops I start.

As for the wine-jargon itself, Searle insisted, he had invented none of it, and gone in search of none either. It had all turned up in newspapers and magazines and direct-mail wine publicity. Not that the virulence of his feelings about food-and-wine snobbery was in any way feigned or worked up. It was traceable ultimately, he said, to the first evening of his honeymoon, which he and Monica had spent at the Confrérie des Chevaliers du Tastevin's 316th banquet in the Cistercian cellars of the Château du Clos de Vougeot:

> We ... found ourselves facing a particularly nauseating Scandinavian couple, both wine and food critics. 'Of some renown,' they swiftly impressed on us, before applying their Godlike attention exclusively to the food and drink. Enchanted by the exquisite subtlety of their analytical nuances, determined that no-one within saliva-spraying range should be deprived of their reflections on the Soufflé de Brochet Truffé Nantua accompanied by a Chablis 'Les Lys' 1964, they totally crushed any attempt at conversation or reflection from the oafish perimeter ...
>
> The male half of the Scandinavian couple swooshed an impressive gulp of ...wine

around his cavernous palate with a sound that for all the world resembled a Parisian clochard washing his feet under a handy hydrant. He then paused, swallowed significantly, rolled his watery blue eyes heavenward, leaned towards us and hissed emotionally, 'Dear God, is it heather, or is it honey?'

As a matter of fact, it was neither – it was corked. After fifteen years' storage, Ronald's indignation emerged as a book. The writing in these extracts, incidentally, shows clearly why Sid Perelman admired Searle almost as much for his turn of phrase as for his drawing.

Shepherding his old work back into hard covers was not his favourite pastime, but in the middle Eighties Searle had to do an awful lot of it. Molesworth resurfaced in 'Compleet' form. The Munchausen drawings, which so far had been published only in America, reached England in 1985, sixteen years late, and reappeared in 1988, this time with R. E. Raspe's original text instead of a 'digest' version. *Ronald Searle in Perspective*, an updated selection from more than four decades of work, came without inbuilt essayistic millstones from well-meaning critics, and was all the more buoyant for it. Some British observers persisted in saying that Searle had become too 'serious', 'meaningful', 'portentous', 'pretentious' – there are so many critical jargon words to denote something that tickles a part of your brain you wanted left alone, or insults some other part you hoped deserved flattery. In France, as ever, the story was different. Under the title *45 Ans De Dessins*, the book won the favour of France's patron saint of book-reviewing, Bernard Pivot. Not only

Above left: 'War & Patriotism', *The Great British Songbook,* compiled by Kingsley Amis and James Cochrane, London, 1986

Searle has consistently taken the Poor Bloody Infantry's view of warfare. The stricken Tommy here, like Searle's father, wears a sergeant's stripes. The condition of his left leg may pass unnoticed at first.

Above right: 'Punishwoment', *Ronald Searle's Non-Sexist Dictionary,* London, 1988

Anything labelling itself 'Non-Sexist' announces itself as potentially sexist, and Searle purists seem to prefer his jokes not to base themselves on verbal patterns: which made this a controversial volume in spite of itself.

did Pivot recommend the album on his television show *Apostrophes*; he also chose it, in consultation with *'son équipe'*, as one of the twenty best books of the year. In France this is rather like receiving the Papal imprimatur and a Book of the Month Club nomination at the same time, and Pivot went on to crown the honour by adding a plug for *Parler en Vin*, the French edition of *Winespeak*, into the bargain.

Searle was glad to receive these encouragements as he had just emerged from four months of stressful grappling with the text and drawings of his war book, which would take another fifteen months to find its way into the bookshops. At least he knew that, whatever should happen to it there, it would retain its unquestionable intrinsic importance as the only contemporary pictorial record of its time and place. No such claim would be made, he was convinced, for the short-term reissue with which he had to deal in the meantime – a volume suggested by Tessa Sayle and rejoicing in the self-explanatory name of *Ronald Searle's Golden Oldies*. Tessa Sayle's commercial instinct was to prove perfectly sound, but the book was full of material Ronald himself could scarcely bear to re-examine. His introduction rumbled with heavy irony and distaste, tinged even with a bitterness left over from the recent return of the old nightmares:

> When I joined this motley throng [of cartoonists] through having plucked the magical (until then relatively unheard) chord of black humour, my juvenile originality was accepted by editors and public alike only because, however outrageously sick or gruesome, it was always safely and cozily British. None of your Transylvanian rubbish but good, heroic stuff carried back by one of our boys from a Jap prison camp, bless him ...
>
> And yet ... the shock of recognition ... can these wrinkled oldies be those I once loved? But, of course! Those hysterical visual acrobatics, the witty anachronisms and the delicate literary nuances, the talking dogs, a desert island scene ...
>
> Obviously there are bound to be insensitive ones for whom such graphic originality is mere dross. This collection, then, is not for them. Preferring to place my faith in those multitudes who still remain addicted to the sparkling cliché and the polished pun, I reach for my daily half-bottle of champagne *blanc de blanc perlant* and toast them for their discrimination in acquiring a treasury of Golden Oldies that will, hopefully, keep me in socialist bubbly next year as well.

Short of placing a sticker on the cover reading 'YOU DO NOT FLATTER THE INTEL-LIGENCE OF EITHER OF US BY BUYING THIS BOOK', he had done his best to disown it. But of course it did very well.

What was undeniable was that, in October 1985, R. W. F. Searle (and his signature, now completely consonant with his drawing style) could raise a glass in celebration of fifty years in print. Half a century of drawing for reproduction – would the worthy Morley Stuart have believed what he had let loose upon the world? In almost the same moment, the girls of the 'real' St Trinnean's were holding a reunion lunch in Edinburgh – a roomful of fellow-sufferers from the Searle creation. He sent wine and flowers, and a short speech, to be read by Cécilé McLachlan (née Johnston), whose blushes were not spared by the text supplied: 'It all goes to show what can happen to an unsuspecting boy of twenty-one, far from home, lost in the fleshpots of Kirkcudbright, when he is invited in for a slice of haggis, a steaming cup of Glenlivet *and* allowed to hold the hands of the daughters of an Edinburgh family, who were pupils at St Trinnean's, to boot ...'

The date chosen for the publication of *To the Kwai – and Back* was Ronald's sixty-sixth birthday. His drawings had passed through the essential processes of chemical conservation and went on show at the book's official launch, at the Imperial War Museum (co-publishers with Collins), two days later. Countess Mountbatten of Burma opened the exhibition, but the artist himself was not present. A media circus populated by old comrades, journalistic colleagues and all manner of random revenants – that was not the kind of engagement he contemplated accepting any more. He was sufficiently represented by the book, which commanded a universal respect. 'The Poetry,' as *The Listener* said, 'is in the pity.' Five days later, the British Museum put on show a large selection of Searle's medal designs, but again he was not there. He had not visited England in nearly twelve years, and would not do so under any kind of spotlight. Instead, the following month, he made a very short visit to see his ninety-one-year-old mother in her retirement' home in the Midlands, a journey he has since repeated. But one has the feeling that when these visits are no longer needed, Searle's links with Britain will have perished. It would be wrong to pretend that the only consequences of the estrangements of 1961 have been positive ones, for Ronald Searle or anybody else. His relations with his children – even his daughter Katie, with whom he is in constant touch – remain problematical. He has a grandson, Johnnie's son Daniel, whom he has never seen. These are abiding sadnesses.

Some reunions Ronald could stand. In September 1985, after a thirteen-year break, he had returned to New York, and all the old friends – John Locke, Frank Zachary, Barbara Nicholls, Jimmy Owens and his wife Lola – and new ones like Steve Heller, Art Editor of the *New York Times Book Review*, who in addition to offering Searle work had called him, in his compendium of graphic satire *Man Bites Man*, 'a formidable "master" of modern caricature ... a satiric magician'. There were Searles all over town in 1985, in the *New York Times* poster campaign organized (by a firm with the splendid name of Bozell Jacobs Kenyon Eckhardt) around the theme of 'reader involvement' – frog can't get to princess because she's reading the *New York Times*, and so on. This was another award-winner, though Searle never saw the trophy. Perhaps the shade of Rube Goldberg is waiting to deliver it.

Since that time, the Searles have been, in David Arkell's words, 'virtually impossible to budge'. In spring, they make a medical trip to Paris, one of which, in 1988, disclosed a tiny speck of something not quite trustworthy in Monica's right breast. Disgusted but accepting, she disappeared at once into the Clinique de Belvédère for an operation to render the area spotless. She was ill for a month, but two years later all was clear. Described by Martin Amis as a 'ludicrously well-preserved woman' in 1978, Monica is clearly heading for some sort of world record in this form of ludicrousness. The house she has designed is perfectly adapted to the Searles' rigorous programme of work-or-play, with no half measures. A sort of spiralling warren, it combines memories of the Lost Boys' domain in *Peter Pan* with something of the feel of a lighthouse. Monica cannot derive the fullest enjoyment from her own sun-terraces, since her long years of treatment have left her skin extremely photosensitive; but the long view over to the distant Mont Ste Victoire is no less imposing on a duller day. Ronald's studio is of the kind that shuns natural light, preferring a battery of almost surgical-looking bench-lamps. All the modern technologies are deployed in the household (and many are of Japanese manufacture, it is interesting to note), so long as thunderstorms are not knocking out the electricity supply. The fax machine has been the most welcome of recent additions: roughs may now be dispatched to editors, and the process of approval and adjustment speeded by up to a week.

When it comes to work itself, Searle sketches in fountain pen, but draws his finished versions in stubbornly non-technological steel nib in a pen-holder. Desclozeaux sends him all manner of odd steel nibs from the flea-markets of Paris – including those elegant but possibly impractical ones, common once but now scarce, which mimic in simple outline the shape of the Eiffel Tower. Searle's inks are a story in themselves. For decades, he used one that was not ink at all but a wood-stain: 'Stephens' Liquid Stains: Ebony'. It was used in calligraphy classes at the Cambridge Art School, and block-makers at the *C.D.N.* liked it because it was much blacker than any ink commercially available at that time. Actually a very deep purple, it mellowed with time to a pleasant brown, which stayed fixed so long as the drawing did not remain in strong daylight. Alas, this has meant that some enthusiasts who have only one Searle work to admire, and insist on admiring it in a frame on the wall, have noticed a certain fading as years go by. Ronald was still using the ebony stain at the time he left England – his Art Editor at *Punch*, Bill Hewison, kept the bottle he left behind out of curiosity – and *Holiday* magazine, on the instructions of Frank Zachary, even had a special printing ink created for the reproduction of the drawings: it was called 'Searle Purple'. In the end, Ronald went over to Indian ink 'because it was more or less immediately waterproof', and thus less liable to run if watercolour was laid over it immediately afterwards. He has fixed, latterly, upon 'Super Yang-tsé Encre de Chine', though he still possesses bottles of the Stephen's Ebony in two sizes, marked '1/9d' and '1/3d'. Henry C. Stephens Limited were so delighted to learn, back in the Fifties, what marvels were being wrought with their product that they photographed one of Searle's Leicester Galleries exhibitions to prove to their own satisfaction that it was true.

Searle's most recent books have followed to some extent the jargon-bashing formula

Right: 'Author identified in ink on title-page', *Slightly Foxed – But Still Desirable*, London, 1989

It will be interesting to see how confusing the book-dealers' life gets when, in a few years' time, copies of this book begin to turn up which need to be described in its own terms. In the jacket, leg and foot of the thunderstruck researcher here is just a hint of the 'shaggy' style of Ed Koren, one of the American cartoonists Searle admires.

established by *Winespeak*. Because his *Non-Sexist Dictionary* and bibliophile-speak collection *Slightly Foxed – But Still Desirable* have worked to a pattern involving word-play, the drawings have tended to take a lead from their captions, which is not the ideal Searle way of working. Some of his most successful images have been so exclusively propelled by the graphic impulse that he has not decided, or realized, until the last moment what the (wordless) joke was going to be. An outstanding example is the *New Yorker* cover of a cat sitting with gnomic satisfaction at a table spread with gorgeous Victorian puddings and confections in the Mrs Beeton style. It was only when this gastronomic array was nearing completion that it occurred to Searle to put a fish in a 'thinks' bubble above the cat's head. What is interesting about these latter-day albums, though, is the re-emergence of Man portrayed in his own right once more rather than through the medium of animal metaphor. This comeback has been confirmed during 1990 in the *New Yorker*, in the first 'gag' cartoon Searle has had published there for more than two decades. The scene is a 'normal' bathroom, where a man is standing at the washbasin, toothbrush in hand – but from the water in the sink there protrudes an arm, its hand brandishing a fine medieval broadsword. Bemused by this suburbanization of Arthurian legend, mocked by the heroic, the bloke in his pyjamas stands and gawps. The tactics of the drawing are fascinating. The bathroom accoutrements are drawn just about as 'straight' as you could expect from Searle after a lifetime of graphic idiosyncrasy. The upthrust arm is shapely, its grip conventional upon what is in every sense a beautifully drawn sword. The situation itself may be an impossibility, but it presents itself as 'true' and harmonious. Now look at the witness to the event, the man with the toothbrush. His head and neck are run together in a horrible boneless-looking lump, more like the stump of a limb than anything cranial.

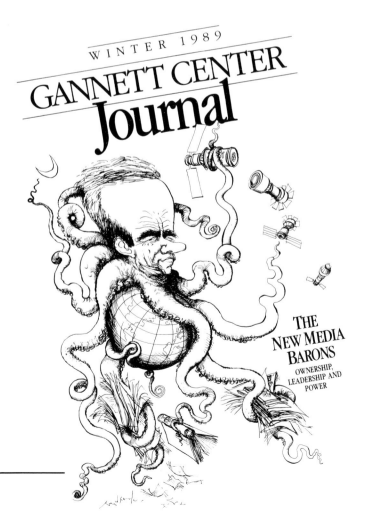

Left: Gannett Center Journal cover, 1989

Rupert Murdoch as the all-grasping media magnate: the TV Guide, *bought from Walter Annenberg, may be glimpsed in his south-eastern tentacle. The* Journal, *self-described, is 'a quarterly forum for scholars, practitioners and informed commentators to discuss topical themes of enduring importance to the mass media and the public'. Its editorial offices are at Columbia University, New York.*

His stupefied features, perched on the rim of his face, are instantly recognized, by any reader of Philip Larkin, as graffiti corresponding to a 'tuberous cock and balls'. The whole aspect of this man, considered by the standards of order prevailing elsewhere in the room, is deformed, anomalous and pathetic. Yet *he* is our representative here; he carries the great human burden of doubt; he is the one who is asking 'what has gone wrong?', when a look in the mirror might tell him. And the funny thing is that we don't doubt the existence of any of it: the tidy bathroom; the sturdy, unghostly vision of the arm; and the man with his obscene vegetable face, stopped in the middle of his routine of expectations.

All through Searle's mature work, Man, the bringer of order, has it taken away from him before he starts. Doomed to play God in a godless universe, he isn't up to it. His own grandiose myths return to mock him while he's still in his pyjamas. It *is* a bleak humour, but that is what makes it so generous; it is brought back from some very dark places in the mind. What happens to it as it travels down Searle's arm and out through his pen cannot be known. If Searle knew himself, he would probably be content at last to stop drawing, which it is clear he never will. Somewhere on the way to that scratching on the page, a more tender impulse mixes in – the urge towards beauty, in all its silliness; for what is beauty but the heavenly display of light that keeps the pig-man oblivious of his own filth? That urge has always been there. It is the one thing Searle does not question. We would be mad to ask him to.

One more thing about that washbasin. It is, of course, a *left* hand that holds the sword.

Right: Untitled, *New Yorker,* 15 January 1990

Searle's first 'gag' (or situation) cartoon in the New Yorker *for more than two decades ('my fault', says the artist).*

Notes

Key: RS: Ronald Searle. RD: Russell Davies. OS: Olive Searle: *C.D.N.: Cambridge Daily News.*

Much of the material in Chapters 1 and 2 was developed from interviews with Ronald Searle, 19/20 February 1990, and from a large file of 'Cambridge notes' prepared by him for his children.

Chapter One

ALFRED HUNT: a photograph exists of Alfred, in a mounting clearly labelled 'Texas photo'.

MISS CARVER: two of her paintings (views of Yarmouth) in possession of OS.

MISS GREEN: later Mrs Yelf. Letter to RS, 17.6.75.

'BULLER' SEARLE: at his death, was said by the *C.D.N.* to have been 'an Eastern Counties boxing champion from 1922 to 1923' (19.4.67).

KAPITSA: Dr Pyotr, FRS, died 8.4.84 aged eighty-nine. 'He was given much credit for the success of the first two Sputniks in 1957' (*Times* obituary, 11.4.84).

HUMO(U)RS OF HISTORY: by Arthur Moreland. Drawings from *The Morning Leader*, published by the *Daily News*, undated in British edition.

PETERSFIELD: still a student lodging-house today, as its many doorbells proclaim.

'CAMP BOOK': prepared by Central School masters. RS's copy in possession of OS.

Chapter Two

FINKLEBAUM: letter, *C.D.N.*, 28.8.39.

JOHN NICHOLSON: became Principal of Bolton College of Art; retired 1967.

MORLEY STUART: letter dated 22.10.35.

C.D.N.: paper changed its name in 1962 to the *Cambridge News*, and in 1969 to the *Cambridge Evening News*, which it remains.

BATEMAN: Henry Mayo, 1887–1970.

LOW: Sir David, 1891–1963. See *David Low* by Colin Seymour-Ure and Jim Schoff, Secker & Warburg, 1985. RS's appreciation of Low, *Guardian* (Manchester), 21.9.63.

GORDON FRASER GALLERY: review, *C.D.N.*, 28.5.36. RS cartoon, 30.5.36.

GRANDPARENTS: George Hunt d.10.4.34. Minnie Hunt d. 7.4.47. James Searle d.18.4.36. Harriet (Fordham) Searle, d.1.2.31.

ROBINSON: William Heath, 1872–1944.

'TURKEYS': cartoon, *C.D.N.*, 5.12.36. 'Fan Mail', 2.1.37.

CORNFORD: John, 1915–36, poet; first Englishman to enlist against Franco; killed in action.

PRESS BALL: report, *C.D.N.*, 20.2.37. Elrick: 27.2.37.

'CRITICS': of Cambridge, cartoon, 21.8.37 (No. 93 in series).

SKETCH CLUB: report, *C.D.N.*, 21.9.37.

RAVERAT: Gwendolen Mary, née Darwin, 1885–1957. *Period Piece*, 1952.

'BLUE TOES': *Cartoonist Profiles*, 1970, p. 16.

CHARIVARIA: *C.D.N.*, 26.11.37, programme copy from RS.

IF MEN PLAYED CARDS: also produced as a short film by Paramount-Famous-Lasky in 1929, and as a sketch in the 1943 film *Star-Spangled Rhythm.*

'ROBINS CLUB': *C.D.N.*, 20.12.37.

NOT WHAT THEY SEEM: *C.D.N.*, 14.3.37. 'The musical interludes were pleasant interludes' (*sic*).

HOBSBAWM: Eric, letter to RD, 5.4.90.

KREISLER: Fritz, 1875–1962, violin virtuoso.

VAUGHAN WILLIAMS: Ralph, 1872–1958, composer.

SAYERS: Dorothy Leigh, 1893–1957, daughter of a Fenland minister; writer.

OLIVER: Vic, 1898–1964, Viennese-born radio comedian and musician, married to Churchill's daughter Sarah.

'SEVEN AGES OF JOURNALISM': *Granta*, 8.6.38.

LOW: *Ye Madde Designer*, Studio Ltd, 1935.

STEVEN SPURRIER: *Illustration* etc., published 1933.

CARICATURES OF TODAY: with an introduction by Randall Davies, Studio Ltd, 1928.

BEAUMONT: C.W., *Design for the Ballet*, bought by RS December 1937.

JOOSS: Kurt, died California 1979, at the age of seventy-eight.

DRAWING SOCIETY: exhibition, *C.D.N.*, 20.5.38.

EDUCATION COMMITTEE: letter, dated 15.6.38.

'LAUTREC': *Cartoonist Profiles*, 1970, p. 17.

SKETCH CLUB: report, *C.D.N.*, 20.9.38.

'MISERY': RS interview with RD, 19.2.90.

MEYLER: Désirée, d.1989. In later life, the author of several fictions, some of them billed as 'Arcadian novels': *Fled is that Music* (1971), *The Gods are Just* (1973), *The Green Days* (1974), etc.

TRENCH-DIGGING: *C.D.N.* reports, 29.9.38, 30.9.38.

'WOODCUT ARTISTE': *C.D.N.*, 16.12.38.

'GOOD ARTIST': *Granta*, 1.3.39.

STUART: review of W. Henry Brown book, *C.D.N.*, 'Table Talk', 18.3.39.

SHAW: George Bernard, 1856–1950, playwright and polemicist. Hannen Swaffer, 'Dean of Fleet Street', 1879–1962.

'SOME RESERVE': RS in 'Top of the Ladder' programme in series 'Under-20 Parade', BBC Sound Archive; recording made 9.1.52.

'JOINING UP': cartoon, *C.D.N.*, 22.4.39.

'SGT-MAJORS': cartoon, 13.5.39.

EXAM PANIC: RS to RD, fax communication, May 1990.

'CAMP HERO': cartoon, 12.8.39.

FORAIN: Jean-Louis, 1852–1931, a mouthpiece for extreme anti-Dreyfusard and anti-Semitic opinion.

'BLACK CLOTH': *C.D.N.*, advertisement, 30.8.39.

Chapter Three

Although some incidents here are described by RS in his *To The Kwai – And Back*, I have tried as far as possible not to overlap with the details of that account. Medical details from RS's personal chronology. Drawings, theatre notebooks, files of *The Exile* and items of equipment all inspected at Imperial War Museum. Copies of documentation either from IWM or RS's own files.

'LIGHTER SIDE': cartoons, *C.D.N.*, 16/23/30.9.39, and 7.10.39.

'MAN WITH A LOAD OF MISCHIEF': by Ashley Dukes.

WIGGINS: letter to RD, 18.4.90.

NORWICH CASTLE: exhibition reviews, *Eastern Daily Press* 4.1.41; *Studio*, March 1941; *C.D.N.*, 6.2.41.

JOHNSTON: Cécilé, letter to RD, 23.4.90. RS letter to C. Johnston, 5.6.41.

'THE REAL ST TRINNEAN'S': title of a memoir by Miss C. Fraser Lee, the headmistress (W. Brown, Edinburgh, 1962).

'MY PROPER CEILING': RS to RD, by fax, May 1990.

'EAST ANGLIAN CUNNING': *To The Kwai – And Back*, p. 9.

SOBIESKI: a useful account of the voyage is given in *With the Cambridgeshires at Singapore* by William Taylor (Trevor Allen Bevis, 1971).

'SCRIBBLED ON': *To The Kwai – And Back*, p. 31.

ORDER OF THE DAY: quoted by W. Taylor, as above.

'SLANT-EYED': see Russell Braddon, *The Naked Island* and *The Piddingtons*.

LETTER: RS to Cécilé Johnston, dated 'January 7, 1942. At sea – still.'

WAVELL: his Order, 4.2.42, quoted in *The War Illustrated*, Vol. 5, No. 121, p. 490.

LILLIPUT: Singapore story from *The St Trinian's Story*, 1959.

C.D.N.: sketches, 17/18.2.42. Robin Goodfellow: 14.2.42. Malaya Postings: 26.3.42.

JOHN STEWART: John Stewart Ullmann, b.1919. See his *To the River Kwai*, Bloomsbury 1988.

HILTON TRANCHELL: profiled by Searle/Kaye Webb in *News Chronicle*, 19.6.52.

'TROUBLE CAME': RS in *ARK* magazine (no. 10), 1954.

ROCKS INCIDENT: this version from BBC *Omnibus*, 'A Step in the Jungle', 1975.

DUTCH EXPERIENCE: RD interview with Klaas Kooy, Paris, 29.4.90.

'ROCK BOTTOM': *To The Kwai – And Back*, p. 123.

'MIND WORKED': BBC *Omnibus*, 1975, as above.

BRADDON: quoted from David Arkell, 'The Several Lives of Ronald Searle', *PN Review*, No. 50 (Vol. 12, No. 6), 1986. Fuller version published *Listener*, 19.6.75; transcribed from BBC *Omnibus*, as above.

MALARIA: source consulted was *Essential Malariology* by Leonard Jan Bruce-Chwatt, Emeritus Professor of Tropical Hygiene, University of London.

SPROD: George, returned to Australia after his British career, currently resides in Sydney.

'911 DAYS': quoted in RS's personal chronology, supplied to RD.

CAMPION: Bernard. His account of the *Exile* experience appeared in *Guzz* ('RNB's own magazine'), Vol. 1, No. 8, 1946. Also *Yours*, February 1985.

KYOHARA: complete correspondence relating to Kyohara case supplied by RS. Also letter from A. Sunnucks to RD, 29.12.89.

WILLIAMS: Bill, pianist and entertainer, died Bermuda, 12.12.83.

SAITO: General, executed for war crimes. Was said (by correspondent to RS) to have had to be wakened to face the executioner, such was his calm.

DRIBERG: Tom, later Baron Bradwell, 1905–76. Independent MP for Maldon 1942–5; Labour MP for Maldon, 1945–55; Barking, 1959–74.

MOUNTBATTEN: dinner, seating-plan supplied by RS. Narrative given in letter to OS, 18.9.45., and Driberg's *Ruling Passions*, 1977. See also Mountbatten's Personal Diaries.

LETTERS: RS to OS, dated 18.9.45, 1.10.45, courtesy OS.

MENINSKY: letter to RD, 14.4.90.

CHANGI: Singapore Changi Airport today advertises itself as 'One Step Closer to Paradise'.

Chapter Four

LETTERS: RS to OS, dated 1.10.45, 10.10.45 ('Red Sea'), 12.10.45 ('Port Suez docks'), 16.10.45 ('in the Mediterranean').

ARTISTS' ADVISORY COMMITTEE: from information privately supplied to RS, 1982.

ARTICLES: on RS's war story, *Illustrated*, 9.2.46; *London Opinion*, May 1946; *Strand*, August 1946.

SUNNUCKS: letter to RD, 29.12.89.

DRIBERG: account of conference incident from unpublished account by RS, 'Spies I Have Known, No. 1'. Ropeworks article, *Lilliput*, October 1946. Driberg on Changi, e.g. *Reynolds News*, 25.2.51.

ADLER: Colquhoun, etc. see J. Rothenstein, *Modern English Painters*, Macdonald 1974, p. 176 et seq.

'TAXI-DRIVER': RS's description, by fax to RD, 24.4.90.

JOHN BULL: letters and Hidge's reply, 8.5.48 and 29.5.48

KENDON: Frank, 1893–1959. Joined C.U.P. as assistant secretary, 1935; Fellow of St John's, 1948. His letter to Searle undated.

'B . . . Y DOCTORS': quoted by Meninsky, letter to RD, 14.4.90.

RADIO TIMES: see *The Art of Radio Times*, BBC Publications, 1981

'ENIGMA OF THE JAPANESE': BBC Radio, 10.8.47: see *The Art of Radio Times*.

HOGARTH: interview with RD, 14.2.90.

'SCOTTISH DANCING': interviews, RD with Kaye Webb, 6.2.90, and 16.4.90.

BELSKY: Franta, sculptor, born Brno, 6.4.21.

'SCIENTIFIC ELIMINATION': RS interview with RD, 19/20.2.90.

BIRD: Cyril Kenneth, alias 'Fougasse', 1887–1965, the only cartoonist to have edited *Punch*.

PUNCH: see *A History of Punch*, by R.G.G. Price, Collins, 1957.

LETTERS: RS to Bird, 30.4.49 and 9.5.49. Bird to RS, 4.5.49.

KEOWN: quoted from *An Experience of Critics*, p. 52.

FUCHS: Klaus, Special *Leader* Supplement, 18.3.50.

PARIS: quotes from introduction to *A Parish Sketchbook*.

GOOD LUCK CHARMS: described in *A Paris Sketchbook*, p. 64 ('Chez Louisette, Clignancourt'); and *Ronald Searle in Perspective*, p. 8.

LASDUN: Denys, profiled by Webb/Searle, *News Chronicle*, 22.1.53.

ARKELL: *PN Review*, No. 50, 1986; and interview with RD, 8.2.90.

'POUND A DAY': George Sprod, letter to RD, n.d. (May 1990).

VICKY: see *Vicky*, by Russell Davies and Liz Ottaway, Secker & Warburg, 1987. RS appreciation of Vicky, *SIA Journal*, No. 157, March 1966.

Chapter Five

PORTOBELLO ROAD: *News Chronicle*, 20.12.51.

Times: leader mentioning St Trinian's, 1.12.51.

'AWFUL ST TRINIAN'S': RS, BBC Sound Archive Recording, 'Under-20 Parade', 1952.

HUMOUR OF DICKENS: undated News Chronicle Publication, 1952/3, with illustrations by Giles, Vicky, Illingworth, Cummings, Low, Ardizzone, Lancaster etc.

EMETT: Rowland, b. London, 1906.

ST TRINIAN'S: RS comments from reply to a proposal by Clark Gesner for the first act of a St Trinian's musical, 28.5.72.

MANZÙ: Giacomo, sculptor and graphic artist, b. 1908.

LEFT-HANDEDNESS: notes of incident made by RS at the time, 'Grand Hotel e Di Milano, June 1953', copy supplied.

CUTTLEFISH: report in the *Sketch*, 10.2.54.

T-SQUARES: Paul Hogarth, interview with RD, 14.2.90.

'EVERYTHING ONE DID': Louise Henderson to RD, 27.3.90.

RS/MUGGERIDGE: RS letter dated 18.1.54, from *Punch* files, with Muggeridge reply.

RAKES: *The Modern 'Rake's Progress'*, by Low and Rebecca West, Hutchinson, 1934.

MUNNINGS: letter to RS, dated 20 February (1954).

MUGGERIDGE: letters 4.5.54, 25.5.54, 18.3.55, carbons privately supplied.

DEHN: Paul, film review, *News Chronicle*, 1.10.54.

BOURLET: letter from Bourlet & Sons to RS's secretary, 9.12.54. *Evening News* report, 18.12.54.

CANARD: translation of undated *Canard* article supplied by RS in typescript.

ROUSSEAU: Henri, 'Le Douanier', self-taught painter, 1844–1910.

TIMES: on Chelsea Arts Ball, 19.11.54.

VENICE/WIGAN: *Daily Telegraph*, 3.9.55, by Campbell Dixon; *Evening News*, 13.12.55, by Jympson Harman; see also *Evening News*, 25.2.56, and *Picture Post* 7.1.56.

WILD THYME: by Philip Guard and Donald Swann. Starring Betty Paul, Denis Quilley and Jane Wenham.

PANORAMA: BBC Television, 10.8.55. Programme No. 22, last in second series.

BARSLEY: letter to RS, 12.8.55.

JOHN LOCKE: interviews with RD, New York, 8/10.3.90.

WILLIAM SEARLE: *C.D.N.*, 10.7.56. 'Four GPO Engineers Retire'.

PUNCH TABLE: Handwritten notes and table-plan made by RS, 1.2.56.

LETTERS: RS to Brockbank, 10.1.56. Brockbank letter, 15.1.56. Agnew letters, 18.1.56, to Brockbank; 20.1.56 to RS. *Punch* files.

MAYHEW: Henry, 1812–87. *London Labour and the London Poor*, 1851.

FERGUSSON: Bernard. Billed in army advertising as 'The Most Travelled Officer in the Army' (e.g. *Eagle*, 15.2.57).

TREWIN: John Courtenay, 1908–90.

SUEZ: from interviews 19/20.2.90, and RS's contemporary notes.

GRIVAS: Colonel, later General, George; b. 1898. Leader of EOKA rebels.

FERGUSSON: see *The Trumpet in the Hall 1930–58*, by Bernard Fergusson (Collins, 1970), p. 268. Also *Un Coup d'Epée dans L'Eau du Canal* by Jacques Baeyens, Fayard, 1976.

KEIGHTLEY: letter, dated 20.1.57.

SPECTATOR: Brian Inglis to RS, 12.11.59. Proof copy of unpublished reader's letter supplied by RS. Article, 'The Ultimatum', by Erskine R. Childers, *Spectator*, 30.10.59

FERGUSSON: letter to RS, datelined BFPO 53, 11.11.56.

CRAIG: Edward Gordon, 1872–1966. RS: 'We had a correspondence that went on for some years at a great pace until ECG became too tired to continue. I've found a few of his letters. The several hundred others have disappeared since . . .'

TIMES: 10.12.56, p. 10.

PEYNET BOOKS: *The Lovers' Pocketbook* (1954), *The Lovers' Travelogue* (1955), *The Lovers' Bedside Book* (1956) etc.

NEW YORK: letter from RS to Brockbank, 19.5.57. Privately lent.

YOUNG ELIZABETHAN: title changed to *Elizabethan*, May 1958; sub-head 'The magazine for boys and girls' dropped in June.

'TEN WORDS': report in *Daily Telegraph*, 12.10.57.

LAMBS' CLUB: 14.10.57. List of those present courtesy of John Locke/RS. Account of RS's arrest in *New York Journal American* 21.10.57, by 'Louis Sobol' (Irving Hoffman).

FFOLKES: born Brian Davis, 1925–88. Quoted in *Funny*

Way To Earn a Living by Michael Bateman (Leslie Frewin, 1966).

SATURDAY REVIEW: 23.11.57, debate with R. Osborn. *Collier's*: 'Roughly Speaking' ('Rumors and Humors for *Collier's* Cartooners'), Vol. iv, No. 2. Replies, No. 4. Oct/Dec. 1956.

SUNDAY DISPATCH: letter from Walter Hayes to Muggeridge, 19.4.57. Brockbank reply, 24.4.57.

'TIM': interview with RD at *L'Express*, Paris, 1.5.90. See *L'Autocaricature* by 'Tim' (Stock, 1974).

THURBER: RS quote from BBC Radio tribute 'The Private Life of James Thurber', programme in series 'World of Books' broadcast 1.12.61, BBC Sound Archive. Also RS essay on Thurber for *Bulletin de la Monnaie*, 1979.

WILLANS: Geoffrey, 1911–58. RS appreciation, *The Times*, 9.8.58.

MONITOR: BBC Television, broadcast 21.12.58.

LISTENER: review, 1.1.59, by K. W. Gransden.

THIS IS YOUR LIFE: broadcast BBC Television, 12.1.59. Transcripts courtesy of BBC Written Archive.

PFLUG: article, *Graphis*, No. 80, 1958.

HURRA IST ST TRINIAN: Stuttgart TV, 19.4.59.

JOURS DE FRANCE: feature, 30.7.–5.8.59.

EIN ENGLÄNDER SIEHT DEUTSCHLAND: Süddeutscher Rundfunk, Stuttgart, 1960.

NEW YORK HERALD-TRIBUNE: article by Gerald Gottlieb, 10.1.60.

HOLIDAY: Readers' letters, September 1959.

REFUGEES: published *Punch*, 30.12.59, and by Penguin, 1960.

ELECTION: RS comments from *Life* magazine text, 31.10.60.

AUSTIN, TEXAS: 439 *Punch* theatre drawings and 80 theatre sketchbooks are held by the Harry Ransom Humanities Research Center, Iconographic Collection, University of Texas at Austin.

BEYOND THE FRINGE: *Punch* theatre drawing, 17.5.61; latterly illustrates cover of *Beyond the Fringe and Beyond* (Virgin Books, 1990).

ADVERTISING AGE: 8.5.61. 'Ad Tries to Imitate the Inimitable RS.'

Chapter Six

ARKELL: from *PN Review*, No. 50 (Vol. 12, No. 6), 1986. Revised version of article appears in Arkell, *Ententes Cordiales* (1989).

BENIN HEAD: Sale, Sotheby's, 20.11.61.

RS LETTERS: to Hewison, 13.10.61, 20.10.61. To Hewison from New York, 8.3.62.

YUKON INCIDENT: RS notes, headed 'Curious coincidences, strange encounters (cont'd)'. Unpublished.

DICKENS: Doris Dickens quoted in *John o'London's*, 6.9.62.

RS ON DICKENS: *Exempla Graphica* A61, 2.12.65. 'The Impossibility of Illustrating Dickens', by RS, *John o'London's*, 20.9.62.

RS ON KEOWN: to Hewison, 19.2.63, and RD interview.

'FACE LIFT': published *Punch*, 13.3.63.

RONALD GRAY: dated 30.8.63. Rabel died 27.8.63, in Cherry Hinton, Cambridge.

GRAPHIS: Ben Shahn article, No. 109, 1963.

RS ON 'ANATOMIES': RS notes for Bremen exhibition of 'Anatomies', October 1964. Typescript supplied.

SWEET SMELL OF SUCCESS: 1957. Directed by Alexander MacKendrick. Written by Clifford Odets and Ernest Lehman. Also starred Burt Lancaster.

HOFFMAN: from RS interview, 19/20.2.90.

GROUCHO MARX: from BBC Sound Archive interview, dated 24.7.64.

MENDEL: interview with RD, Paris, 2.5.90.

HORSLEY: RD interview with Miss Horsley, 23.1.90.

T.L.S. REVIEW: 13.10.66.

SOUPAULT: Philippe, 1897–1990. Obituaries, *Le Monde* and *The Times*, 13.3.90.

WINCHELL: Walter, column syndicated in e.g. *Miami Herald*, 11.12.66.

DIVORCE: report, *The Times*, 17.2.67.

WILLIAM SEARLE: *Cambridge News*, 19.4.67. 'Cartoonist's father dies at 71'.

TIME: 'Milestones' entry, 14.7.67. Letters from RS and M. Stirling, 21.7.67.

RS ON ANIMALS: RD interview, 19/20.2.90.

COWARD: anecdote from RD interview; see also 'Thirty Years after St Trinian's', by Martin Amis, *Sunday Telegraph Magazine*, 5.2.78.

SINÉ: Maurice Sinet, b. Paris, 1928. Georges Wolinski, b. Tunis, 1934.

'IL CELEBRE ARTISTA': from unidentified Italian newspaper cutting headed 'Pupe e Pupazzi', RS files.

JIMMY OWENS: RD interview, New York, 10.3.90.

LINE-UP: broadcast BBC2, 2.7.69

CARTOONIST PROFILES: 'Sound Off!' by RS, in Vol. 1, No. 3, Summer 1969.

DESCLOZEAUX: RD interview, Paris, 30.4.90.

RAUCH, TOPOR, KERLEROUX: Hans-Georg Rauch, b. Berlin, 1939. Roland Topor, b. Paris 1938, of Polish parents. Jean-Marie Kerleroux, b. Besançon, 1936.

'PROFONDÉMENT CHOQUÉ': article by Raymond Cogniat, *Le Figaro*, 6.2.73.

LAUTREC: BBC Television *Monitor* film, 1960.

ARKELL: from *PN Review*, No. 50, 1986; and RD interview.

MOLESWORTH: letter from Molesworth to RS, 11.1.70,

received 24.1.70. RS reply same date.

SCHWARZENBERG: article, *Observer*, 7.1.90; file of undated cuttings (*Monde, Canard* etc) supplied by RS.

BARBARA NICHOLLS: RD interview, New York, 12.3.90. Letter from RS, 10.7.70.

PERELMAN: résumé of Perelman notes from RS files. See Dorothy Herrmann, *S. J. Perelman, a Life* (Simon & Schuster, 1986).

'SMALL IS MY CINEMA': originally published by the *New Yorker*; reprinted in *The Rising Gorge* (Simon & Schuster, 1961).

BRUCE LUNCH: accounts from Herrman (see above); Mary Blume; and RS, by fax, 7.5.90.

'COLOUR': RS to Michael Bateman for 'Atticus', *Sunday Times*, 31.12.67.

FORLANI: 'Un Anglais à la Nationale', *Paris-Match*, 3.2.73.

'DOCUMENTS SUR L'ARTISTE'. RS: 'It has always fascinated me to see how glass, by placing distance between the viewer and the object, can endow crap with interest, authenticity, respectability, and even academic authority.' RS notes on the *vitrines*, unpublished.

DICK DEADEYE: according to the 1978 Searle monograph and RS's own annotations, he worked on this film for four years.

BBC: *Omnibus*, broadcast BBC1, 15.6.75.

LISTENER: review by David Pryce-Jones, 19.6.75.

Chapter Seven

DE HOOGHE: Romeyn, born Amsterdam 1645, died 1708.

HEARTFIELD: RS letter to Gertrud Heartfield, 20.10.77. Her reply, 21.11.77.

GROSZ: RS essay for *Bulletin du Club Français de la Medaille*, 1978. Design for Grosz *Gedenktafel* and reporting of ceremony, *Der Tagesspiegel*, 4.12.77.

AMIS: for *Sunday Telegraph Magazine*, 5.2.78.

SHAW: Irwin, born Brooklyn, 1913, best known for novels *The Young Lions* and *Two Weeks in Another Town*.

MONIKA, etc: programme transmitted TF-1, 5.4.78.

BOXER: Mark, review, *New Statesman*, 17.11.78.

BLYTHE: review, *Listener*, 14.12.78.

HOLMES: review, *The Times*, 24.11.78.

LAURA PERELMAN: This version from RS typescript. Story appears in *I Saw a Ghost* ... ('Eye-witness accounts by the famous of supernatural encounters'), compiled by Ben Noakes (Weidenfeld, 1986).

WOLFE: Tom, review of *The Situation is Hopeless, New York Times Book Review*, 8.3.81.

CANADIAN AWARD: RS comments and file of correspondence with LaPalme, by fax to RD, 2.6.90.

POST: RS comments on postal systems, by fax to RD, 2.6.90.

NORMAN: Philip, in *Sunday Times*, 17.10.82.

WINE: RS typescript dated October 1983, and marked 'Note apropos *Winespeak* for someone or other.'

CHÂTEAU: this note from RS press-release ('Why my book, *Winespeak*?'), dated 10.9.83.

LIRE: edition of Jan. 1985. *Apostrophes* transmitted 18.12.84. Letter to RS from Service de Presse of Denoël, 15.1.85.

PITY: review by Denis Thomas, *Listener*, 13.3.86.

'THINKS' BUBBLE: *Radio Times* interview with Mel Calman, 12.6.75.

'TUBEROUS': from 'Sunny Prestatyn', in *The Whitsun Weddings*, 1964.

Bibliography

1. Albums of drawings by Ronald Searle

Forty Drawings (Cambridge University Press, 1946; Macmillan, 1947). Foreword by Frank Kendon.

Le Nouveau Ballet Anglais (Editions Montbrun, 1946).

Hurrah for St Trinian's! and Other Lapses (Macdonald, 1948). Foreword by D. B. Wyndham Lewis.

The Female Approach, with Masculine Sidelights (Macdonald, 1949). With a letter from Sir Max Beerbohm.

Back to the Slaughterhouse and Other Ugly Moments (Macdonald, 1951).

Weil noch das Lämpchen glüht (Diogenes, 1952).

Souls in Torment (Perpetua, 1953). With Preface and short dirge by C. Day Lewis.

Médisances (Editions Neuf, 1953).

The Female Approach: Cartoons (Knopf, 1954). Introduction by Malcolm Muggeridge.

The Rake's Progress (Perpetua, 1955; new edition, as *The Rake's Progress: Some Immoral Tales*, Dobson, 1968).

Merry England, etc. (Perpetua, 1956; Knopf, 1957).

The Penguin Ronald Searle (Penguin, 1960).

Which Way Did He Go? (Perpetua, 1961; World Publishing, 1962).

From Frozen North to Filthy Lucre (Viking, 1964; Heinemann, 1964). Remarks by Groucho Marx. Commentaries by Jane Clapperton.

Searle in the Sixties (Penguin, 1964).

Pardong, M'sieur: Paris et autres (Denoël, 1965).

Searle's Cats (Dobson, 1967; Greene, 1968; revised edition with re-drawings, Souvenir Press, 1987).

The Square Egg (Weidenfeld & Nicolson, 1968; Greene, 1968).

Take One Toad: A Book of Ancient Remedies (Dobson, 1968).

Hello – Where Did All the People Go? (Weidenfeld & Nicolson, 1969; Greene, 1970; as *Tiens! Il n'y a personne?*, Jean-Jacques Pauvert Editeur, 1969).

Hommage à Toulouse-Lautrec (Editions Empreinte, 1969; as *The Second Coming of Toulouse-Lautrec*, Weidenfeld & Nicolson, 1970).

Filles de Hambourg (Jean-Jacques Pauvert Editeur, 1969; as *Secret Sketchbooks: The Back Streets of Hamburg*, Weidenfeld & Nicolson, 1970).

The Addict: a Terrible Tale (Dobson, 1971; Greene, 1971).

I Disegni di Ronald Searle (Garzanti Editore, 1973).

Gilbert & Sullivan: A Selection from Ronald Searle's Original Drawings from the Animated Feature Film 'Dick Deadeye' (Entercom Productions, 1975).

Dick Deadeye (Jonathan Cape, 1975; Harcourt, 1975). Based on Searle's drawings.

More Cats (Dobson, 1975; Greene, 1976).

Searle's Zoodiac (Dobson, 1977; as *Zoodiac*, Pantheon, 1978).

Ronald Searle (Rowohlt, 1978; Deutsch, 1978; Mayflower Books, 1979). Introduction by Henning Bock. Essay by Pierre Dehaye.

The King of Beasts and Other Creatures (Allen Lane, 1980; as *The Situation Is Hopeless*, Viking, 1981).

Von Katzen und anderen Menschen (Eulenspiegel Verlag, Berlin DDR, 1981).

Ronald Searle's Big Fat Cat Book (Macmillan, 1982; Little, Brown 1982).

The Illustrated Winespeak: Ronald Searle's Wicked World of Winetasting (Souvenir Press, 1983; Harper, 1984).

Ronald Searle in Perspective (New English Library, 1984; Atlantic Monthly Press, 1985).

Ronald Searle's Golden Oldies 1941–1961 (Pavilion Books, 1985).

To The Kwai – and Back: War Drawings, 1939–1945 (Collins, in association with the Imperial War Museum, 1986; Atlantic Monthly Press, 1986).

Something in the Cellar: Ronald Searle's Wonderful World of Wine (Souvenir Press, 1986; Ten Speed Press, 1988).

Ah Yes, I Remember It Well . . . Paris 1961–1975 (Pavilion, 1987; Salem House, 1988).

Ronald Searle's Non-Sexist Dictionary (Souvenir Press, 1988; Ten Speed Press, 1989).

Slightly Foxed – But Still Desirable: Ronald Searle's Wicked World of Book Collecting (Souvenir Press, 1989).

2. *Ronald Searle as compiler/editor/contributor*

The Biting Eye of André François (Perpetua, 1960). Editor, and author of introduction.

Toulouse-Lautrec: A Definitive Biography by Henri Perruchot, translated by Humphrey Hare (Perpetua, 1960; World Publishing, 1961). Editor.

Cézanne: A Definitive Biography by Henri Perruchot, translated by Humphrey Hare (Perpetua, 1961; World Publishing, 1962). Editor.

La Caricature: Art et Manifeste. Du XVIe siècle à nos jours (Editions Skira, 1974), co-editor with Claude Roy and Bernd Bornemann. With 'some reflections' by Ronald Searle.

3. *Collaborations*

Paris Sketchbook, with Kaye Webb (Saturn Press, 1950; Braziller, 1958; revised edition, Perpetua, 1967).

The Terror of St Trinian's; or Angela's Prince Charming, with 'Timothy Shy', alias D. B. Wyndham Lewis (Parrish, 1952; reprinted, Ian Henry Publications, 1976).

Down with Skool!, with Geoffrey Willans (Parrish, 1953; Vanguard, 1954).

Looking at London, and People Worth Meeting, with Kaye Webb (News Chronicle Publications, 1953).

How to be Topp, with Geoffrey Willans (Parrish, 1954; Vanguard, 1955).

Whizz for Atomms, with Geoffrey Willans (Parrish, 1956; as *Molesworth's Guide to the Atomic Age*, Vanguard, 1957).

The Dog's Ear Book: with Four Lugubrious Verses, with Geoffrey Willans (Parrish, 1958; Crowell, 1958).

The Big City; or, The New Mayhew, with Alex Atkinson (Perpetua, 1958; Braziller, 1959).

The Compleet Molesworth, with Geoffrey Willans (Parrish, 1958; reprinted, Pavilion, 1984).

Back in the Jug Agane, with Geoffrey Willans (Parrish, 1959; as *Molesworth Back in the Jug Agane*, Vanguard, 1960).

USA for Beginners, with Alex Atkinson (Perpetua, 1959; as *By Rocking-Chair across America*, Funk, 1959).

Russia for Beginners, with Alex Atkinson (Perpetua, 1960; as *By Rocking-Chair across Russia*, World Publishing, 1960).

Refugees, 1960, with Kaye Webb (Penguin, 1960).

Escape from the Amazon!, with Alex Atkinson (Perpetua, 1964).

Anatomie eines Adlers: Ein Deutschlandbuch, with Heinz Huber (Desch, 1966; as *Haven't We Met Before Somewhere?*, translation by Constantine FitzGibbon, Heinemann, 1966; Viking, 1966).

The Great Fur Opera: Annals of the Hudson's Bay Company, 1670–1970, with Kildare Dobbs (McClelland & Stewart, 1970; Greene, 1970).

Paris! Paris!, with Irwin Shaw (Harcourt, Brace, Jovanovich, 1977; Weidenfeld & Nicolson, 1977).

4. *Books illustrated by Ronald Searle*

Co-operation in a University Town by W. Henry Brown (Co-operative Printing Society, 1939).

White Coolie by Ronald Hastain (Hodder & Stoughton, 1947).

Life Interests by Douglas Goldring (Macdonald, 1948).

Tanker Fleet by W. E. Stanton Hope (Anglo-Saxon Petroleum Co., 1948).

Turn But a Stone by Gillian Olivier (Hodder & Stoughton, 1949).

This England 1946–1949, edited by Audrey Hilton (Turnstile Press, 1949).

Meet Yourself on Sunday: a Mass-Observation book (Naldrett Press, 1949).

Meet Yourself at the Doctor's: a Mass-Observation book (Naldrett Press, 1949).

A Long Drink of Cold Water by Patrick Campbell (Falcon Press, 1949).

The Inconstant Moon by Noel Langley (Arthur Barker, 1949).

A Short Trot with a Cultured Mind by Patrick Campbell (Falcon Press, 1950).

Stolen Journey by Oliver Philpot (Hodder & Stoughton, 1950).

The Piddingtons by Russell Braddon (Werner Laurie, 1950).

The British Inn by Bernard Darwin and others (Naldrett Press, 1950).

Life in Thin Slices by Patrick Campbell (Falcon Press, 1951).

An Evening at the Larches by Harry Hearson and J. C. Trewin (Elek, 1951).

The Naked Island by Russell Braddon (Werner Laurie, 1952).

London – So Help Me! by Winifred Ellis (Macdonald, 1952).

The Diverting History of John Gilpin by William Cowper (Chiswick Press, 1952; King Penguin, 1954).

An Experience of Critics by Christopher Fry and others, edited by Kaye Webb (Perpetua, 1952; Oxford, USA, 1953).

Six Animal Plays by Frank Carpenter (Methuen, 1953).

It Must Be True by Denys Parsons (Macdonald, 1953).

The Journal of Edwin Carp by Richard Haydn (Hamish Hamilton, 1954).

Patrick Campbell's Omnibus (Hulton Press, 1954).

Modern Types by Geoffrey Gorer (Cresset Press, 1955).

The Investigator: A Narrative In Dialogue by Reuben Ship (Sidgwick & Jackson, 1956).

Mr Rothman's New Guide to London (Rothman's of Pall Mall, 1958).

The St Trinian's Story: The Whole Ghastly Dossier, compiled by Kaye Webb (Perpetua, 1959).

A Phoenix Too Frequent by Christopher Fry (Oxford University Press, 1959).

The Anger of Achilles: Homer's Iliad, translated by Robert Graves (Doubleday, 1959).

Great Restaurants of America by Ted Patrick and Silas Spitzer (Lippincott, 1960).

A Christmas Carol by Charles Dickens (Perpetua, 1961; World Publishing, 1961).

Great Expectations by Charles Dickens, abridged by Doris Dickens (Michael Joseph, 1962; Norton, 1962).

Oliver Twist by Charles Dickens, abridged by Doris Dickens (Michael Joseph, 1962; Norton 1962).

The Thirteen Clocks and The Wonderful O by James Thurber (Penguin, 1962).

The Savoy of London by Lucius Beebe (Lund Humphries/Savoy, 1964; revised reissue, 1979).

Those Magnificent Men in Their Flying Machines; or, How I Flew from London to Paris in 25 Hours, 11 Minutes by Allen Andrews and William Richardson (Dobson, 1965; Norton, 1965).

The Adventures of Baron Munchausen by R. E. Raspe and others, with introduction by S. J. Perelman (Pantheon, 1969; reissued without introduction, Harrap, 1985; new edition, with introduction (copyright 1948) by John Carswell, Methuen, 1987).

Those Daring Young Men in Their Jaunty Jalopies: Monte Carlo or Bust! by Jack Davies, Ken Annakin and Allen Andrews (Putnam, 1969; with title reversed, Dobson, 1969).

Monte Carlo or Bust! by E. W. Hildick (Dobson, 1969). Novelization.

Scrooge by Leslie Bricusse (Aurora Publications, 1970).

Mr Lock of St James's Street: His Continuing Life and Changing Times by Frank Whitbourn (Heinemann, 1971; first issued as an export booklet by Lock's [the Hatters], 1948).

The Subtle Alchemist by George Rainbird (revised edition, Michael Joseph, 1973).

Too Many Songs by Tom Lehrer: With Not Enough Drawings by Ronald Searle (Pantheon, 1981; Eyre Methuen, 1981).

The Great British Songbook compiled by Kingsley Amis and James Cochrane (Pavilion, 1986).

5. *Other works*

A list of books in which Searle's drawings have incidentally appeared would take up enormous space; but the following have a bearing on the text:

The Humour of Dickens, chosen by R. J. Cruikshank 'with illustrations by modern artists' (News Chronicle Publications, undated [1952]).

With the Cambridgeshires at Singapore by William Taylor (Trevor Allen Bevis, 1971). Foreword by the Reverend Canon Noel Duckworth.

The Cartoon Connection by William Hewison (Elm Tree Books, 1977).

Man Bites Man: Two Decades of Satiric Art, edited by Steven Heller (Hutchinson, 1981). Foreword by Tom Wolfe.

Ententes Cordiales by David Arkell (Carcanet Press, 1989).

Index

Roman numbers refer to text, italic numbers to illustrations.